weird
english

weird
english

evelyn
nien-ming
ch'ien

HARVARD UNIVERSITY PRESS
Cambridge, Massachusetts, and London, England

2004

Library of Congress Cataloging-in-Publication Data
Ch'ien, Evelyn Nien-Ming.
Weird English / Evelyn Nien-Ming Ch'ien.
p. cm.
Includes bibliographical references and index.
ISBN 0-674-01337-9 (alk. paper)
1. English fiction—20th century—History and criticism.
2. Language and languages in literature.
3. English fiction—21st century—History and criticism.
4. Dialect literature, American—History and criticism.
5. Dialect literature, English—History and criticism.
6. Languages in contact—English-speaking countries.
7. American fiction—History and criticism.
8. English language—Foreign elements. 9. Multiculturalism in literature.
10. English language—Variation. 11. Minorities in literature.
12. Speech in literature. 13. Languages, Mixed. I. Title.

PR888.L35C47 2004
823′.9109—dc22   2004040509

To my parents,
Lawrence Tien-Tso and Anne Pei-Yu

And in memory of my grandmother,
Inez Cheng-Li Liao Ch'ien (1906–2001)

Acknowledgments

My communities at the University of Hartford and the Hartt School of Music gave me the space and peace of mind to finish this book. And those at Harvard University and the University of Virginia inspired me to start it.

A special thanks to Elaine Scarry, Michael Levenson, Amy Edgar Sklansky, Ken Shih, Richard Rorty, Eric Lott, and Caroline Rody, who read early drafts and provided much help and support. Cora Diamond, Martin Gustafsson, and anonymous reviewers for Harvard University Press delivered extremely helpful comments in later stages.

Lindsay Waters believed in the book from the outset and provided constant encouragement. Maria Ascher edited the final text with an expert hand. A final thanks to Thomas Wheatland, Tim Jones, Richard Tonachel, Rob Stilling, and Colleen Lanick for their hard work in editorial matters, production, sales, and publicity.

Contents

weird
english

Introduction

A man absorbed with writing was absorbed not just with
words but with symbols and, through the act of writing
with the brush, with a form of painting and thus the
world itself.

—Wayne Senner, *The Origins of Writing* (1991)

In 1995 I rode a soft-bed train car to Harbin,
China, a city on the Sino-Russian border. It
was minus-forty degrees Fahrenheit when my friends and I—
three Michelin-man figures decked out in a total of eighteen
sweaters—trudged through crisp snow toward the ticket window
for the *bing deng* (ice lantern) show. The air transformed our
breath into fine dustings of snow on the fleece of our earflaps,
and the spit of bystanders froze into flattened spheres of ice
when it hit the ground. My friends peeled off a hundred feet before we got to the window and concealed themselves behind a
huge snow sculpture. I continued on, alone. At the ticket window I said, "San" ("three"), in my best imitation of the slurred re-

gional accent. I handed over the money, grabbed the tickets, and rejoined my snow-covered Caucasian friends, who would not have passed for native Chinese. Though the wind muffled the sound, we heard the ticket seller banging on the window and cursing in Chinese. It was now clear to him that I was a foreigner who had just helped fellow foreigners evade the extra ticket costs that outsiders usually paid.

Joining the queue of ticket holders, I couldn't enjoy this victory against a system that set its prices according to physiognomy. I had violated an unwritten code of honor. My imagined community chastised me for my deception. Despite being an American visiting China for the first time, I had a lingering feeling of solidarity with a community that my parents had held on to, albeit solely in their imagination. My name, too, was a constant reminder of this invisible membership. Could a past I had never experienced, through some karmic magic, influence my behavior? Or was it simply guilt that kept me from celebrating this small victory? Can the immigrant's dilemma, passed down to generations who have grown up thinking of themselves as natives, educate us about the inherent social obligations that extend beyond boundaries of physically immediate communities and encompass all of humanity, if only in an imaginary way?

Children as Countries

Much the most important thing about language is its capacity for generating imagined communities, building in effect particular solidarities.

—BENEDICT ANDERSON, *Imagined Communities* (1991)

My parents united their children through their names.[1] Alone, each of our names is only a third meaningful; but when the last character in each of our names is arranged from oldest to youngest,[2] we spell out the first three characters of the phrase "Zhong Hwa Ming Guo" ("Taiwan, Republic of China").[3] By giving us such names, my parents signified that we were at least as valuable as a country and a republic.[4] To them, our names represented the symbolic equivalent of a country and a community.[5]

The etymology of a name can evoke imagined communities, training the products of diasporas to live in the imagination. Our histories and their symbolic bundles, our names, can connect us to more than one nation, and we can be connected to communities both distantly and proximately imagined.[6] When do we forfeit our histories—when we can no longer speak to our relatives in their native tongue, or when we can no longer imagine them? If we can imagine their lives, their emotions, their language, their dreams—are we not still related? How do we re-embody this relationship so that it does not fade into artifact but has living blood?

Missundastood

Toys L Us.

—Chinatown cartoon from *The Simpsons* (2002)

Quiet, or I'll chop you off.

—*Chocolate Inspector,* www.flubtitles.com (2003)

A Shree Muskateens.

—Chinese translation of "The Three Musketeers,"
www.flubtitles.com (2003)

With increasing frequency in literature, readers are encountering barely intelligible and sometimes unrecognizable English created through the blending of one or more languages with English. Currently these literatures are classified as ethnic or minority literatures, and their vernaculars are objects of cultural rather than literary study. This book aims to show that weird English constitutes the new language of literature and that it brings new literary theory into being. I will examine both weird forms of English and the authors' bi- or polycultural status and context influencing this English. The chapters that follow offer observations and analyses of linguistic activity in bicultural communities, to supplement the political analyses existing in these areas.[7]

The weirding of English has been an ongoing phenomenon throughout history. English is, like other languages, a hybrid, and its original influences include Latin, French, and German. In this book I will highlight recent phenomena of hybridity in print literary culture, since many of the authors treated here are transcribing what used to be an exclusively oral use of hybrid English. In the later twentieth century and the early twenty-first, literary authors are performing the act of weirding English on a political level; they are daring to transcribe their communities and thus build identities. Benedict Anderson, commenting on this transition from oral to written language, asserts that print identity is a commodity of power. "Today," he writes, "the Thai government actively discourages attempts by foreign missionaries to provide its hill-tribe minorities with their own transcription-systems and to develop publications in their own languages; the same government is largely indifferent to what these minorities *speak*."[8] Vernaculars used by weird-English authors have existed for decades, but the act of transcribing establishes the community-speak in a permanent way. (It is also crucial to acknowledge the form in which vernaculars have traveled to print.)[9]

Writers like Paul Beatty, Irvine Welsh, Derek Walcott, Li-Young Lee, Junot Díaz, and Lois Ann Yamanaka write in vernaculars that have only recently become cool, instead of a freaky linguistic indulgence. The appreciation of and engagement with vernacular is riding on the back of an ethnic-awareness tsunami that is crashing into the establishment.[10] Today, varieties of English are codes for communities—the less orthodox and more subversive, the stronger the impact, as shown in the examples below:

> I am work hard my whole life, and fierce besides.[11]

> More albinos, more cross-eyed niggers, more tígueres than you'll ever see. And the mujeres—olvídate.[12]

> Oh, you know—like in "She's oomphy—toomphy—just my moomphy," and he sang it, in case Arun didn't know this popular Hindi film song.[13]

> Oh-ho-ho. *Hazukashii!* I'm so old. They call me granny at the school![14]

> Mother dubs me Alexi-stop-spleening-me!, because I am always spleening her. If you want to know why I am always spleening her, it is because I am always elsewhere with friends, and disseminating so much currency, and performing so many things that can spleen a mother.[15]

Many of the above writers use vernaculars with strength and confidence, demonstrating strategic intent behind its use. The use of weird English is a calculated effort. For polycultural writers, weird English is not simply the temporary adoption of a spelling disorder,[16] but a conscious appropriation of hybridity. I contrast this self-consciousness with the accidental misspellings of children. For example, in *Early Spelling* Gunther Kress includes an example of a child who Englishes loanwords in a dictation exercise: the child writes "robabe yoget" for "rhubarb yogurt," "crem fresh" for "crème fraîche," "blanchd armens" for "blanched almonds." Kress writes, "This child-speller has 'normalized' the spelling of these words, and has in effect turned them into 'English words.'"[17] In contrast, weird-English writers denormalize English out of resistance to it, and form their own language by combining English with their original language. In immigrant communities where weird English is exclusively an oral phenomenon, pidgins and misspellings may have meant a lack of education or fluency. But for weird-English writers, the composition of weird English is an active way of *takin' the community back.*

Although English, and language in general, have often been the subject of analysis—with striking emphasis for Oulipo (constraint-based texts), modernism, language poetry, slam poetry, spoken word, and countless forms of x-pear-yee-mental literature—the weird-English forms I describe in this book are new forms of polycultural expression.[18] In these forms of English, words are used to compose structures other than sentences; poems are strings of repeated words that compose a mantra mantra mantra mantra, and narratives are constructed from mis-ordered words words ordered mis-; novels are transcribed streams of consciousness like Faulkner's *The Sound and the Fury* dreams of writes when he dreams like collage words falling falling falling.

Because weird English possesses the extra dimension of a foreign language, it requires not only interpretation but also translation. Weird English revives the aesthetic experiential potential of English; we see through the eyes of foreign speakers and hear through their transcriptions of English a different way of reproducing meaning. This can happen on an acoustic and visceral level. We can reexperience English sounds as sounds and not words. Martin Gustafsson, in "Entangled Sense," writes about experiencing language as sound. He describes the aesthetically appealing situation of finding an environment where all the languages spoken are completely foreign and unintelligible: "Think what a relief it can be to spend some time in a country where a language is spoken which you do not understand at all; you are not forced to hear what people say, but can lie in an environment of pure sound."[19] Gustafsson's imagery resonates with the strong acoustic sensibility that is prompted upon hearing weird English. Cultural emphasis on the visual component of language can subdue the significance of the acoustic component.

This account of the acoustic aspect of language implies that human beings have a relationship with language that is satisfying beyond its function of delivering meaning. Humans derive more from language than simply information connected to words or symbols. Language can be an aesthetic affirmation of our socialization—for example, in certain cultures we might imagine the percussive sounds of language as having the pace of a human heartbeat, or word arrangements that emphasize or destabilize the rhythm of breathing, or letters and characters as design patterns. Weird English highlights these aesthetic aspects of linguistic presence in human life.

Thus, language as an experience has dimensions unconnected to the transference of information. These dimensions can change the way in which meaning is transferred. If I write letters F A R A P A R T so they have to be read slowly, the experience of the meaning could generate an affective reaction that might be sensual, clean, or stuttery.[20] There are no rules ahead of time to control the subjective experience in this case; some people might interpret the distance between letters differently, as maybe a design or set of clues leading to another meaning altogether. If I write several words on a blackboard, perhaps a transliteration of Chinese phrases such as *jiu rou peng you* ("fairweather friend[s]") or *yi san bi yi san gao* ("there's always a higher mountain to climb"), readers might misinterpret this as an example of language poetry or force a coherence on this set of words that the writer did not intend. Weird English wants to do more with English than communicate *what* the subject is; it also wants to show *who* the speaker is and *how* the speaker can appropriate the language. Efforts to incorporate all these elements in language can result in destabilizing or disrupting the transmission of meaning. In emphasizing the aesthetic, weird-English writers depart from the conventions that guide meaning-making and thus interrogate their value. Philosophers have explored this destabilization theoretically, albeit in the context of logical sentences rather than entities such as weird English. But the conclusion is similar: linguistic invention is proof that rules are guides to whether something will have meaning. Martin Gustafsson has written: "It seems to me . . . the philosophical idea that the meaningfulness of a language depends on the existence of a fixed framework of rules could seem plausible only within a relatively homogeneous culture characterized by printed language. So maybe the kind of destabilization involved in weird-English literature means, in a way, a sort of return to a pre-print situation, in the sense that the idea of capturing language within a fixed framework of rules will again seem, at best, mildly absurd."[21]

Thus, weird English functions to overturn the idea that all language operates according to rules, because weird English explicitly creates its own rules. Its intelligibility doesn't depend on

existent rules. Also, weird English contrasts with linguistic entities such as nonsense and bad English because it generates the
invention of new rules. The invention of the rules happens after
the creation of the language. The game happens; the rules follow. Weird English pushes the invention of rules, whereas a linguistic entity such as nonsense discourages rule creation. Cora
Diamond describes Gustafsson as positing that

> what comes first is saying something meaningful; the
> rules are posterior descriptions and determine no prior
> limits on what can be meaningfully said. He calls this the
> Primacy of Meaningful Expression. So there might be a
> rule already in place—[say,] that the length of a river is
> given in spatial terms (as in "The Nile River is 2,200 miles
> long"). But this rule does not make it the case that "The
> Nile River is two weeks long" is meaningless. That sen-
> tence might be used in some context to say how long it
> takes to go down the Nile in a speedboat. We can't, he
> says, first decide what rules are in force, and then use
> those rules to decide what, if anything, a given utterance
> means. On the contrary, we can get clear what rules (of
> the type that interests him) are relevant to what is being
> said only by way of understanding what is being said. So
> Gustafsson wants to make a sharp distinction between
> rules laying out what counts as senseful utterance and
> rules prescribing the forms of "standard English," which,
> most significantly from his point of view, have nothing to
> do with the meaningfulness of what is uttered.[22]

Furthermore, we learn about new registers of meaning when we
destabilize rules. Gustafsson shows that rules do not control the
amount of meaning that seeps through the linguistic entity that

is offered up by speakers/writers. As a philosophical and linguistic entity, weird English is a subset of and an innovation in the category of experimental English. It is clearly a vernacular—comprises more than *simply* funny uses of letters or words, rap, "Waste Land–like" poetry, works in the style of *Finnegans Wake,* or antireferential linguistic compositions such as language poetry. Weird English is the kind of language creation happening now—vernacular transcription that has a built-in self-consciousness of its political, social, and metaphorical implications, as well as aesthetic value.

This book documents well-executed and notable cases of extraordinary play with English: from the hyper-selfconscious vernacular usage of Vladimir Nabokov to the overtly courageous use of Spanglish that exists in the work of Junot Díaz. Outside literary studies, we can look to the world that inspires literary play. The linguistic innovations of certain populations have spawned critical attention in the form of books, articles, and videos: *Crazy English* (1998), by Richard Lederer; *A Fresh Look at American English* (2001), by Wallace Goldstein; *The Story of English* (a six-video set on global English); a cover article in the *Atlantic Monthly* on global English (2000);[23] and humorous critiques of English jargon, such as *Junk English* (2000), by Ken Smith. Countless websites examine the way in which English is being appropriated by other cultures: www.flubtitles.com inventories odd subtitle translations in Chinese films, and www.engrish.com catalogues samples of humorously incoherent Japglish.[24] In reaction, one can find many items on the Internet—such as "On How to Avoid Writing Chinglish," by Ji Shaobin—which attempt to illuminate and correct grammatical misdemeanors in English.

Language acquisition and misacquisition inspire writers to subvert rules of grammar and spelling—and for weird-English writers today, it is chic to do this purposefully, to bring life to English. Two of the writers discussed in this book, Vladimir Nabokov and Maxine Hong Kingston, composed their novels before the Internet became an integral part of worldwide existence. Their tone quality contrasts with that of the younger generation of writers, who trade on the originality of their vernacular rather than feeling as if they need to translate and accommodate the reader. (Both Nabokov and Kingston self-consciously translate throughout their books; see Chapters 1 and 2.)

In literature, the conscious manipulation of English as subject matter is a balancing act of intelligibility and experiment. The best uses of weird English are terrible in their intelligibility, because they demonstrate that certain lives are linguistically disenfranchised and thus that some communities are excluded from mainstream discourse. To see, to read, to hear this awakens us to the voices that hide in the dark, waiting for ears to hear them. Certain features are shared in all of these instincts to create weird English:

1. Weirding deprives English of its dominance and allows other languages to enjoy the same status;
2. Weird English expresses aesthetic adventurousness at the price of sacrificing rules;
3. Weird English is derived from nonnative English;
4. The rhythms and structure of orthodox English alone are not enough to express the diasporic cultures that speak it.

Writers like Lois Yamanaka, Irvine Welsh, Jonathan Safran Foer, Derek Walcott, Edwidge Danticat, Touré, and Li-Young Lee, who adopt voices that diverge from standard English, are continuing a tradition begun by James Joyce, William Faulkner, Gertrude

Stein, Louis Chu, T. S. Eliot, and others—but with specific intentions, separate and different from those of the modernists.[25]

Particular authors deploy weird English with memorable radicalness. In *Trainspotting*, Irvine Welsh writes entirely in dialect. Standard English is too cramped, too civilized, and too repressed for the characters in his books. *Trainspotting* is radical because of the language, not simply the narrative. The language in this book is its performance of postcolonial poverty. Drugs are auxiliaries to the attitude. Presenting a palliative to theoretical postcolonial writing, which is frequently wandery or jargon heavy, Welsh's character Rent in *Trainspotting* provides the subjective component so crucial to seeing the realities and effects of colonialism: "It's nae good blamin it oan the English for colonising us. Ah don't hate the English. They're just wankers. We are colonised by wankers. We can't even pick a decent, vibrant, healthy culture to be colonised by. No. We're ruled by effete arseholes. What does that make us? The lowest of the fuckin low, the scum of the earth. The most wretched, servile, miserable, pathetic trash that was ever shat intae creation. Ah don't hate the English. They just git oan wi the shite thuv goat. Ah hate the Scots."[26] As if to underscore the self-hatred and self-perceived ugliness that accompanies a brutalized culture, as well as the lack of any form of nostalgia for one's own cultural life, Rent continues:

> Life's boring and futile. We start oaf with high hopes, then we bottle it. We realise that we're aw gaunnae die, withoot really findin oot the big answers. We develop aw they long-winded ideas which jist interpret the reality ay oor lives in different weys, withoot really extending oor body ay worthwhile knowledge, about the big things, the

real things. Basically, we live a short, disappointing life; and then we die. We fill up oor lives wi shite, things like careers and relationships tae delude oorsels that it isnae aw totally pointless. Smack's an honest drug, because it strips away these delusions. Wi smack, whin ye feel good, ye feel immortal. Whin ye feel bad, it intensifies the shite that's already thair. It's the only really honest drug. It doesnae alter yir consciousness. It just gies ye a hit and a sense ay well-being. Eftir that, ye see the misery ay the world as it is, and ye cannae anaesthetise yirsel against it.[27]

The vernacular reflects the narrator's refusal to be educated in the ideals of the colonizing culture—his voice is unpolluted, unbrainwashed by the dominant culture. The vernacular affirms the passage's content of antiromanticism in an honest form of representation.

The dialect of *Trainspotting* restores energy to English, remaking the profane into a musical language and training the reader to be open to new speech. The film *Trainspotting* cushions the viewer by using subtitles during certain parts of the film, where dialect is used—until, of course, the viewer learns the dialect.[28] My students attest that the novel *Trainspotting* is better comprehended when paired with the movie *Trainspotting* because the written language stymies them.[29] For some students the book by itself is unintelligible unless they read it aloud; the narrative requires hearing because of its consistently unorthodox spellings. In many cases, spoken-word format can capture the accents, as well as the anger that seeps through a verbal rendering and gets lost on the page (even capitalizations and exclamations !!DON'T FULLY DO THE JOB!!).

Welsh's book *Marabou Stork Nightmares* experiments with dialect but choreographs the interactions between characters. Mixed font sizes, diagonal letter arrangements, and white spaces accrete spatial meanings, indicating proximity or distance of voices in the narrative. Various fonts also designate the identity, location, volume, and other coordinates and features of the speaker.

> Thank you but no fuckin thank you Bev-ih-leey, chuck. Bring back Patricia Devine. Come back Patsy, Patsy De Cline, all is forgiven . . .
>
> Suppose you'd like to know what's goin on in ma mind.
> DEEPER
> DEEPER
> DEEPER————————————Peace.[30]

This approximation of Welsh's font and design arrangement displays his ability to convey physical space through writing. Welsh combines the modernist sensibility of manipulating words to generate images, to do something other than straightforwardly convey meaning, with the simultaneous weirding of English: "Bev-ih-leey . . . ma mind." These activities are different; the modernist sensibility reaches for the antireferential qualities of language poetry, whereas the weird-English writer challenges the possibility of saying anything according to the rules that dominate conventional English. Such writers challenge the existence of a normative standard for English.

Sharing the detonating quality of Welsh's prose, Lois Ann Yamanaka's voice shocks with its content and dialect:

> My madda always saying she the lucky one. She got ten thousand wishes for her whole life. Thass plenny enough

wishes, if you ask me. Far as wishes go, no mo' too much going around far as I can see.

She use her first one when I was born. She wish me dead.

Kill um, God. Kill this fuckin' thing.

She saying this soft up until the time the doctor yelling at her to "Oosh, girlie, oosh." Then yelling at the nurse to "Strap this girl's arms down."

Thass when my madda started swinging and yelling at him to "Kill this fucking piggie" she get stuck up her Japanee trap.[31]

Later in the story, the narrator, a child who is harassed and sexually molested by her uncle, wishes for her own death. Yamanaka forces the reader inside a subjectivity that is honest and vulnerable. The content of the passage also reveals that the young narrator has internalized the superstitions embedded in her culture.

Focusing on the linguistic aspects of the narratives of weird-English writers reveals levels of truth, self-truth, group truth; likewise it reveals deceit, self-deceit and group deceit. The weird-English writers I discuss in this book have love affairs with language and their characters. They are loyal to their communities, yet strive for assimilation. Looking at their works, I try to uncover their subjectivities and separate them from the larger politicizable trends they often get lost in. In these literary explorations, questions explode. Is there a weird-Englishy linguistic self in reality, or is it a purely imaginative projection? Can these selves be real if weird English is a transition language, one infected by its ghost original language and still evolving? For example, Nabokov's Pnin hovers between imagination and reality; he is outside both the Russian and the American communities, with no relationship of reciprocity to confirm his existence. Meanwhile Díaz's Yunior also feels culturally marginalized and overwhelmed by his detachment from Santo Domingo.

Narratives provide a space for semi-imaginary selves and communities to exist. For example, Arundhati Roy's passages seem to emanate from an autistic anticonsciousness, and Kingston's writing becomes make-up-as-we-go-along-language. Theory also allows for the rise of weird Englishes that could not exist in reality. In much postcolonial criticism, for example, weird English veers into babble, and this graduation into unintelligibility reveals the precariousness of transacting with an imaginary community or a sublimated desire for a community. Though a freeform style of English, weird English is not exclusively the language of the individual's imagination; at times it is a group code that systematically disables and decenters the individual. In Chapter 5, on the unintelligibility of postcolonial writing, I show how linguistic decentering is manifested as freefall jargon and endless digression, with linguistic meaning teetering on the line between cogence and unintelligibility. These examinations of authorial linguistic experimentation perforate the analysis in each chapter.

Linguistic Melancholia

> Displacement, as an abstract concept, becomes the tangible home.
>
> —ANDRÉ ACIMAN, *Letters of Transit* (2000)

For my parents, China is fixed in 1949. The development of this relationship to China continues internally, privileging interiority and memory over the physical world. This dreamlike, hallucinatory quality associated with interiority pervades the works of the authors discussed here. This interiority, symbiotic with memory, generates automatic writing that must in turn be regenerated with living speech. For all these writers, their English is interpolated by a language of the past and reworked into their literature; their imagined communities invoke a ghosted language. The past is like a shadow that detaches itself from the body and clings to the new linguistic body to sustain itself. Eventually, the author separates from the shadow and assimilates into a new culture.

The importance of embodying language cannot be underestimated. This book, which examines the unorthodox English that is created by immigrant and postcolonial writers who are bilingual or polylingual, must be attuned to the positioning of language as melancholic but also as agency-affirming and playful. The members of my family have always seemed to accept one another's tendencies toward restlessness and nomadism, and we have become dependent on each other to check these tendencies. Bruce Chatwin may have been right when he said that restlessness is a part of an individual's anatomy or biological makeup; this at first seemed to apply to my family and supplied me with an adequate explanation. But I have come to realize that restlessness may also arise from uneasiness about the environment—a deep-seated uneasiness that can never be conquered. For exiles, restlessness is part of their temperament; their souls linger with indecision between two cultural spaces. They worry that they will never reencounter the feelings of being native to a place.

This book—like the writing of the authors it treats—requires embodiment. Within each chapter I enact reembodiment by reconstructing the authors' positions with respect to English. There are also questions to be answered in the process of reconstruction. Where does this resistance to orthodox language begin? The linguistic anarchists feel banished and bereft when they lose their first language. Their pain initially catalyzes the process of linguistic defiance, invention, recuperation, and enfranchisement.

In the mid-1990s, a sociological study in rural Virginia examined a large influx of Cambodian and Vietnamese immigrants who were suffering from depression; one of the symptoms was inarticulateness and muteness. The problem with diagnosing the disease was that its presence could not be expressed, thus condemning the afflicted to internal exile. This state of exile is reified as linguistic muteness.

This continuum includes immigrant and postcolonial writers, whose exile can be reified as linguistic exile. Like the war poets who were at a linguistic loss in describing the war, immigrant and postcolonial writers face the redescription of their worlds in a language which did not have all the vocabulary they require. Such writers must constitute themselves as writers in English through their writing.

An original language seeks reembodiment, though it is always partially unembodied because of its plural origins. Thus, the subject material of such writers is not simply a narrative but an effort to reembody language: its historical residue, its syntax, its grammar, its tone, and its sentiment. Maxine Hong Kingston and Junot Díaz speak about ghosts and shadow warriors; Salman Rushdie, Arundhati Roy, and Vladimir Nabokov always include a figure shrouded by the past—Moor, Baby Kochamma, Professor Pnin. The shadow quality of a former culture manifests itself concretely in language. In examining the work of postcolonial and immigrant writers, we can view the development of these writers' English. Their positioning with regard to English is fraught with conflict.

Down widda Brown, Mellow widda Yellow

The empire is still around and I'm sick of f—king psychological imperialism.

—JOE YANG, a New York banker (2002)

The literature of weird English makes extensive use of vernaculars, the raw material of the different types of analyses related to ethnic or immigrant study. Although vernaculars and pidgin speech were once dismissed as an undignified representation or parody of ethnic groups, now the use of accented English has aesthetic capital. Juliana Spahr, in *Everybody's Autonomy,* writes that although "the nonstandard language practices of second-language speakers tend to get defined as mistake instead of as deviance,"[32] artists rebel against this hostile reception of accented English. For example, she writes that Theresa Cha, in her book *Dictée,* asserts the act of stuttering as a defiant action: "By writing in the stutters and misspellings of a second-language speaker, she resists the cultural hegemony of language acquisition that smoothes over the stutter, the atypical pronunciation."[33]

Amid the stuttering, we see a newly confident use of vernaculars, happening simultaneously with the burgeoning of ethnic pride. Jeff Yang, the CEO of Factorinc.com, an Asian marketing company, said in 2000: "It is cool to be Asian now. It wasn't when I was in school, but now kids are *in* when they are Asian."[34] Affirming his view are the proliferating presence of Asian-character tattoos and the increasing popularity of Asian languages among college students. Lisa Yun, a professor at the State University of New York at Binghamton, has observed that Asian American students are affectionately calling each other "coolies," reclaiming the term and purging it of its evil connotations by uttering it with confidence and invincibility.[35]

The changing status of vernaculars—from parody to a new rhetoric of coolness or deviance, or deviance as coolness, or from an aesthetically negative to an aesthetically positive status—affects its use in literature. Interpretation of a literary work that is written in a vernacular requires a sense of the vernacular's political and social role in relation to that work. A vernacular is part of aesthetic choice and design; it is not simply transcription.

Marilyn Halter, in *Shopping for Identity*, a book about the marketing of ethnicity, notably mentions the cultivation of certain speech patterns and naming practices as trends in America: "Although cultivating a foreign accent may not yet be a sign of true Americanness, relearning one's ancestral tongue, eating ethnic cuisine, displaying ethnic artifacts, fostering a hyphenated identity, and even reverse name-changes (back to the old-country original) have become the American way."[36] Independent of Halter's assertion, certainly the trend of ethnic cool counters the racism of the past several decades.[37] English departments, bookstores, and libraries are classifying books according to ethnicity in an effort to create audiences and communities around the topics of ethnicity.

The literary examples in this book will focus on weird English as an ethnically driven phenomenon. In this book, I examine how weird-English writers become conscious of language as a practice of their ethnicity. They state in essays and interviews outside their work that their polylingual backgrounds influence their writing in English. They maintain that their cultural status causes their divergence from orthodox English. They argue that their literary English is not just stylistically different but also linguistically different from orthodox English. In some cases the weirdness is less linguistically accessible, but still present. For example, in an interview with Ha Jin, Anchee Min told him that although one of his books was composed in fairly orthodox English, "it felt very Chinese; it was very Chinese."[38] Jhumpa Lahiri confesses that her work is often a scrupulous translation, but it is so fluidly translated that its polycultural elements do not exist within her use of language.

The authors discussed in the following chapters are novelists who sustain a practice of linguistic polyculturality. In their writing, they implicate another language by calling upon the grammatical and linguistic structure of their original language. Each chapter will explore a facet of weird English. In this introduction, I map out different theoretical aspects of weird English that will be developed later in the book. Each chapter is a literary case study that takes a particular author as illuminating one or two aspects of weird English. Proceeding from Nabokov, to Kingston, and then to Díaz, I show how the production of weird English moves from a *metaphorical* relationship with the original language to a *literal* one, in which the original language is mixed with English. The authors are generally discussed in chronological order; the pre-Internet authors are examined first. The first chapter concentrates on how Vladimir Nabokov positions himself with respect to English, tracing the development of his English from the invisible but influential foundations of "unreal estate" and showing how this leads to a relationship with language as pedophilia. Nabokov, an immigrant who developed one of the most highly original styles of English, maintains a debt to Russian as providing the groundwork—and at times the structural apparatus—for his literary works. In the chapter titled "Chinky Writing," I examine the way Kingston compares Chinese and English in her works—the way Chinese penetrates her English, from larger narrative structures to individual words and sentences—contorting English to produce the cadences, rhythms, and sounds of Chinese. I also question her earlier emphasis on the ideograph as a way of conceiving Chinese from a non-Chinese perspective. I then look at the writing of Arundhati Roy, who uses language to design a political vision celebrating the virtues of the small—a term encompassing the powerless, children, nature, and those entities in the world that are under threat by the encroaching corporatization of the world. Like Roy, Junot Díaz invests language with the power to influence political and social vision. He forcefully incorporates Spanish into his mainly English texts, showing concretely the linguistic violence that Spanish inflicts on English and vice versa. Instead of contorting English to fit Spanish, he demonstrates the inadequacy of English by substitution rather than metonymy or metaphor. He makes Spanglish an American language. Finally, I examine the weirdness of postcolonial writing by comparing Rushdie to Homi Bhabha.

Screw Inscrutability

Language is like a radio. I have to choose a specific station, English or Japanese, and tune in. I can't listen to both at the same time. In between, there is nothing but static.

—KYOKO MORI, *Polite Lies* (2001)

Recently, at a dinner party in SoHo, a twenty-two-year-old Russian immigrant wanted to know my opinion about an architectural structure made of "glass cotton." After a moment, I realized he meant "fiberglass."

Though weird-English authors may be fluent, they can still tap into the activity of learning a language. They resemble philosophers who converse with facility in English but still view themselves as being *in the process of learning the language* of rhetoric and interrogation.[39] In *Philosophical Investigations*, Ludwig Wittgenstein's criticism of Augustine on the topic of learning to name objects opens his set of meditations about language as a *practice*. Language learners, like philosophers, mistrust themselves with the new vocabulary; their narratives are narratives of grasping, of contortion, of pain, art, irreverence, and creativity. The outlaw writers I discuss here refuse to follow the law in any form, and their writing turns into innovative, experimental uses of language, diction, style, and content. These authors instinctually fracture or morph traditional English in their writing. They move outside the laws of English that create new versions of the language. It is this movement of defiance against a lawfully bound linguistic strategy that results in linguistic anarchy, or weird English.

Doris Sommer claims that immigrant writers command a different kind of interpretation and that immigrant texts resist mastery of reading: "By marking off an impassable distance between reader and text, and thereby raising questions of access or welcome, resistant authors intend to produce constraints that more reading will not overcome. . . . It is the rhetoric of selective, socially differentiated understanding. Announcing limited access is the point, whether or not some information is really withheld. Rebuffs may not signal genuine epistemological impasses;

it is enough that the impasse is claimed in this ethico-aesthetic strategy to position the reader. . . . The question, finally, is not what 'insiders' can know as opposed to 'outsiders'; it is how those positions are being constructed as incommensurate or conflictive."[40] Sommer labels these writerly rebuffs as gestures indicating "unavailability"; they offer readers lessons in their own limits and cause them to be less presumptuous. She says that "worrying" is important for readers and that the "more difficult the book, the better."[41] Her stress on practicing caution while reading is praiseworthy, but it does not serve as a theoretical foundation upon which to approach all, or even most, minority writing. She suggests, for instance, that authors purposely deflect readers with certain authorial techniques, a difficult proposition to believe of all minority writers:

> The asymmetry of positions restricts a reader's travel from one place to the other, despite the fantasies of mutuality that imagine efforts to understand an ethnically inflected text compensate for a writer's burden to perform in an imperial language. "Ideal" or target readers for particularist texts are, then, hardly the writer's co-conspirators or allies in a shared culture, as we have presumed in our critical vocabulary. They are marked as strangers, either incapable of or undesirable for intimacy. Discrimination here admits that social differences exist in social positionality, and that different degrees of understanding are consequences, or safety requirements. But from the demarcated positions on a chart where only the powerful center can mistake its specificity for universality, these "marginal" or "immigrant" texts draw boundaries around that arrogant space. Instead of pandering to "competent"

> readers with guided tours, the texts, in a "Cordelia effect"
> (like Bartleby's too), cripple authority by refusing to sub-
> mit to it.[42]

Sommer suggests that immigrant writers have internalized a hierarchy and refuse to submit to it in their writing. I agree, in
part, with the idea that such writers absorb surrounding structures—but I don't think that they necessarily rebuff, rebuke, or
suggest lack of availability in their writing as a result. Rather, I
see them as less conscious of their audience, and more aware of
the language and the art they are producing. These activities are
separate. I will show in my readings of weird English that appeals for community are embedded in the writing. The tonality
of these texts is not about unavailability.

What Sommer reads as "unavailability" is what I read as temporary, willed autism by authors who alternately move in and
out of the community and experience some madness, perhaps,
in the process. Their imaginary communities can be so difficult
to sustain that they sometimes lose sight of or contact with
them. Sommer realigns the reader with the text but does not
put pressure on the idea of repeated rupturing in translational
acts. Neither does she comment on the pathology of creating
versions of English that are not entirely translatable, that are on
some level intensely individualistic, hyper-stylistic, and resistant
to a stable production of meaning. Immigrant and postcolonial
writers resist the mastery of their interpreters and translators
but they are still not masters of the linguistic creatures they
have made. Their elaborate, and sometimes possibly affected,
language is not only a stylistic device and a barrier to the mastery they resist but an indication of their own separation from
the text as well.

The slow evolution of the disjunction between referent and meaning in literature corresponds with its changing role: formerly, it affirmed the sturdiness of communities and homes; now, the genre of a text is frequently contested, and it is within a text that the sturdiness of the physical world is interrogated. Fantasy, travel, and dislocation undergird the world of immigrant and postcolonial writers, who still remain suspended from meaning. The burgeoning genres of immigrant and postcolonial literature are "terms" in the process of developing meaning. Though literary exile with relation to modernism is a common theme, alienation (as in post–World War I literature)[43] is not necessarily the primary consciousness of the immigrant writer or postcolonial writer, who also partakes of global citizenship. The authors considered in this book negotiate from their sense of exile to relocate themselves in the world, sometimes leaving an exiled text behind them.

Although weird-English writers experiment with English, they do not ultimately want to be labeled untranslatable, for their concerns are eminently social. These writers know that being on the margin of communities starts when they are considered inscrutable or untranslatable. They also know that those who call them untranslatable are excusing themselves from engaging in acts of interpretation. Language deficiency alone does not prohibit interpretation; in some contexts the words "I don't understand" constitute antisocial behavior (or can mean "I don't want to understand"). Behaviors can be understood without words; for instance, we can interpret the behaviors of pets without language. This is not to say that nonlinguistic interpretation is ideal; it is just to say that interpretation is a phenomenon that goes beyond linguistic expression. Vital to the act of interpretation is the simultaneous formation of community, which fixes language just as language affirms community.

The subtleties of the culture manifest themselves in the host of details that are involved in learning a language: the pitch, intonations, accents, and use that must be dismantled and reorganized to master new linguistic techniques. Edward Sapir wrote that "embedded in languages are qualities that reflect the temperament or genius of a certain race" and that language is the "intuitive science of experience."[44] In other words, language records and organizes experience in a systematic way so that it can be delivered in an efficient way. Furthermore, it captures temperament because it is the material of personalities.

Experience and personality are both continually in flux; thus, so is language. Since language is a portable commodity, it does not, Sapir says, "indefinitely set the seal on a common culture when the geographical, political, and economic determinants of the culture are no longer the same throughout its area."[45] When any of these factors change, particularly geography, "drift" may occur (the term is Sapir's): "The drift of a language is constituted by the unconscious selection on the part of its speakers of those individual variations that are cumulative in some special direction."[46] Thus, the contortion or mutation of language directly reflects a contortion or mutation of experience.

Immigrants know that translators between communities are ambassadors of ideologies and intimacy. One glance at the development of communities and their tendency to migrate to their closest equivalent reveals this: the community ties between Europe and America are much closer than America's bond with any Asian country. *Immigrant writers want readership.* They do not rebuke efforts of interpretation. They dare readers to trust a sure translation. Minorities want interpretation. The September 11 crisis left Cantonese populations in New York City bereft of community outside Chinatown; crisis centers asked for *translators.* "Translation" is a buzzword to energize interpretation in areas *beyond* language, to set community etiquette in motion. The resistance of the mainstream population to interpreting this culture and the preference for marginalizing it isolate this community from the greater New York community. Furthermore, becoming part of the mainstream community can mean negating one's own capacity or desire to serve as an interpreter between communities. Often, Chinatown success stories do not return to Chinatown to live but will move to suburban areas;[47] thus, interpretation gets cut off between communities before potential ambassadors can facilitate intercommunity exchange. The problem of interpretation and translation has become a subject for writers; Jhumpa Lahiri's *Interpreter of Maladies* and Chang-rae Lee's *Native Speaker* and *A Gesture Life* indicate by their titles that language, interpretation, and translation are the issues of the moment because they express the emergence of community that is happening now.

Immigrant writers thus experience a linguistic exile from their original language, and in appropriating English they can engage in a reconstitution of identity that absorbs the mainstream conceptions of their marginalized culture. For a writer to resist succumbing to this pathology of self-hatred, the appropriation of English must be a very self-conscious activity; learning English is not simply learning words but conceptualizing the political force of the words in relation to one's own culture. Thus, immigrant writers such as Nabokov, Kingston, and Díaz are extraordinarily aware of the role that English plays in their lives and of their positions with respect to English.

Postcolonial writers also exhibit highly self-conscious relationships to English because of its status in their cultures. Their identity problems may be similar to those of immigrant populations in that they must resist an appropriation of certain psychic material that can get transferred in the learning of English.

In *Postcolonial Transformations,* Bill Ashcroft interrogates the question of whether people who are learning English as a second language will necessarily be converted to English-speaking culture.[48] He suggests that the distinction between *langue* and *parole* opens us to the idea of transformative conversations between learner and native speaker.[49] We can conceive of these conversations as transactions of knowledge (even though they may be subliminal transactions) that increase the possibility of interpretability and translatability simply by being an occurrence of community impact. English can be appropriated by a learner without the accompanied acceptance of the rules of English-speaking culture. Nevertheless, postcolonials must contend with tension in their homeland surrounding the use of English, while immigrants may feel the economic necessity of learning English against an aesthetic preference for their first language. Furthermore, weird-English writers vary in background, race, and agenda. But they share a repeated interest in defining and theorizing about English, because they have a kind of outsider status that gives them some expertise as people who can see English as "art," since they can communicate efficaciously in other languages.

Mon Homme Derek

I think the ultimate question to a writer is: "What language do you think in?" I think in English; I do not think in French Creole. I imagine if I had a dream, the conversation that I would dream in would be in English, unless the dream was particularly about a certain thing. So if I think in English, my instinct is to write in English because that is the language of my thoughts.

—DEREK WALCOTT

Derek Walcott is often called a postcolonial writer, but the breadth of his work defies clean categorization. Walcott is versatile, multi-voiced, and multi-toned. Most significantly, he is free. Walcott's writing provides illustration of the degrees of weirdness one could have in English, and he mixes words in his poetic language with the instinct of a weird-English writer. A reading of his poetry reveals a consistent vacillation between employing English, English patois, and French patois. An overview of his poetic trajectory identifies the varying degrees of commitment a weird-English writer can have to weirding English.

Walcott is also conscious of the postcolonial and immigrant dilemma and of the linguistic conflicts that become political. In the poem "A Far Cry from Africa," he describes the quelling of a Mau Mau uprising by British colonials, and does so with haunting internal pain. Witnessing the mass slaughter of people, he realizes he is between two cultures, unable to escape the paralysis of being unable to take sides. In the last stanza of "A Far Cry from Africa," he writes:

> I who have cursed
> The drunken officer of British rule, how choose
> Between this Africa and the English tongue I love?
> Betray them both, or give back what they give?
> How can I face such slaughter and be cool?
> How can I turn from Africa and live?[50]

The last line can be read in two ways. The first sense is rhetorical: it is an emotional cry. The second sense is methodological: Walcott asks for a recipe on how to continue with the burden of history. But in any case, Walcott's own existence is obliterated; there is no place he can go if he refuses attachment to British or African history.

Whereas Walcott unravels internal emotional conflict in the poem quoted above, he stages linguistic conflicts in "Sainte Lucie," "Parang," and "Blues." "Sainte Lucie" is fertile with French and French patois amid English: "Pomme arac, / otaheite apple, / pomme cythère, / pomme granate, / moubain, / z'ananas, / the pineapple's / Aztec helmet, / pomme, / I have forgotten / what pomme for / the Irish potato, / cerise, / the cherry, / z'aman / sea-almonds / by the crisp / sea-bursts, / au bord de la 'ouvière. / Come back to me, / my language." Walcott's doubling of English and French—as if each object demands a different language from him—is illustrated line by line, as he switches from French to English and back again. By the end of the poem, French has returned to him, and he writes the fourth section in more complex and fluid French, transcribing a Creole song he remembers from the past.

In "Parang" his cultural confusion manifests itself linguistically as switch-hitting between proper English and dialect. The title refers to a fast and formal musical dance form in Trinidad, and the poem clearly has a swaying beat to it. The beat peters out by the end of the poem, where the fiddler appears almost to leave the atmosphere of Trinidad and arrive at a place of reflection. At the opening of the poem, the fiddler recalls the immediate and physical dance floor, where he remembers bawling "in a red-eyed rage" and singing about "the wax and the wane of the moon / Since Adam catch body-fever." But later he leaves the visceral for the ethereal: the poem finishes with the fiddler pondering "the breast of the naked moon." Notably, "Parang" opens with heavy dialect, but the dialect dissipates and more recognizably orthodox poetic wording accumulates as the poem proceeds. The poem begins, "Man, I suck me tooth when I hear / How dem croptime fiddlers lie, / And de-wailing, kiss-me-arse flutes / That bring water to me eye!" But it ends with dreamy Yeatsian lines written in almost completely standard English: "Young men does bring love to disgrace / With remorseful, regretful words, / When flesh upon flesh was the tune / Since the first cloud raise up to disclose / The breast of the naked moon." Such lines illustrate the versatility, or maybe the ambiguity, of Walcott. He can harness the vernacular but also move outside it. He can speak in vernacular but not completely commit to it.

The poem "Blues" appropriates the rappable beats of the street, showing the departure of Walcott from the swing of Trinidadian parang. "A summer festival. Or some / saint's. I wasn't too far from / home, but not too bright / for a nigger, and not too dark." The rigorous scheme of enjambment, in combination with the three-stress meter, keeps the rhythms alive and vital. The poem describes a fight in the West Village of Manhattan; the participants aren't hurt, just badly bruised: "You know they wouldn't kill / you. Just playing rough, / like young America will. / Still, it taught me something / about love. If it's so tough, / forget it." The conclusion is abrupt and hard like the rest of the poem. Repeated beatings, even if you survive them, will break you. So forget it.

Walcott writes in dialect but he doesn't live there. His obsession with Odysseus is well documented in his poetry, and his linguistic travels are Odyssean in their range, daring, and emotional cost. In "Sea Grapes," he writes, in iambic pentameter (after composing the rest of the poem in free verse): "The classics can console. But not enough." Eventually he becomes more optimistic about literature's ability to feed an individual. In his later poetry, particularly in "Upstate," Walcott reveals what twenty years in a new country contributes to the capacity to reposition oneself to a language: "I must put the cold small pebbles from the spring / upon my tongue to learn her language, / to talk like birch or aspen confidently." He can, at this point, embody his new home and learn its language. These lines align linguistic assimilation with geographic commitment, with an ability to speak for, consume, and inhale the atmosphere of the land one lives on.

Possible Translations

> Since subjects competent in several languages tend to speak only in one language, even where the latter is dismembering itself, and because it can only promise and promise itself by threatening to dismember itself, a language can only speak itself of itself.
>
> —JACQUES DERRIDA, *Monolingualism of the Other* (1998)

When weird-English writers transgress the world of the first language by becoming emotionally oriented toward a new linguistic world, their relationship to language becomes epistemological, not simply pragmatic. They can regard language as part of a corpus of accumulated knowledge rather than as simply a necessary practice to retain community ties. When they discover that their language was never "theirs" to begin with, they are awakened to the arbitrariness of identity and of their given language, which they called their "mother" tongue. Sometimes the failure to overcome their attachment to their past language can result in voicelessness. Maxine Hong Kingston describes herself as "invisible" and focuses on the problem of Asian Americans losing their voice—becoming mute—instead of adopting the language of the new culture. This paralysis disables the weird-English writer, preventing him or her from assimilating, even surviving in, a new culture. The authors in this book, by their very authorship, have succeeded in relinquishing a sense of possession over a particular language.

Jacques Derrida, in *Monolingualism of the Other,* emphasizes the "prosthesis of origin." Our native language is, he stresses, accidental. One's native language is always "other" because language is always "other." Derrida's book separates certain features of language from the idea of property: "When I said that the only language I speak is not mine, I did not say it was foreign to me. There is a difference. It is not entirely the same thing."[51] Derrida separates the idea of foreignness from the idea of belonging or citizenship, thereby configuring language as neutral territory which becomes contested property only when a population is invested in such an effort. "Because the master does not possess exclusively, and naturally, what he calls his language, because, whatever he wants or does, he cannot maintain any relations of property or identity that are natural, national, congenital, or ontological, with it, because he can give substance to and articulate [*dire*] this appropriation only in the course of an unnatural process of politico-phantasmatic constructions, because language is not his natural possession, he can, thanks to that very fact, pretend historically, through the rape of a cultural usurpation, which means always essentially colonial, to appropriate it in order to impose it as 'his own.'"[52] Several moves are made in this passage, which echoes the kind of thinking in Harold Bloom's *The Anxiety of Influence* about the chain of appropriation and reappropriation that occurs in poetic history. However, this kind of reasoning is subliminal to the passage—which maps out the appropriation of language not in a literary way but in a political way. Languages are bartered politically—they are passed around without any substantive embodiment once they are "detached" from their culture. Despite this vulnerable position, language can protect itself because of its limitations: "One cannot speak of a language except in that language. Even if to place it outside itself. Far from sealing off anything, this solipsism conditions the address to the other, it gives its word, or rather the possibility of giving its word, it gives the given word in the ordeal a threatening and threatened promise: monolingualism and tautology, the absolute impossibility of metalanguage."[53] It is through metalanguage that translation and inclusion of imaginary communities is possible. Thus, the idea of a solipsistic, private language is not only ontologically impossible but the negation of linguistic activity. This larger argument is undergirded by smaller but no less important claims about linguistic possession. Derrida wants to ensure that the term "foreign" is not immediately associated with the idea of "not-mine," and furthermore that "intimate" does not imply "mine." In Derrida's terms, any claims of "my" language are misleading; his constant refrain is "I have but one language—yet that language is not mine." His claim seems natural; after all, one cannot make possessive claims about something that does not *naturally* occur as property and does not logically exist as a privately owned thing. Still, Derrida says that we can master language, although he speaks of always surrendering to language.[54] In other words, we have a relationship with language that mirrors our bonds with human beings. Nabokov and Rushdie often invoke language as a muse, a lover, or a phenomenon with a distinct otherness with which an individual *cultivates* a relationship. For example, Nabokov speaks longingly of Russian as if it were an ex-lover: "For more than a year I have had no relation with my Russian muse."[55] This relationship is like any other: it is characterized by feelings of possessiveness, occasional surrender, compromise, and sentimentality. The weird-English writer, having experienced a long-distance relationship with home, is already familiar with all of these feelings. Such writers know how to negotiate with language as a consolation for exile, which inflicts "a double movement in its victims, toward simultaneous atomization and homogenization and thus a wearing down of the potential for agency."[56] This double movement can manifest itself in the language use of exile-outlaw weird-English writers, who often express a lack of command over their expression, as if language were an unruly other—albeit an intimate significant other. This feeling of a lack of agency, of self and language possession, is juxtaposed with an acute ability to mimic and to invent sounds.

Resurgences of agency manifest themselves in the composition of new languages and dialects. Rushdie has also said that he invents dialects to keep the relationship alive (as we will see more fully in Chapter 5). Arundhati Roy has a relationship of *savoir faire* with language: "I don't sweat the language," she says. In her novel *The God of Small Things,* she cultivates intimacy with language: she specializes in forming secret words, children's pidgin, and the language of lovers: "Littleangels were beach-colored and wore bell-bottoms. Littledemons were mudbrown in Airport-Fairy frocks with forehead bumps that might turn into horns. With Fountains in Love-in-Tokyos. And backwards-reading habits."[57] For Roy, the issue between the big (the powerful) and the small (the vulnerable) is a repeated theme, and she uses different voices to communicate this, as we will see in Chapter 3.

Derrida elaborates on the idea that language is never constant but always changing to adjust to new uses and expressive needs. "We only ever have one language" that is "not at one with itself."[58] Within this "one language" reside a plurality of voices, and perhaps even vocabularies. For Derrida, this means that "no such thing as *a* language" exists.[59] Language is always plural, or descended from plurality; whatever language we speak is always an eclectic creature, rather than a set of rigid discourses. For example, polylinguals don't have a one-to-many relationship with different languages; they have a one-to-one relationship with the *entity* language, which may be a composite of many languages. "For the classical linguist, of course, each language is a system whose unity is always reconstituted. But this unity is not comparable to any other. It is open to the most radical grafting, open to deformations, transformations, expropriation, to a certain a-nomi and de-regulation. So much so that the gesture—here, once again, I am calling it writing [*écriture*], even though it can remain purely oral, vocal, and musical: rhythmic or prosodic—that seeks to affect monolanguage, the one that one has without having it, is always multiple."[60] For the weird-English writer who begins to know a new culture along with the old, the resulting language will be a conflicted language, a language that defies being counted, or expressed as the sum of two or more languages. Instead, it is a hybrid that seeks to emulate the structure of speaker and monolanguage. *It is a hybrid seeking a monogamous relationship with the speaker.* This phenomenon describes the writer who is caught between languages. For example, Vladimir Nabokov experienced a conflict of interest when he tried to abandon his Russian for English. He wanted to quell the urge to hybridize his language so that he could develop perfect English—he couldn't be faithful to more than one linguistic muse. He contrasts with Rushdie, who celebrates linguistic polyphony and polygamy. One might go so far as to say that Rushdie enjoys an orgy of languages, but he does so at the price of instability.

The developing language appropriates new vocabularies but retains its own singularity; it acquires linguistic debris and pieces of old consciousness. Hybrid languages are thus flecked with borrowed words and phrases, resulting from play with more than one language. Rushdie seems to enjoy this especially. In *The Ground beneath Her Feet*, he writes what he calls "polyglot trash talk": "'Chinese khana big mood hai' (translation: I want a plate of noodles) or 'Apun J. R. R. Tolkien's Angootiyan-ka-Seth ko too-much admire karta chhé' (translation: I like J. R. R. Tolkien)."[61]

Language is more than the words that are used to create meaning.

A Limitless Language

> Because there is no natural property of language, language gives rise only to appropriative madness, to jealousy without appropriation. Language speaks this jealousy; it is nothing but jealousy unleashed. It takes its revenge at the heart of the law. The law that, moreover, language itself is, apart from also being mad. Mad about itself. Raving mad.
>
> —JACQUES DERRIDA, *Monolingualism of the Other* (1998)

Implicit in the use of language is the search for an arena in which it is meaningful. Using language is a means of searching for a community, and when the community is intangible or inaccessible, or the immediate communities dissatisfy, language can become a tool to find a new one.[62] Eva Hoffman expresses her disorientation at discovering a new set of signs and signifiers: "The words I learn now don't stand for things the way they did in my native language."[63] Wittgenstein showed that we cannot discern meaning without discovering use; so if we look at the communities that form through language, we see a meaning and an intention.

We discover use when we see how different cultures emphasize different vocabulary to express their ordering of priorities or community "goods." For instance, cultures whose systems of justice are based on shame emphasize words relating to pride and shame more than cultures whose systems of justice are based on law. Alasdair MacIntyre discusses this phenomenon in *After Virtue,* exploring the way in which the justice system in ancient Greece revolved around shame. And we can imagine how one could fix shame as a reference point from which to analyze the gravity of certain crimes. For instance, in ancient China, "loss of face" could justify (in certain Chinese courts) acts of revenge. Presumably this was also true in India; Rushdie, in his novel *Shame,* tells of a father who kills his daughter because she dishonors the family by dating a white boy. The language of justification for such acts—"shame," "reputation," "honor"—reveals the inseparability of language and culture within societies.

Thus, language can expose the moral sense of a community. Some philosophers believe it also affects the moral sense of individuals. "Human beings," wrote Iris Murdoch, "are obscure to each other without language and in certain respects which are particularly relevant to morality."[64] Humans can become mutual objects of attention or have common objects of attention, through the elaboration of a common vocabulary. "Attention is a kind of seeing, and the result is that we develop language in the context of looking: the metaphor of vision again."[65] It is important to note Murdoch's link between the event of perception and the invention, or inventive use, of vocabulary. Nabokov realized that language could shape moral sense, but he did so after surrendering to the rules of agreement: not until 1946 did he report that he had begun to feel "acclimated" to English.[66]

The phenomenon that Wittgenstein describes as permeating life and language with rules is agreement. Whereas in logic the rules are defined and necessary, disputes about language often occur, and in section 240 of *Philosophical Investigations* he says: "Disputes do not break out (among mathematicians, say) over the question whether a rule has been obeyed or not. People don't come to blows over it, for example. That is part of the framework on which the working of our language is based (for example, in giving descriptions)." In the following section he reframes the same assertion: "'So you are saying that human agreement decides what is true and what is false?'—'It is what human beings *say* that is true and false, and they agree in the *language* they use. That is not agreement in opinions but in form of life.'" In practice, this means that meaning between people is not derived from linguistic rules. We can imagine sentences that, according to certain principles, seem like nonsense but in fact have meaning. Martin Gustafsson writes, for example, that the sentence "Caesar is a prime number" can be interpreted in ways which render it nonsensical, but also in ways which imbue it with meaning. It depends on the interpreter and the interpreter's frame of reference. If "Caesar" can mean anything from a Caesar salad to a Roman emperor, it is flexible enough as a linguistic entity to create a variety of meanings. One of my philosophy classmates once imagined a situation where "Caesar" was the name of a very attractive prospective date, in which case "Whoa, Caesar is a *prime* number!" is a recognizable expression of approval.

This view contrasts with that of Augustine, who believed there was something inexorable about language rules, something more fundamentally operative to language rules than language itself. Following Augustine, Wittgenstein remarks: "If language is to be a means of communication there must be agreement not only in definitions but also (queer as this may sound) in judgments. This seems to abolish logic, but does not do so."[67] In other words, although in logic or mathematics we might judge a result to be true or false based upon a rule, we cannot apply the same concept of a rule to language, which we have already asserted to have the phenomenon of agreement as its rule.

This being the case, humans cannot rely on a fixed framework of language to understand its use. In section 32 of *Philosophical Investigations*, Wittgenstein says: "Someone coming into a strange country will sometimes learn the language of the inhabitants from ostensive definitions that they give him; and he will often have to guess the meaning of these definitions; and will guess sometimes right, sometimes wrong." Wittgenstein continues to challenge the idea that we have a grasp of language before we use it. Language is not the physical output of mental thoughts we already have; it is a physical activity that we train ourselves to do, in order to survive. We simply *have language*.

With every transplantation to a new community, immigrant writers, removed from their community, must gain—in acquiring a new language—a new comprehension of what counts as agreement. But if their first language was not English—which is the case for every author discussed in this book—then they will be following more than one form of life, and thus more than one phenomenon of agreement. Their activity within a new community may be completely cut off from their old community; but it is more likely that they will merely gain distance from their first tongue in order to learn the second (to retrain) and then they will be able to combine or play with both languages. This is manifested, for example, in Nabokov's use of Russian meter in sections of *Pale Fire*, in Rushdie's mimicry of Indian run-on words in *The Moor's Last Sigh* ("Cashondeliveri"), in Kingston's Chinese-accented English in *China Men*, in Díaz's mix of Spanish and English in *Drown*, and in Roy's backward writing. There can be an irreverence to this playing with languages, to this multivalence. "All immigrants and exiles," says Eva Hoffman, "know the peculiar restlessness of an imagination that can never again have faith in its own absoluteness." The mind is constantly searching, never able to "take any set of meanings as final."[68]

Finally, polylingual writers may be uncertain about which language is best for their own self-expression. Although Rushdie is conversant and practically fluent in several languages, some writers, like Nabokov, acquired English through hard work and ingenuity (he claimed that eavesdropping helped him to study accents while he was writing *Lolita*). Although Nabokov wrote English so well that one would have difficulty discerning his foreignness, subtle aspects of his tone and linguistic distance—and characterization—are foreign; and once the reader knows that he was not a native speaker of English, this knowledge illuminates these subtleties. For writers in a new language, the abode may be not a home but a temporary spot—a "place" of sorts, but not a home. This kind of relationship to language might describe Nabokov's first brush with English, although later he seemed to claim America—and with it, American English—as his home.

Still, a mixture of feelings remains in weird English. Memories may interrupt transition to a new culture. But language is an eclectic inventory of such experience. Weird-English authors show the depth and inexorability of linguistic commitments and forms of life. They are unable to fully surrender any of the worlds of their languages, but juggle them in their struggle to create meaning.

Impossible Autobiographies

> People without roots are aware of them, like an amputated limb.
>
> —EVA HOFFMAN, *Lost in Translation* (1990)

Since weird-English writers are building their worlds from words, it is understandable that they credit language with having spatial properties. According to Elizabeth Klosty Beaujour, bilingual—and presumably polylingual—writers "feel that their languages have volume, that they take up space, and that there is a physical distance in their heads between the languages that they master. . . . Bilingual writers who feel that they are thus inhabited by 'linguistic space' tend to use geographical and geological imagery to express their sense of the physical distance between the languages inside their heads."[69] Some of them will call languages "worlds" or "lands" or even "layers," according to Beaujour. Writers who translate their own work may imagine a vertical movement through the layers. Beaujour cites François Cheng, who discusses his apprenticeship as a translator of poetry from Western languages into Chinese and vice versa; she says he has been able to "establish a system of subterranean mental canals that free him from the imprisoning mirrors of the languages, mirrors that impeded his work."[70] For polyglot writers, this sense of having linguistic space spurs them to recreate it materially, to record their imaginary space in the physical realm.

For weird-English writers, any home they have is an imaginary one. They use their verbal art to keep their imaginary community alive, and often language itself serves as insulation from insecurities. The urge to retain the images of their community becomes more pressing as their images of home become enfeebled. Denied a physical or geographic home, the weird-English writer reconfigured as exile creates, according to Svetlana Boym, "a portable home away from home, which an émigré ferociously guards [and which] preserves an imprint of his or her cultural motherland." She continues: "The exiles might be bilingual, but rarely can they get rid of an accent. A few misplaced prepositions, a few missing articles, definite or indefinite, betray the syntax of the mother tongue." While in the traditional biography of the imagined community of a nation exiles are the ones who "lost their souls," in the postmodern story exiles embody the dream of "mad polyphony, for which every language is a foreign one."[71] This polyphony results in hybrid writing. For weird-English writers striving to keep their home and culture alive, one of the most capacious resources is writing. This section has two purposes: to elaborate the notion that language may become material geography or space for polylingual writers, spatial worlds which they navigate; and to show that because the writer's notion of realism is larger than the physically immediate, his or her writing is a departure from autobiography and is not constituted by it. Nabokov also invokes the image of a house with reference to language, stating that learning English was "like moving from one darkened house to another on a starless night during a strike of candlemakers and torchbearers."[72]

Trinh T. Minh-ha writes that this constant movement makes a patchwork autobiography—generally considered the province of such writers—impossible:

It is often said that writers of color, including anglophone and francophone Third World writers of the diaspora, are condemned to write only autobiographical works. Living in a double exile—far from their native land and far from their mother tongue—they are thought to write by memory and to depend to a large extent on hearsay. Directing their look toward a long bygone reality, they supposedly excel in reanimating the ashes of childhood and of the country of origin. The autobiography can thus be said to be an abode in which the writers mentioned necessarily take refuge. But to preserve this abode, they would have to open it up and pass it on. For not every detail of their individual lives bears recounting in such an "autobiography," and what they chose to recount no longer belongs to them as individuals.[73]

Writers who construct narratives of displacement cannot, according to Minh-ha, write autobiographies, because the details of their displacement are not theirs to begin with, and the material of the autobiography is drawn from a community imagination rather than an individual one. Just as Rushdie admits to constructing "errata" in *Midnight's Children* to convey the way in which memory works and to "individualize" the historicizing of Saleem, so other writers who create a narrative from a communal pool of facts must be described as rewriting a history rather than constructing an autobiography. The content of the imagination is just as real as the surrounding physical environment. Maxine Hong Kingston has said: "What I feel I've done is push autobiography into a larger form; realism has to include the life of the imagination. I've also taken fiction and pushed it into a more truthful form than it has ever been before. . . . I don't mind having my work called 'autobiography.' There's been a lot of critics who've tried to lambaste autobiography as a lesser form, that it's something that amateurs write. But when I write biography,

I'm writing about people who have amazing lives of the imagination. And so if I am to write their lives truly, then I have to use techniques of fiction in order to write a true life."[74]

Kingston's way of bridging past and present is to create voices out of the silence, as well as to create an English-speaking voice to translate untold experiences by immigrants. She does not claim to be a transcriber, however; she describes herself as occupying a space between strict biographer and fiction writer: "Our usual idea of biographies is of time-lines, of dates and chronological events. I am certainly more imaginative than that; I play with words and form."[75] Kingston's work has provoked several critiques that focus on "Asian American" as a historically developed concept. This further emphasizes the significance of time in comprehending the dilemma of the immigrant writer, specifically the Chinese American writer. For Kingston and other writers, home—the domain in which they are most comfortable—is a complicated mixture of physical reality and memory.

Because of these common features, a biographical account of each author is required, so that we have the empirical matter for analyzing their works. Sometimes the autobiographical component is quite direct; sometimes it is extremely subtle. For example, in Rushdie's novel *The Ground beneath Her Feet,* the date on the first page is that of his exile; furthermore, in this novel and in *The Moor's Last Sigh,* the protagonist bears an uncanny resemblance to the author. *The Woman Warrior* presents itself as autobiography, but Kingston asserted later in interviews that fiction and (her) reality often merge in the book.[76] Their sense of outsideness seems to compel, or catalyze, some autobiographical form of release that becomes something else—that needs to become something else in order to be narrative.

Susan Suleiman provides the example of Holocaust writers

who wrote in a language other than their native tongues and conveyed, despite their perfect command of English and correctness of grammar, a certain distance from their textual language with "subtle marks of foreignness."[77] She says that there is a difference between "works that were written 'at home,' in the native language, addressed to an implied native audience, and works that were from the start and in their very composition split off from the writer's first language or public. Among the latter, the most 'homeless' are memoirs written not only far from home, but in a foreign tongue (one experienced as foreign); they are 'in translation' from the start, with no original."[78]

Once authors discover the freedom of homelessness, they may expand linguistic territory as a nomad might expand geographic territory. The temptation to expand language is irresistible. Trinh T. Minh-ha says: "Writers who, in writing, open to research the space of language rather than reduce language to a mere instrument in the service of reason or feelings, are bound like the migrant to wander. . . . They disturb the classical economy of language and representation, and can never be content with any stability of presence."[79] Thus, weird-English writers may derive special comfort in destabilizing linguistic boundaries, since they have already broken geographic ones. The weird-English writer, refashioning language, is already outside the community. "For a number of writers in exile," Minh-ha writes, "the true home is to be found not in houses, but in writing. . . . Exile, despite its profound sadness, can be worked through as an experience of crossing boundaries and charting new ground in defiance of newly authorized or old canonical enclosures."[80] By virtue of having struggled with the status of exile, they are alive to the ways in which language can transgress the borders of agreement subservient to a community. For them, knowledge of language as "other" can lead to a disengagement from the origin, a realization that a sense of "favorite" can be arbitrary, or tied to the familiar. But this is not because one language is more "mine" than another language.

Imaginative Acts Are Painful and Neurotic

> In dreams our recently dead
> still survives,
> he even enjoys good health
> and recovered youth.
> Reality displays
> his dead body.
> Reality retreats not an inch.
>
> —WISLAWA SZYMBORSKA, "Reality," from *People on a Bridge,*
> trans. Adam Czerniawski (1986)

Immigrant and postcolonial writers have to be particularly determined about their efforts to preserve their imagined homelands because such worlds are intangible (their discourse not being dominant) and feeble, compared to the robust environments that can overwhelm them. Such writers often invest more passion in the process of imagining than someone whose home is physically immediate. (Imagine that you have to imagine what you consider home for the rest of your life.) For these writers, getting the environment "right" is crucial to reducing anxiety. Getting the details right is just as important for comfort in an imagined home as it is in a home that is physically immediate. But they are distanced from any immediate physical reassurance that the details are right—that the tables and chairs are properly matched, that the sofa is soft, that the curtains hang just so.

Fecund and detail-oriented, imagination is primed for artistic creation. Nabokov emphasized details so greatly in his university classes that his exams became notorious for their questions, which were chiefly directed to the meticulous reader. He was famous among his university students for emphasizing particulars over thematic topics: "In my academic days I endeavored to provide students of literature with exact information about details, about such combinations of details as yield the sensual spark without which a book is dead."[81] This addiction spilled over into Nabokov's personal life. As a lepidopterist, he obsessed over the fine points of butterfly coloring and wing shape. He confessed that literature and lepidoptery quelled his anxiety because within these fields one could concentrate on detail for detail's sake: "I discovered in nature the nonutilitarian delights that I sought in art. Both were a form of magic, both were a game of intricate enchantment and deception. . . . Few things indeed have I known in the way of emotion or appetite, ambition or achievement, that could surpass in richness and strength the excitement of entomological exploration. And the highest enjoyment of timelessness—in a landscape selected at random—is when I stand among rare butterflies and their food plants."[82] Although Nabokov calls the details of art "nonutilitarian," he acknowledged that there is an ordered structure in which those details are presented. He adhered to a standard of completeness and precision in his aesthetic productions, researching every subject he wrote about with endless perfectionism. "Query: can anyone draw something he knows nothing about? Does there not exist a high ridge where the mountainside of 'scientific' knowledge joins the opposite slope of 'artistic' imagination?"[83] Nabokov wrote with knowledge of both the scientific and the artistic. His work on butterflies revealed attentiveness to proportional accuracy and carefully recorded changes he observed in his studies of butterflies. His mercilessness toward a particular author exposes his dislike of imprecision: "The butterflies are certainly inept. The exaggerated crenulation of hindwing edges, due to a naive artist's doing his best, . . . is typical of the poorest entomological figures of earlier centuries."[84] Nabokov showed how descriptions of natural phenomena could be brought to life in all their details: "There comes for every caterpillar a difficult moment when he begins to feel pervaded by an odd sense of discomfort. It is a tight feeling—here about the neck and elsewhere, and then an unbearable itch. . . . He hangs himself by the tip of his tail or last legs, from the silk patch, so as to dangle head downwards in the position of an inverted question mark, and there is a *question*—how to get rid now of his skin. One wriggle, another wriggle—and zip the skin bursts down the back, and he gradually gets out of it working with shoulders and hips like a person getting out of a sausage dress."[85] Nabokov was aware of the problem of making "written" time match "experiential" time. In a passage describing the transition from pupa to butterfly, he confesses that his play-by-play description might take a few minutes to read, though the full transformation of pupa to butterfly in human time requires days. But he escapes the problem of remaining true to "human" time by locating the narrative sensibility inside the pupa. From this intriguing temporal perspective, Nabokov could bring to life a striking natural phenomenon and draw in the reader without losing credibility.

As if identifying with the victorious imago,[86] Nabokov captures the tone of triumph in the evolution of caterpillar to butterfly. He finishes: "It is really at last a glorified molt" and the "butterfly creeps out." Though "she is very damp and bedraggled, . . . those limp implements of hers that she has disengaged gradually dry, distend, the veins branch and harden—and in twenty minutes or so she is ready to fly."[87] Nabokov often imported the language he used to describe butterflies into his novels: Lolita, too, is described as "bedraggled" and "limp."[88] When Nabokov worked at the Museum of Comparative Zoology at Harvard, his wife, Véra, hoped that the butterfly work would lead to a renewed period of writing for her husband. Nabokov worded this less benignly: he felt "like a drunkard who in his moments of lucidity realizes that he is missing all sorts of wonderful opportunities."[89] But Nabokov admitted that he identified with the acts of transformation that created butterflies. He believed that he had to undergo, like the pupa, a waiting period in which he could develop his inner strength before emerging with perfect English.

Nabokov transposes his state of exile onto that of a pupa—an example of the sustained mental imaging derived from tenacious powers of imagination. Such powers are honed after extensive practice. Weird-English writers are practitioners of sustained imaginative acts—in particular, those which require a capacity for role-play (placing oneself within society, even within a cocoon) or mimesis. These skills help with artistic endeavors, especially writing. Elaine Scarry discusses how writing, unlike other arts, is specifically mimetic: "Each of the arts incites us to the practice of all three acts: immediate perception, delayed perception, and mimetic perception. But painting, sculpture, music, film and theater are weighted toward the first, or (perhaps more accurately) they bring about the second and third by means of their elaborate commitments to the first; whereas the verbal arts take place almost exclusively in the third."[90] Scarry details how writing is not only a mimesis of perception; it actually mimics "the structure of production that gave rise to the perception, that is, the material conditions that made it look, sound, or feel the way it did."[91] Mimicry is the reproduction of past experience, so it is an exercise of memory as well as of imagination.

Writing is the material equivalent of this mental reproduction (or series of mental reproductions). Wittgenstein, another polyglot, also notes the interdependence of the visual and the verbal. In order to enhance our reading, he says, we have to visualize. There is a sense in which we have to imagine in order to read correctly, or visualize *while we read:* "If you are reading something aloud and want to read *well,* you accompany the words with vivid images. At least it is *often* like that. But sometimes what matters is the punctuation, i.e. your precise intonation and the duration of your pauses."[92] In fact, all of the writers discussed here are expressive about being conscious of their thought processes as full of images. Their visual powers are increased in order to compensate for the instability of the changing visual landscape; their verbal exercises reflect the compensatory workings of their imaginations. Their language is saturated with the sensory residue that the concrete worlds can't hold steady, or simply don't include. For these writers, language as a phenomenon is an experience of *all* the senses, not just one at a time. Nabokov confirms this position: "I don't think in any language. I think in images. I don't believe that people think in languages. They don't move their lips when they think. It is only a certain type of illiterate person who moves his lips as he reads or ruminates. No, I think in images, and now and then a Russian phrase or an English phrase will form with the foam of the brainwave, but that's about all."[93] Nabokov's assertions are intuitive: we often think faster in images than in words (think of the old adage about a picture equaling a thousand words), and writing is derived from acts of image transmission: this is more obvious in Asian languages than European ones. For example, the character for "door" in Chinese evokes the shape of a door; the character for "mountain" mimics the silhouette of a mountain (three lines connected by a common line across the bottom, with the middle line reaching the highest point); and the character for "mouth" is quite illuminating—it is an open square. Thus, writing is undoubtedly related to image making and makes use of the human ability to process images, as Steven Pinker notes in *The Language Instinct* (2000). For example, Kingston asserts that her writing is generated by images:

> I am very visual. The visions, the images, come first. I find the words for them afterwards. I'm not an ear writer, the way I think James Joyce is a sound writer. But there's a narrative impulse in me, too. *China Men* started out, for example, when I kept seeing an image of a white triangle, I didn't know what to do with it. But I learned that it was because of something my father kept mentioning when he talked about stowing away on a ship from Cuba to come to New York. He was in a crate. He talked about looking through cracks when he was hiding, and he could see this triangle of white trouser legs.[94]

Arundhati Roy adds to the chorus, claiming that the inspiration for *The God of Small Things* was not an idea or a character but an image—"the image of this sky blue Plymouth stuck at the railroad crossing with the twins inside and this Marxist procession raging around it."[95]

All of the writers, in fact, clearly and definitively—even vehemently—say that images motivate their writing, and even state that they are building structures in their books. Roy, in *The God of Small Things,* manipulates English letters to form designs, to write backward, to separate words. This is such a frequent practice that I devote a large part of Chapter 3 to the way she structures words, sentences, and paragraphs. She attributes her architect's background to her affinity for design: "I would start somewhere and I'd color in a bit and then I would deeply stretch back and then stretch forward. It was like designing an intricately balanced structure, and when it was finished it was finished." Díaz also speaks about how "the architecture of his collection was important to him."[96] Rushdie describes *Midnight's Children* as being inside-out: "The shape the book gradually adopted was the shape of the attempt to impose shape on what seemed formless, which is why the book sort of has the meat on the inside and the skeleton on the outside, because the skeleton was gradually imposed on the book."[97]

Their interest lies in the recreation of a world, and they want to synthesize the verbal and visual in the act of reproduction. In contrast, other writers dismantle the act of perception into each of the five senses. They transcribe each of the five sensory processes separately. For example, James Joyce showed how sound could create its own separate world: "ineluctable modality of the audible . . . Crush, crack, crick, crick."[98] His ability to divide sensory worlds caused other writers to question how they presented the senses in narrative. Should writers blend the auditory, visual, and tactile in order to recreate reality, or should they present each as a separate modality? In Joyce's case, the focus was on individual senses and their "modalities." But weird-English writers yearn to synthesize. Kingston recalls a period in Chinese history when a poet could "write and sing and paint" his poem. "See how integrated that is? All those parts of your body are connected. You're not fragmented. Even now, the poets still do calligraphy."[99]

In their new environments, immigrant writers cope with the lack of certain amenities once accessible to them. But these absences leave them with physical spaces that demand acts of imagination and recreation. For them, writing is the material analogy of their acts of recreation in an environment which they find empty, and these acts mirror the process of writing. As Elaine Scarry points out,

> Verbal art, especially narrative, is almost bereft of any sensuous content. Its visual features, as has often been observed, consist of monotonous small black marks on a white page. It has no acoustical features. Its tactile features are limited to the weight of its pages, their smooth surfaces, and their exquisitely thin edges. The attributes it has that are directly apprehensible by perception are, then, meager in number. More important, these attributes are utterly irrelevant, sometimes even antagonistic, to the mental images the work seeks to produce (steam rising across a windowpane, the sound of a stone dropped in a pool, the feel of dry August grass underfoot), the ones whose vivacity is under investigation here.[100]

Thus, the vacuity of sensory detail in the physical environment can enhance the imaginative capabilities. Writers who nostalgically wish to recreate their original homes in their minds may surrender to makeshift homes in their physical world in order to maximize the potential for imagining. Without a physical home as an obstacle, they can create an imaginary home in their minds that is adequately vivacious. The combination of being outside boundaries and abandoning certain assumptions about language leaves the weird-English author to treat language itself as artistic material, and to stretch its capacity to serve as verbal and visual art.

In the following chapters I show how the features of immigrant and postcolonial writing emerge in the works of Nabokov, Rushdie, Roy, Kingston, and Díaz. Their outsideness makes them compensate by creation: to borrow Edward Said's term, they are "overcharged."[101] Their intensity in constructing literature manifests itself in a love of detail and a satisfaction in pushing the boundaries of literary English, transgressing its traditional uses, and creating new literary worlds.

The Trouble with Writing about Imaginary Communities

Some of my relatives in the United States think my sense of relation to an imaginary community is a little excessive. I can't blame them. Reflection is a cushy way to survive the rupture of diaspora. In contrast, they believe, and live out, the atomistic, individualist subjectivity that the early third millennium in America often seems to demand. The here and now. Short, funky sentences versus elliptical, encompassing declarations. The way in which they talk and write about this subjectivity exposes this ontological difference of being, of seeing one's relation to historical matter. I saw this clearly when reading the answers to an exam question about the concept of the human in Primo Levi's *Survival in Auschwitz*.[102] This is what one student wrote:

> Myself being a third generation Holocaust survivor I really did not learn any thing new in Primo Levy's Survival in Auschwitz. My grandmother and grandfather both survived Aushwitz along with Bergen-Belsen and Dachau. My grandmother escaped and fled to a monastery where she

> impersonated a nun until liberation. And my grandfather
> was in the Partisan underground army. In fact I get my
> name from a relative who was killed at the age of 3 by the
> SS in front of the entire village. My great grandfather re-
> fused to shave his head so the SS grabbed the baby and
> threw him into the air in front of the family and 5 of them
> tried to shoot the baby in the air. They all missed no shots
> hit but the baby fell cracked his head open on the ground
> died instantly. My great grandfather still refused to shave
> his head and they killed him too. The fact that I hear this
> horrible story at least 5 times a year is non-human. And
> the tiny little bit of money they get a month from the Ger-
> man government will never be sufficient payback for in-
> fant target practice.[103]

What is striking about this—other than the narrative itself—is
that it is so graphic and *alive*. It rejects the narrative it recounts
as horrible and violent, yet its style is popular speech; note the
lack of punctuation and the disregard for grammatical rules.
The way in which it is written *is* its art, as if the student wanted
to *create art* in the writing. The account forces itself on the imagination, and the inhumanity is located in the act of narration
itself. The violence to grammatical conventions in the passage
reflects the state of mind of the narrator. This narrative and
imagined community still commits violence from a distance.
Furthermore, the story is built into the identity of the hearer,
who inherited the name of the dead baby. Thus, his name configures immigrant sacrifice in the form of a dead baby, rather
than a rejected nation or country (as in my name). In naming
him, his parents appropriated history differently from someone
like me.

Regardless of the method of appropriation, the idea of imagined communities through names forces a revised conception of self that is ongoing: the self is affirmed through its ties to community.[104] The idea of imagined community is also powerful for the writers discussed in this book. In a passage that resonates with the Holocaust incident described above, Maxine Hong Kingston writes:

> The Chinese magazines had war cartoons. . . . An enemy bayoneted an old man, spurting his blood. A bayonet was a gun that shot knives. An enemy threw two naked babies into the air, and another enemy caught one on his bayonet. The second baby fell to the ground and smashed. A booted enemy stepped on its head. The mother had her arms raised toward the babies. . . . In one panel the huge mother was grimacing, her stomach bloated. She was drinking from a jug. MaMa explained that the Japanese were forcing her to drink water until she burst. They would bounce on her stomach and it would explode. They were torturing her children in front of her, and stopped whenever she drank. If she peed, she had to drink her own urine. The children's mutilation was so gruesome, the cartoonist did not show it.[105]

Kingston likewise remarks on the violence of narrative, of verbal discourse that demands excretion through writing. She feels compelled to record this, just as my student felt the need to erupt during exam-taking. Both imagize through a textual medium. This turn to writing is a reorientation to history; it is a reaction to a past situation when the author was silent, or silenced. For example, Díaz had a childhood speech problem, and Kingston remembers lacking a voice as a young girl. Nabokov felt invulnerable enough in weird English to probe pedophilia;

Roy defined literary madness as a gift; and Rushdie has become the icon of the global linguistic citizen. Through English, language became *their art.*

Such artistic redemption through the invention of language is the subject of this book.

1

A Shuttlecock above the Atlantic

NABOKOV'S MID-LIFE AND MID-GEOGRAPHIC CRISES

I don't seem to belong to any clear-cut continent. I'm the
shuttlecock above the Atlantic, and how bright and blue
it is there, in my private sky, far from the pigeonholes
and the clay pigeons.

—VLADIMIR NABOKOV, *Strong Opinions* (1973)

The 1950s saw the incipient evidence of immi-
grant-speak in the works of Vladimir Vladi-
mirovich Nabokov. His books fascinated readers with their literary virtuosity, but few recognized them as samples of immigrant
vernacular, even though Nabokov insisted that his immigrancy
and unfamiliarity with English drove him to perform acts of literary daring.[1]

Nabokov's language remains distinctive and experimental in a
genre—the novel—that is increasingly estranged from convention. (Among countless examples, one could cite *La Disparition*,
or *A Void*, by Georges Perec, a book written entirely without the

letter *e;* Irvine Welsh's *Marabou Stork Nightmares,* written as if graphically designed; and the *nadsat*-narrated *Clockwork Orange,* by Anthony Burgess.) But his distinctiveness is rarely attributed to a periodically weak sense of English-speaking self. Critics praise his meta-fluency, but Nabokov insisted throughout his life that he was never fluent in English. To read his writing in English with completeness of vision is to recognize his lifelong conflicted and emotional relationship to it.[2]

Certainly Nabokov's writing is symphonic, but his English betrays his struggle to achieve comfort with the language rather than immediate facility.[3] We see a writer-in-progress in the English language, one acutely aware that literary fluency is related to class standing. In fact, fluency often belonged to those with status, and sometimes—for immigrants—determined it. With this knowledge, the Russian-born author eschewed economy-driven everyday language for mannered prose.[4] His English is notable, even extraordinary, because he makes language the catalyst of great emotional crises and the significant other of his life.[5] He imagines English with an emotional life of its own, making his writing exciting for the reader. The method of an immigrant, his continual repositioning of self to English and his love-hate affair with it illuminate the emotional component in the shifting linguistic patterns of his writing.

This repositioning happens from text to text; here the focus will be directed to *Pnin* (1953) and *Lolita* (1955).[6] This chapter will show linguistic crises and repositionings in Nabokov's life. In the novel *Pnin,* the adjacent English and Russian expose a psyche of indecisiveness, fearfulness, and hesitation. *Pnin* illuminates the immigrant need to acquire imaginary estate—the immaterial estate of language. *Lolita* signifies a step beyond imaginary estate: linguistic property is metaphorized as an unruly child.

The metaphors in both novels echo the onset of mid-life crises. Pnin's broken and unstable language signifies impermanence and loss of unfettered commitment; Humbert Humbert's twilight love is a twisted longing for the fluency of youth. In *Lolita* he molests language, metaphorized as a young girl, and calls this book his "love affair with the English language." Whereas *Pnin* shows the cost of lacking fluency, *Lolita* notes the sacrifices in gaining it. Within the two novels, Nabokov's style illuminates his crises with language. Central to this chapter is an emphasis on the emotional crises that accompany the linguistic ones.

Unreal Estate

> I had inherited an exquisite simulacrum—the beauty of intangible property, unreal estate—and this proved a splendid training for the endurance of later losses.
>
> —Vladimir Nabokov, *Speak, Memory* (1966)

> Man exists only insofar as he is separated from his surroundings.
>
> —Vladimir Nabokov, *Pnin* (1953)

Language is the unrealest estate for Professor Pnin, who can't master it. We think of language as patently social, as publicly owned, but Nabokov shows us how Pnin's remarkably asocial language obstructs the formation of social ties rather than binds them.[7] Pnin's language deflects ownership. His utterances can be frightening in their contribution to social damage; Humbert Humbert shares this linguistic destructiveness with Pnin. But Nabokov's asocial language reveals, as a strong contrast, the importance of owning in the acquisition of language: in owning a language, we begin to demonstrate that we own ourselves. His positioning to language reveals that fluency depends on, or is enhanced by, two events: first, language must be viewed as an entity or property, or inspire the desire for ownership; second, language's entity is comparable to the concept of a soul. To recognize this is to recognize the implicit communal debt we share with all humanity.

On some level, language must celebrate the concept of the interior to human beings in communication.[8] If "bad" language destroys, well-spokenness creates: it creates distinctness, soulfulness, interiority, and thus is a discrete, possibly appropriable entity.[9]

In Pnin's case, asocial English is accompanied by glimmers of Russian, which recall occasions of past conventional social success (among them, marriage). In the enclosed spaces of parentheses, Nabokov suggests the possibility of a shadow language that illuminates another dimension of Pnin's character—even suggests (an interior), or (((an interior))). If Pnin could find an interior through the design of words, he might be known to us—or we might feel as if there were someone, a soul, to know.[10] By writing in a distinct way, Nabokov shows us that when we act as if we own language by asserting our *own* style, we perform the act of ownership.[11] We title something, and thus become entitled. In the following sections, I show how parentheses can provide representation for concepts such as interior and exterior. I also show that they can take on another level of linguistic signification and can demarcate a bilingual consciousness and personality.

As an immigrant deprived of any physical property, Pnin engages in a hopeful wish for estatehood himself, for the right to be entitled. But he is the embodiment of someone who can't own his new language, English. Pnin is an inarticulate protagonist with obviously unfluent English. Technically, Nabokov's strategy of introducing this character works against public sympathy: usually, the more beautifully a text is arranged, the easier the entrance into an empathetic trajectory. But Professor Pnin's interior life is impenetrable, obscured by a cacophony of badly arranged word structure and mispronunciation. His English at times is so halting and stilted that it seems unembodied and unemotional, devoid of life and passion. Like many speakers of broken English, he inspires impatience.[12] His robotic responses seem invulnerable and immature simultaneously; on a social level he is unanchored, unadult, even unlinguistic. (Impatience with broken English reminds us that for noise to be literary, it must communicate the intentional and emotional states concurrent with the creation of the language—not simply convey information.) Despite all this, and as a result of Nabokov's linguistic strategies incorporating Russian sounds and sensibility into English, the character Pnin becomes narratively porous.

First, the conceptual organization of a bilingual existence is accomplished by parentheticals, and is accompanied by other suggestions of Russian presence. In redefining the position of the immigrant to English, Nabokov creates a new English, one which is composed of continual live metaphor.[13] He shows how English and Russian have competing claims on an immigrant like Pnin.[14] Second, the weirdness of Nabokov's English occurs on the level of invented vocabulary. Jane Grayson writes: "Nabokov deliberately retains certain Russicisms and selects unusual vocabulary in order to impart an originality and individuality to his style. In his later English production it is not possible to draw any clear distinction between what is 'foreign' or 'non-standard' and what is original and calculated to enrich the scope of the English language."[15] Grayson also suggests that

Nabokov's English is Russianized to be metrical. Below I will present examples of Nabokov's third strategy: the importation of sensual and rhythmic qualities of Russian into English. "The examination of Nabokov's developing English style," writes Grayson, "can be carried beyond mere choice of words and their harmonies to larger units and the rhythmical grouping of words. Nabokov is attentive to the rhythm and harmony of his prose. Rhythmic, even metrical prose is a marked feature of his Russian writing, and he carries this feature over into his English production."[16] This underlying Russian structure of Nabokov's English illustrates a psyche that is still influenced by Russia but also sustained by difficult experience with immigration. In an interesting comparison of Nabokov's feelings toward English and Russian, D. Barton Johnson writes: "It is of interest that Nabokov describes the relationship between the later Russian and the earlier English variants of his memoirs as that of capital letters to cursive."[17] Nabokov's writing contains the repression of Russian, a precursor format to later works by early third-millennium authors who incorporate Russian accents spelled-out in their works.[18] Nabokov's conservatism reveals his expectations for his readers' capacity to absorb Russianisms: he expects low tolerance for Russianized English. But Nabokov's conservatism exposes the emotional struggle that ensues from the incommensurability of languages and the lack of space in which a discursive zone can be developed between these languages and across this incommensurability. Today, Nabokov's work is the artifact of the emotional life we are outgrowing—one that globalism is beginning to cure.

Still, the beginning of recognizing the resistance to English as immigrants' psychic burden is the beginning of sharing this burden linguistically. This means reading weird English as English;

readers become authors of a new English. They share with the author some of the burden of translation. Authors now feel free to enjoy unorthodox English and unpredictably spelled prose. If this continues, linguistic incommensurability between populations could end.

Puhneen's Baaahhd Ahksent

"Alex," he said, "what was the language you studied this year at school?" "The language of English," I told him. "Are you good and fine at it?" he asked me. "I am fluid," I told him. . . . "Excellent, Shapka," he said. "Do not dub me that," I said.

—JONATHAN SAFRAN FOER, *Everything Is Illuminated* (2002)

My English, this second instrument I have always had, is however a stiffish, artificial thing, which may be all right for describing a sunset or an insect, but which cannot conceal poverty of syntax and paucity of domestic diction when I need the shortest road between warehouse and shop. An old Rolls Royce is not always preferable to a plain jeep.

—VLADIMIR NABOKOV, quoted in Jane Grayson, *Nabokov Translated* (1977)

Language designs the structure of our social relations. As implied in earlier passages, linguistic design creates interior/exterior, inclusive/exclusive, inside/out, and other comparable entities. The emotional accompaniment for this structure is dyadic as well: a body is simply cognized as exterior and public, whereas a soul is interior and emotional. Nabokov's language is interior-creating and emotional.[19] The consequence of this is that we might think that Pnin cannot be reached/damaged/hurt through language (((only the Pnin inside is vulnerable))), but the bad accent tells us that he can be hurt; his language can be broken like his physical body. His halting accent and broken language reveal his vulnerability and catalyze our vision of him as human. Language becomes inextricable from the formation of an interior; we see that to injure one part of Pnin's language is to injure his linguistic existence as a whole.

Pnin's awkward immigrant tells us much about language. *Pnin* narrates linguistic dysfunction and the frustration of continually running up against its limits. If fluency is interior-building, lack of it is too public to bear. *Pnin* presents this version of language: a language in pain.[20] Newness is pain; but it is also the beginning of new self-awareness. In *Pnin,* we are treated to a self-conscious version of the physicality of language:

> The organs concerned in the production of English speech sounds are the larynx, the velum, the lips, the tongue (that punchinello in the troupe), and, last but not least, the lower jaw; mainly upon its overenergetic and somewhat ruminant motion did Pnin rely when translating in class passages in the Russian grammar or some poem by Pushkin. If his Russian was music, his English was murder. He had enormous difficulty ("dzeefeecooltsee" in Pninian English) with depalatization, never managing to remove the extra Russian moisture from *t*'s and *d*'s before the vowels he so quaintly softened. His explosive "hat" ("I never go in a hat even in winter") differed from the common American pronunciation of "hot" (typical of Waindell townspeople, for example) only by its briefer du-

ration, and thus sounded very much like the German verb
hat (has). Long *o*'s with him inevitably became short ones:
his "no" sounded positively Italian, and this was accentu-
ated by his trick of triplicating the simple negative ("May I
give you a lift, Mr. Pnin?" "No-no-no, I have only two
paces from here." He did not possess (nor was he aware of
this lack) any long *oo:* all he could muster when called
upon to utter "noon" was the lax vowel of the German
"*nun*" ("I have no classes in after*nun* on Tuesday. Today is
Tuesday.").[21]

Speaking is destruction for Pnin; it is murder. Nabokov felt
that linguistic damage could be violent and explosive: "My complete switch from Russian prose to English prose was exceed-
ingly painful—like learning to handle things after losing seven
or eight fingers in an explosion."[22] Linguistic ravage occurs in
sentences of bad pronunciation, where the message is killed before fully conveyed: "'Important lecture!' cried Pnin. 'What to
do? It is a cata-stroph!'" (*Pnin,* 17). Or in this exchange on the
phone: "'You are,' suggested the voice warily, 'Mrs. Fire?' . . .
'What was that telephone call?' . . . 'Someone wanting Mrs.
Feuer or Fayer'" (31). In self-deprecating moments, Nabokov
writes Russianisms into Pnin's conversation: "I must not, I must
not, oh it is idiotical" (81); "Pnin sighed a Russian 'okh-okh-okh'
sigh, and sought a more comfortable position" (110). Finally,
Pnin's poignant self-description is mispronounced English: "'I
haf nofing,' wailed Pnin between loud, damp sniffs, 'I haf nofing
left, nofing, nofing!'" (61).

In the first case, the emotional impact of the message is damaged en route: "cata-stroph" calls attention to itself as a linguistic unit before its meaning is absorbed. In the second case, the

person Pnin is looking for—Mrs. Thayer—hangs up on him because she can't interpret his accented English. In the third case Pnin is a tragicomic figure with the clumsiness of inarticulate longings. The result is that Pnin seems less a person than a two-dimensional character. Is true drama, then, reserved for the articulate? In Pnin's case, lack of voice also means the lack of presence, which includes dramatic presence. In all of the above cases, the empathy is removed from Pnin and he is left alone, in linguistic exile.[23]

To his credit, Pnin reflects on his English pronunciation, with the intention of correcting his murderous accent: "'My name is Timofey,' said Pnin, as they made themselves comfortable at a window table in the shabby old diner. 'Second syllable pronounced as "muff," ahksent on last syllable, "ey" as in "prey" but a little more protracted. "Timofey Pavlovich Pnin," which means "Timothy the son of Paul." The pahtronymic has the ahksent on the first syllable and the rest is sloored—Timofey Pahlch'" (104). His self-examination provides a dimension to his character, and he becomes more than an unaware, inarticulate cartoon. Pnin manages to convey information through broken English, but Nabokov purposely misspells English words to mimic Russian pronunciation: "'I search, John, for the viscous and sawdust,' he said tragically. 'I am afraid there is no soda,' she answered with her lucid Anglo-Saxon restraint. 'But there is plenty of whisky in the dining-room cabinet. However, I suggest we both have some nice hot tea instead.' He made the Russian 'relinquishing' gesture" (59). Joan's matter-of-fact interpretation does not provide the complete picture of communication—Nabokov adds the homophonically amusing but misspelled words "viscous" and "sawdust" to give the reader a full view of the dialogue. But another critic suggests that Nabokov's transliteration is purposely inaccurate, in order to emphasize that Pnin is being actively misunderstood and mocked by a cruel colleague, Jack Cockerell. Leona Toker writes: "The transliteration 'viscous' for 'whiskey' is fantastic enough—the typical Russian distortion would have been something like 'veeski'—but the substitution of 'sawdust' for 'soda' is impossible: the Russian word for 'soda' sounds much the same as the English one." She adds, "This pseudo-Pninism strikingly differs from the other records of the protagonist's speech," and asserts that the variety of transliter*ations* is due to the variety of transliter*ators*.[24] In her view, the inaccurate transliteration of the above, for example "veeski" for "whiskey," indicates that Jack Cockerell, who constantly mocks Pnin, is the transliterator.[25] "The 'viscous and sawdust' deviation from verisimilitude can be accounted for only as a facetious quotation from Jack Cockerell, who tends to impute to Pnin such impossible mistakes as 'shot' instead of 'fired.' . . . Pnin's failure to understand the humor of comic strips in the same episode is another blatant Cockerellian exaggeration."[26] Cockerell's misunderstanding of Pnin, which we see by his linguistic playfulness (sordid but still somewhat lighthearted), is balanced by a variety of receptions to his accent. Toker continues:

> At the beginning of the novel Pnin's sentences are faithful word-for-word translations for corresponding Russian phrases: "And where possible to leave baggage?" . . .—*A gde mozhno ostavit' bagzah?* Later Pnin inserts carefully stored colloquialisms into his conversation, or speaks in a funny yet credible mixture of solecisms and quotations for a curriculum vitae. . . . By the end of the novel, under the influence of new friendships, his English is considerably improved, though not his pronunciation. . . . The narrator,

who discusses the regularities of the Russian accent . . .
with a precision matching only Pnin's own phonetic analysis of his name and patronymic . . . generally refrains
from transliterating his speech. Among the few exceptions
is the account of the road directions that Pnin, in the
comedy of errors in Chapter 6, gives to Professor Thomas,
taking him for the ornithologist Wynn.[27]

Toker's assertion that Pnin's English improves is hard to justify,
since his English alters according to whom he is addressing. But
she does point out, significantly, that the way in which characters expose their degree of humanity toward Pnin is through language; Nabokov is trying to indicate level of social engagement
through their ability to be linguistically tolerant. Victor's capacity to accept Pnin's English exhibits such tolerance: "Pnin talked.
His talk did not amaze Victor, who had heard many Russians
speak English, and he was not bothered by the fact that Pnin
pronounced the word 'family' as if the first syllable were the
French for 'woman'" (*Pnin*, 105). Still, Pnin's inability to reproduce proper English is a handicap that he admits he cannot simply drop. He also confesses to hearing Russianized sounds even
when they do not exist. "'I still hear,' said Pnin, picking up the
sprinkler and shaking his head a little at the surprising persistence of memory, 'I still hear the *trakh!*, the crack when one
hit the wooden pieces and they jumped in the air. Will you not
finish the meat? You do not like it?'" (106). Regardless of how
his audience receives his linguistic messages, Pnin cannot trust
his own English, and thus his English betrays him and exposes
him to the linguistic bullies in his community. For him, English
is still elusive in pronunciation and unfertilized by experience.
Pnin is even characterized as having a shallow knowledge of Eng-

lish—not simply because he lacks vocabulary but because the words he says do not seem to have any emotional meaning to him. An outsider might assume that his relation to English, being shallow, exemplifies his relation to life. The narrator critiques his use of English, often lacking context or acquired without conceptual organization: "A special danger in Pnin's case was the English language. Except for such not very helpful odds and ends as 'the rest is silence,' 'nevermore,' 'weekend,' 'who's who,' and a few ordinary words like 'eat,' 'street,' 'fountain pen,' 'gangster,' 'Charleston,' 'marginal utility,' he had had no English at all at the time he left France for the States. Stubbornly he sat down to the task of learning the language of Fenimore Cooper, Edgar Poe, Edison, and thirty-one Presidents. In 1941, at the end of one year of study, he was proficient enough to use glibly terms like 'wishful thinking' and 'okey-dokey.' By 1942 he was able to interrupt his narration with the phrase, 'To make a long story short'" (14). Pnin thus stands on the terra infirma of words that have no weight to him. His linguistic exile[28] is a lesson in gradual subtraction.[29] After the subtraction of his Russian identity, his slippery, insecure hold on English leads to a freefall into impermanence for Pnin.[30] His existence reacts to his language; his lifestyle is wandering, unpredictable, explosive, and destructive. Pnin experiences constant relocation, though he wants to rest in one place. His life is a series of unreciprocated commitments: his wife leaves him; he has no permanent residence; he is unable to keep his job. Pnin's fate is left hanging, but the reader has already witnessed the shrinking of Pnin's world at a rapid rate, in proportion to the increase of exilic feelings. Pnin's aloneness is striking.[31] With no supporting community or family, his potential to become a total fiction is frightening; existence that goes unacknowledged may eventually cease to sustain itself. Furthermore, everything that Pnin loves or desires attachment to is ephemeral. One critic describes Pnin as "an exile from his essential self,"[32] and this resonates with Nabokov's own complaints about losing his Russianness. At one point, Pnin self-deprecatingly but jokingly calls himself a "Bachelor of Hearts (Oh, punster Pnin!)" (151), and the narrator's parenthetical aside seems cruel and reductive.

Pnin's language is often a search for a permanent and reliable form of rightness in the world.[33] English cannot give Pnin the social stability he needs, the community he requires; and thus it must be supplemented by Russian. This happens because he is fundamentally unable to socialize through English. His use of it seems awkward and stilted, and at times the narrator injects comments of criticism that denigrate his speech. But as Pnin the character acclimatizes to the culture of America, he realizes that he can't rely on the Russian parentheticals to offset the weight of English, and this leads to his psychic instability. Immigrants like Pnin are tragedies in the making. They carry a few radiant fragments from other worlds with them, but these become dull from lack of use—old anachronistic shards that had meaning only in the past, discardable in a new world.

Nabokov plays with our ability to empathize by confusing us.[34] In the book, the language of love, of hate, and of intense feeling can create an effect opposite to that which was intended. We also realize that empathy can be attached to so many different factors that, if we are not properly guided by a narrator, the world created by the text can be disorienting. Why, for instance, does Nabokov have Pnin say "I haf nofing!", as opposed to "I have lost everything!" or some other properly unhappy version of the statement? Obviously, Nabokov wants to be loyal to the accent he has been transcribing so carefully all along, but the accent's appearance with peculiar strength at this moment is evidence that Nabokov is almost testing our level of empathy. In the entire novel, the narrator has been calling attention, in a derisive sort of way, to Pnin's deficiency in English, and in this quotation we are torn between humor at the pronunciation as transcribed and pathos for the character. Pnin's Russianness[35] is an object of ridicule throughout. Clearly the narrator does not attribute to him the status of being taken seriously, seriously enough so that his anguish can even be acknowledged.

Thus, we encounter the problem of characterization in Nabokov: rather than focusing on the emotion that language conveys, he embarks on games with meaning and context. For instance, Pnin calls his landlady "John" versus the proper "Joan"; and even in cases where he is involved in tragedy, the aesthetic presentation of his English is so caricatured and jarring that it interrupts the flow of empathy—although not sympathy—from reader to character. Pnin is belittled into a cartoon by the language he produces, but we experience the horrifying observation that it is possible to ignore, or regard with less importance, human suffering if it is expressed in a cultural context different from our own. We realize that Nabokov can create a barrier to the understanding of a character by erecting a language barrier; we realize that the linguistic mistakes that Pnin makes affect not merely our judgment of language but also our judgment of Pnin's emotional state. In our sphere of moral visibility, those who are ignorant of their linguistic ineptness are pathetic in their distress. They can be so unglamorous or unsightly that we deny them proper moral attention. Nabokov brings to the surface this stinging moral truth (tempered by the fact that we are reading fiction, in which we don't get the complete view and it's safely presumed we don't). He shows us that our moral attentiveness is allied to our aesthetic attentiveness but doesn't reside there. It resides, he reminds us throughout *Pnin,* in language, the focus of his book. For Pnin, a professor of Slavic literature whose lover works under "Dr. Rosetta Stone" (*Pnin,* 44), a paper existence between parentheses is inevitable.

A Shuttlecock's Bilingual Parentheticals

> Now, what about the language which describes my inner
> experiences and which only I myself can understand?
> How do I use words to stand for my sensations?—As we
> ordinarily do?
>
> —LUDWIG WITTGENSTEIN, *Philosophical Investigations* (1953)

Turning his back on this reception of broken English in 1950s America, Nabokov shows that Pnin's broken English obscures our vision of him. He creates Pnin's dimensions; a Russian dimension is generated with the use of parenthetical asides and other methods of linguistic implication. Nabokov implies that there is an interior left untranslated, that the English side of Pnin is only his surface, his exterior. Nabokov also finds that the combined cultures can fuse to create a new English, albeit a weird one.

For a long time, Nabokov couldn't make up his mind whether he wanted to be Russian or American. He likewise hesitated for several years between his two muses, Russian and English. He was suspended between two worlds: imaginary Russia[36] and unreal America.[37] As mentioned earlier, his ambivalence materializes in the ubiquitous usage of parentheses. (((In this section I will argue that his frequent use of parentheses signifies indecisiveness, ghostliness, and interiority, among other things.))) In

Pnin the reader is bombarded with English and Russian phrases that appear in various forms: English with Russian in parentheses; Russian with English in parentheses; and English in a bad accent.[38] The author conceives of parallel universes where interpretation can take place in English or Russian. Nabokov flip-flops between English and Russian—alternatively, (Russian phrases) or (English phrases). To reiterate: the problem for Pnin is psychic instability. The schizoid existence is not only a language issue, as we have seen in earlier passages, but an existential one generated by language. Does Pnin have knowledge of the world? Does he feel that no one finds him—through language or not—worthwhile? Is our moral behavior based on the fact that we can understand language? Can we see humanness without it? The unsturdiness of Pnin's language exposes these flaws in morality—that what we consider as perfectible cannot be. It is a linguistic creation, and thus a human one.

Nabokov's portraits of Pnin are not, then, mockable. They function as commentaries on how we view humanness; they are pictures of what constitutes the human for us and what does not count as human. Nabokov makes us wonder about our own pictures and sounds, and how we shape them into a concept of humanness. Are we compendiums of our culture—or are we nonhuman, puppet-like packages regurgitating culture? Can we, for example, see beyond the "encyclopedia of Russian shrugs and shakes" that constitutes Pnin and see a person? Can we separate the linguistic entity of Pnin and see Nabokov underneath?

> It soon transpired that Timofey was a veritable encyclope-
> dia of Russian shrugs and shakes, had tabulated them,
> and could add something to Laurence's files on the philo-
> sophical interpretation of pictorial and non-pictorial, na-

tional and environmental gestures. It was very pleasant to see the two men discuss a legend or a religion, Timofey blossoming out in amphoric motion, Laurence chopping away with one hand. Laurence even made a film of what Timofey considered to be the essentials of Russian "carpalistics," with Pnin in a polo shirt, a Gioconda smile on his lips, demonstrating the movements underlying such Russian verbs—used in reference to hands—as *mahnut'*, *vsplesnut'*, *razvesti*: the one-hand downward loose shake of weary relinquishment; the two-hand dramatic splash of amazed distress; and the "disjunctive" motion—hands traveling apart to signify helpless passivity. And in conclusion, very slowly, Pnin showed how, in the international "shaking the finger" gesture, a halfturn, as delicate as the switch of the wrist in fencing, metamorphosed the Russian solemn symbol of pointing up, "the Judge in Heaven sees you!" into a German air picture of the stick—"something is coming to you!" (*Pnin*, 41)

The detail of this description is so precise that it seems like a lesson to Americans in Russian gesture, even though it is a caricature. What drives it is a highly emotional exchange—so emotional that it generates physical energy—that brings us closer to Pnin.

Russian references thus make Pnin alive. The translation from character to person occurs here through the use of a different language. Seeing Nabokov's parentheticals as physical and psychical representations of Pnin is also crucial to bringing Pnin to aliveness, as well as illuminating the conflict between languages that Nabokov experienced. Through parenthetical additions, readers can witness the translation and interpretation that Nabokov undertakes inside the novel. The presence of Russian also exposes Pnin's psyche: the continuous parenthetical addition of Russian signifies this demand for balance through language. Russian expression is naturally incorporated into the text, as if to remind the reader of the weirdness of appropriated English—for example, "Yes, this I will buy" (99) and many other instances of untraditionally disorderly English. For example, at a train station Pnin engages in dialogue with a rail attendant, asking a series of questions: "Where stops four o'clock bus to Cremona?" (18) and "Where possible to leave baggage?" (18). After the agent answers his questions, Pnin then asks another question with a bit of narrator presence: "'Quittance?' queried Pnin, Englishing the Russian word for 'receipt' *(kvitantsiya)*." Pnin's persistent questions continue, but finally climax in an awkwardly worded interrogative: "'And now,' said Pnin, 'where is located the public telephone?'" (18). In the first of several examples of English accompanied by Russian parentheticals, similar awkward word arrangement is echoed by his ex-wife, Liza: "Yes, she never doubted that Timofey was a darling *('Nu kakoy zhe ti dushka')*. . . . And now where was the bathroom? And would he please telephone for the taxi?" (57). Pnin's awkward English causes him to return to Russian, as if to remind himself of the comfort that fluent language offers. So he incorporates a number of Russian words in his daily English speech. On almost every page of *Pnin* a Russian word or phrase appears, or a piece of English that has been clearly influenced by Russian. The following examples of parenthetical "other" language (sometimes English, sometimes Russian) suggest the dual consciousness of bilingualism—the echo or shadow existence that competes with the live linguistic ego: "Another Gogolian person, in Miami, offered 'a two-room apartment for non-drinkers *(dlya trezvih)*, among fruit

trees and flowers'" (75). Later, another set of Russian parentheticals is incorporated with the feel of subtitles in a Russian-
immigrant scenario that a narrator is describing: "However
(odnako), it really is hot here *(i zharko ahe u vas)!* I think I shall
now present myself before the most luminous orbs (*presvetlïe
ochi*, jocular) of Alexandr Petrovich and then go for a dip
(okupnutsya, also jocular) in the river he so vividly describes in his
letter" (122–123). At moments where a Russian parenthetical does
not elaborate or add information to the English already present, the parenthetical becomes an aesthetic aside, as if to indicate that the aesthetic qualities of Russian—its sounds and
rhythms—justify its insertion into the text: "By stupidity *(po
gluposti)* I came out with an unprotected head" (126). Pnin also
calls upon Russian in sentimental moments or moments of
strong emotion: "All the more vexing *(tem bolee obidno)* that
his mother . . ." (127).[39] Or: "*'Huliganï,'* fumed Pnin . . ." (73).[40]
Or: "drinking himself to death *(govoryat, spilsya)*" (183). These
fragments of Russian can be revealing—for the reader, Pnin's
Russian life becomes his expressive life, not simply his articulate one.

Linguistic competence may determine social relations, but
emotional lives remain intact regardless of the level of fluency.
Still, language becomes an area of contestation between immigrants when emotional connections do not exist: "It would be
hard to say, without applying some very special tests, which
of them, Pnin or Komarov, spoke the worse English; probably
Pnin; but for reasons of age, general education, and a slightly
longer stage of American citizenship, he found it possible to correct Komarov's frequent English interpolations, and Komarov
resented this even more than he did Pnin's *antikvarnïy liberalizm*"
(72).[41] Nabokov adds that Pnin's reaction is on the same cultural

plane: "'Look here, Komarov' (*Polushayte, Komarov*—a rather discourteous manner of address), said Pnin" (72).

In the novel, entire poems are transcribed in Russian throughout, and a description of how they are to be read publicly is also included, with an addition of a brief literary critique: "I have marked the stress accents, and transliterated the Russian with the usual understanding that *u* is pronounced like a short 'oo,' *i* like a short 'ee,' and *zh* like a French 'j.' Such incomplete rhymes as *skazal-glaza* were considered very elegant" (181).[42] Sometimes the reader may feel that Nabokov does not find the exact word he needs in English, that he must appeal to both languages to provide a full sense of the irony of his descriptions: "It is always painful for a sensitive *(chutkiy)* person to see another in an awkward position" (183).[43] Nabokov reverses the parentheses on occasion, using Russian with English parentheticals, for many of the same reasons he uses English with Russian parentheticals. But his use in both cases suggests he must absolutely use the Russian language.

In the following examples, Pnin's Russian expressions are retranslated back into English. On this level, Pnin's aesthetic presence becomes stronger when he employs Russian. The reader is forced to confront and first encounter Russian transliteration before seeing the parenthetical English definition. (This is the forerunner of contemporary works like Safran Foer's *Everything Is Illuminated,* where all the words are Russianized.) In these passages, Pnin has an overwhelming urge to speak in Russian. He has to use it; he cannot wait for the translation into English, or he cannot translate his phrases into English and must rely on the Russian. We see these uses of Russian on the level of imperative exclamation: "*It* was there, *slava Bogu* (thank God)! Very well! He would not wear his black suit—*vot i vsyo* (that's all)" (19); "'Nu, nu, vot I horosho, nu vot'—mere verbal heart props—and she cried out: 'Oh, he has splendid new teeth!'" (53); "'What a gruesome place, *kakoy zhutkiy dom,*' she said" (54); and "Suddenly he heard her sonorous voice ('Timofey, zdrastvuy!') behind him" (53). This also includes details such as: "Timofey Pnin settled down in the living room, crossed his legs *po amerikanski* (the American way), and entered into some unnecessary detail" (33).

Russian appears in slang or colloquial phrases that sometimes translate awkwardly into English: "*Nu, eto izvinite* (Nothing doing)" (47); "*Gospodi, skol'ko mï im dayom!* (My, what a lot we give them!)"—"them" being the benighted American people (71); "*V boyu li, v stranstvii, v volnah?* In fight, in travel, or in waves?" (73); and "The barn was full of *dachniki* (vacationists) and disabled soldiers from a nearby hospital" (179). In describing the customs of a Russian community, the narration of *Pnin* becomes inundated with Russian phrases, such as "All this was due ('Yes, I see, *vizhu, kampus kak kampus:* The usual kind of thing')" (53); "('*sidite, sidite!*' don't get up)" (131); "'*Tshay gotoff* (Tea's ready),' called Susan from the porch in her funny functional Russian; 'Tomfey, Rozochka! *Tshay!*'" (132); "'*Moyo pochtenie* (My respects),' said both men" (126); "*Kak horoshi, kak svezhi* (How fair, how fresh)" (147); "Hot *pirozhki* (mushroom tarts, meat tarts, cabbage tarts) . . . *ryabinovka* (a rowanberry liqueur)" (152); "'*Avtomobil, kostyum-nu pryamo amerikanets* (a veritable American), *pryamo Ayzenhauer!*' said Varvara" (121).

Gratuitous usage alludes to the ghost of a bond with a community that still asserts itself against English: "*amerikanski* electricity" (77); "*botvinia* (chilled beet soup)" (129); "the Garden Strawberries, *zemlyanika,* and the other cultivated species, *klubnika* (Hautbois or Green Strawberries)" (132); "*bezkorïstnïy* (disinterested, devoted)" (143).

Occasionally, Pnin will comment on the different customs of American and Russian culture—for example, in terms of address. "In reviewing his Russian friends through Europe and the United States, Timofey Pahlch could easily count at least sixty dear people whom he had intimately known since, say, 1920, and whom he never called anything but Vadim Vadimich, Ivan Hristoforovich, or Samuil Izrailevich, as the case might be, and who called him by his name and patronymic with the same effusive sympathy, over a strong warm handshake, whenever they met: 'Ah, Timofey Pahlch! Nu kak? (Well how?) A vï, baten'ka, zdorovo postareli (Well, well, old boy, you certainly don't look any younger!)!'" (105). The underlying emotional quality of this social exchange can be felt in the sensual qualities of the language. Nabokov's sense of irony surfaces in Russian: "Pnin used to always be embarrassed by Liza's 'pshihooslinïe' (psychoasinine) interests" (50). In many cases, Nabokov will interject a literary allusion that is more readily available to Pnin in the original Russian; and at times he will combine a Russianism (as in the alliterative pairing of "mute mirth") within the reference: "Pnin, rippling with mute mirth, sat down again at his desk: he had a tale to tell. That line in the absurd Russian grammar, 'Brozhu li ya vdol' ulits shumnih (Whether I wander along noisy streets),' was really the opening of a famous poem" (67). Or: "Plïla I pela, pela I plïla . . . She floated and she sang, she sang and floated" (79). The narrator plunges into soliloquy shortly after: "Of course! Ophelia's death! Hamlet! In good old Andrey Kroneberg's Russian translation, 1844—the joy of Pnin's youth, and of his father's and grandfather's young days! And here, as in the Kodstromskoy passage, there is, we recollect, also a willow and also wreaths. But where to check properly? Alas, 'Gamlet' by Vil'yama Shekspira had not been acquired by Mr. Todd, and was not represented in Waindell College Library, and whenever you were reduced to look up something in the English version, you never found this or that beautiful, noble, sonorous line that you remembered all your life from Kroneberg's text in Vengerov's splendid edition. Sad!" (50). Pnin also engages in lengthy literary analyses. Jane Grayson writes that this occurs on the narrative level, as well as on the level of words:

> One distinctive feature of Nabokov's English is a preference for precise terms and recherché vocabulary. This preference grows with continuing practice in the language. When revising an earlier English version, he frequently replaces a simple English word with a more unfamiliar or specialized equivalent. . . . He frequently substitutes the rare word for the familiar, the elaborate for the simple. Taking a general view of this development, it would almost seem that Nabokov, in order to establish an individual style and stamp it with difference and distinction, was deliberately choosing to step out of the ordinary in his use of words and quite deliberately preferring the extraordinary. The attempt to clarify this general observation and identify the nature of "extraordinariness" in the words he chooses would lead to analysis under such headings as Latinate words, technical terms, and purpose-built and invented word forms. . . . Obviously, though, these compartments are not watertight; some scientific terms are Latin in origin, and conversely many Latinate words are used by Nabokov to give an erudite or technical flavor to his prose.[44]

Grayson writes that some examples that appear in *Pnin* include "crepitate," "auroral," and "palpated." In English and Russian, Nabokov insists on the eccentric. As readers, we may not understand the words, but the attitude—the writer's attitude—is present. This preference for the original and eccentric is linked with a desire to carve out an American identity, as well as a hesitancy to leave Russia altogether.

Nabokov's American Constitution

As Nabokov moves away from writing *Pnin,* he makes decisive moves to sever ties with Russia. Although Nabokov seems, in *Pnin,* to feel the weight of writing in Russian, he vehemently declared that he would never return to Russia:

> I will never go back, for the simple reason that all the Russia I need is always with me: literature, language, and my own Russian childhood. I will never return. I will never surrender. And anyway, the grotesque shadow of a police state will not be dispelled in my lifetime. I don't think they know my works there—oh, perhaps a number of readers exist there in my special secret service, but let us not forget that Russia has grown tremendously provincial during these forty years, apart from the fact that people there are told what to read, what to think. In America I'm happier than in any other country. It is in America that I found my best readers, minds that are closest to mine. I feel intellectually at home in America. It is a second home in the true sense of the word.[45]

But nostalgia for Russia had its limits: politically, Nabokov wanted to dissociate himself from what he saw as the will toward the bourgeois and conservative. He spoke of it mainly with reference to literature and politics: "I have sufficiently spoken of the gloom and the glory of exile in my Russian novels, and especially in the best of them, *Dar* (recently published in English as

The Gift); but a quick recapitulation here may be convenient. With a very few exceptions, all liberal-minded creative forces—poets, novelists, critics, historians, philosophers, and so on—had left Lenin's and Stalin's Russia."[46] His meditations on exile frequently reveal a hatred of the Russian system and all oppression; he expressly discredits the country's cruelty, censorship, and dictatorship in many of his interviews in *Strong Opinions*. This resistance to censorship also translated into affection for eccentricity—especially eccentricity connected to exile.

Nabokov brought Russia to America in forms outside fiction, but his writing of *Lolita* signifies the end of his obsession to import Russian culture into his American writings. In his lectures on literature, he began to focus on non-Russian features in writing: "Nabokov gave a series of six general lectures on Russian writers when he began his Resident Lectureship at Wellesley. . . . All the lectures concentrated upon the 'Westernness' of each writer, as if to establish and underscore the intrinsic émigré quality of all Russian literature."[47] Nabokov appeared to associate Westernness with creativity and free expression, and implied that artistic genius required this context of freedom: "It is really wonderful to be living at least in a country where there is a market for such things."[48]

Nabokov's transition to American happens on corporeal, linguistic, and political levels. He says, "I am as American as April in Arizona," and elsewhere remarks, "My weight went up from my usual 140 to a monumental and cheerful 200. In consequence, I am one-third American—good American flesh keeping me warm and safe."[49] His love of America is itself quite "American": he often speaks of its landscape or its environmental riches in his most fervent expressions of attachment: "I dream of going to spend my purple-plumed sunset in California, among the larkspurs and the oaks, in the serene silence of her university libraries." At age forty, he even tried to enlist in the army during World War II. The American influence on Nabokov's personality surfaced in public, in fiction, and sometimes in his lectures. His battle with censorship, his correspondence with Stanley Kubrick, and his cross-country adventures were the trappings of a successful American writer. Nabokov wasn't ungrateful for the pragmatic benefits of being American: "I do feel a suffusion of warm, light-hearted pride when I show my green USA passport at European frontiers."[50]

His conflict during his new loyalty is expressed in terms of his muses.[51] He says of Russian: "I have lain with my Russian muse after a long period of adultery" and "I shall take three months' vacation with my ruddy robust Russian muse."[52] He also discusses English in terms of a feminine counterpart: in *Strong Opinions,* he calls English "my little American muse."[53] His new muse, English, is the subject of his next book, *Lolita.*

English: Nabokov's Second Muselet

So the fantasy of a private language, underlying the wish
to deny the publicness of language, turns out, so far, to
be a fantasy, or fear, either of inexpressiveness, one in
which I am not merely unknown, but in which I am powerless to make myself known; or one in which what I express is beyond my control.

—STANLEY CAVELL, *The Claim of Reason* (1979)

How ludicrous these efforts to translate
Into one's private tongue a public fate!

—VLADIMIR NABOKOV, *Pale Fire* (1962)

Lolita, a narrative about a charming muselet[54] whose American nature is almost cartoonish, signals Nabokov's shift in interest from Russian emigrant life to American culture. Nabokov's parentheticals are no longer indications of Russian translations but bespeak an alter ego who is ironic and humorous: "My very photogenic mother died in a freak accident (picnic, lightning) when I was three, and, save for a pocket of warmth in the darkest past, nothing of her subsists within the hollows and dells of memory, over which, if you can still stand my style (I am writing under observation), the sun of my infancy had set."[55] In this case, the parentheses contain the alter ego of Humbert Humbert. We see that within the parentheses is the text that Humbert Humbert wants to hide from "observation"; inside these curls is the evil (and funny) Humbert Humbert, while outside them is the Humbert that is trying to be appropriate in front of a jury, trying to convince them of his innocence. At times, parentheticals function as addendum; there are more French than American parentheticals, and Russian words do not exist. But much of the time the reader senses that Humbert Humbert seeks a more intimate, more tolerant audience when ensconced inside the parentheses than he does when outside them. The parentheses are more than editorial additions; they reverberate with irony or emotion: "A few more words about Mrs. Humbert while the going is good (a bad accident is to happen quite soon)" (*Lolita,* 79); "She groped for words. I supplied them mentally ('*He* broke my heart. *You* merely broke my life')" (279). After Charlotte Haze is killed, Humbert Humbert offers his own visual imagery for his role: "I had actually seen the agent of fate. I had palpated the very flesh of fate—and its padded shoulder. A brilliant and monstrous mutation had suddenly taken place, and here was the instrument. Within the intricacies of the pattern (hurrying housewife, slippery pavement, a pest of a dog, steep grade, big car, baboon at its wheel), I could dimly distinguish my own vile contribution" (103). The Nabokov in parentheticals is a freed man: from his position of exile, he wrote as if uncensored by self-consciousness. America allowed Nabokov a literary license that he had not had before. He could reinvent a story of exile in America; release a weird mixture of envy and respect; clothe it in disdain; and incarnate it in Humbert Humbert. Nabokov once said he was the dictator in the world he invented, and in *Lolita* the narration seems to veer between sheer satire and lifelike dialogue. Writing *Lolita* caused him to recreate his American experience; he had to immerse himself in the project of being American in order to understand America: "I lacked the necessary information—that was the initial difficulty. I did not know any American twelve-year-old girls, and I did not know America; I had to invent America and Lolita. It had taken me some forty years to invent Russia and Western Europe, and now I was faced by a similar task, with a lesser amount of time at my disposal. The obtaining of such local ingredients as would allow me to inject average 'reality' into the brew of individual fancy proved, at fifty, a much more difficult process than it had been in the Europe of my youth."[56] Still, Nabokov managed to research American adolescence thoroughly, and, as an exile, could succeed in acting on "individual fancy" or, as he referred to it, his "favorite habit—the habit of freedom."[57] His comprehension of "individual fancy" helped shape *Lolita;* Nabokov had the insight to see the potential for perversity that could reside in artistic creation. He transposed this insight onto a story that would illustrate the connection between artistic creation, freedom, and fluency. Humbert Humbert is the dark persona of the exile, whereas Pnin, who asks very little of life, redeems the exile with his dreams and longings.

Nabokov uses the word "ersatz" to describe his sense of his own English, and writes to a friend: "I am afraid my imitation English has let me down."[58] Nabokov never held a spontaneous interview because he felt that he spoke "like a child."[59] Instead, he left his interviewers with index cards providing answers to the questions that they would have sent beforehand. He insisted to interviewers that in all his endeavors in which English was involved, he had to rewrite everything.

English was Nabokov's naughty child, his Lolita. His twisted muse eventually subordinated his former Russian muse though it did not eliminate her—a linguistic transition that Elizabeth Klosty Beaujour describes as "not the absolute suppression or replacement of the first language, but rather a rearrangement of the linguistic layers, a shift in subordination."[60] Still, Nabokov experienced this new loyalty as painfully demanding a withdrawal from his former Russian muse: "On my walk, I was pleasantly pierced by a lightning bolt of inspiration. I had a passionate desire to write, and write in Russian, and I must not. I don't think that anyone who has not experienced the feeling can really understand its tortuousness, its tragic aspect."[61]

Nabokov admits, however, that his English is new, comparable to the emerging butterfly from a pupa that has undergone a metamorphosis: "The re-Englishing of a Russian re-version of what had been an English re-telling of Russian memories in the first place, proved to be a diabolical task, but some consolation was given me by the thought that such multiple metamorphosis, familiar to butterflies, had not been tried by any human before."[62] For Nabokov, the subordination is one in which a greater passion subdues a lesser one. *Lolita* is an esoteric love affair with a language that in concept seems anachronistic. The temporary ban on *Lolita* in the decade after it was published probably amused Nabokov, because he was trying to describe and make alive in *Lolita* something completely unrelated to the matter of incest: loving to learn a new language.

Nabokov states in the afterword to *Lolita* that the novel is a love affair with English. John Hollander wrote a review of *Lolita* that extends this idea: "But in *Lolita,* the word-play leads back to love-play always: it is a little like an extended trope or the pathetic fallacy; in which verbal hocus-pocus makes the obsessive object light up, in intellectual neon, everywhere." He continues in later passages: "*Lolita,* if it's anything 'really,' is the record of Mr. Nabokov's love affair with the romantic novel, a today-unattainable literary object as short-lived of beauty as it is long of memory."[63] Decades later, Hollander's critique was reaffirmed and extended by Thomas Frosch: "The most valuable insight about *Lolita* that I know is John Hollander's idea of the book as a 'record of Mr. Nabokov's love affair with the romantic novel, a today-unattainable literary object as short-lived of beauty as it is long of memory.' I would add that parody is Nabokov's way of getting as close to the romantic novel as possible and, more, that he actually does succeed in re-creating it in a new form, or one that is contemporary and original, not anachronistic and imitative." Frosch later asserts that the linguistic is at the forefront in Nabokov's love-play: "His displacement of the formula from the literary to the linguistic is instructive. Indeed, both in theory and practice, he is always moving the linguistic, the stylistic, and the artificial to center-stage."[64]

If *Lolita* is Nabokov's expression of love for English, the author certainly picked a strange medium for that love. But Humbert Humbert shares some traits with Nabokov, although of course he is morally Nabokov's opposite. He is a dandified outsider who has refined tastes. But these tastes are highly exaggerated in *Lolita,* and Humbert Humbert is conscious of being a foppish mystery to Dick Schiller, describing himself as a "fragile, *frileux,* diminutive, old-world, youngish but sickly, father in velvet coat and beige vest, maybe a viscount" (*Lolita,* 273).

If *Lolita* is a love affair with English, Humbert Humbert is the metaphor for an uneasy middle-aged love. His prose is tense with discomfort in the environment, constantly shifting and adjusting to external shocks, or commenting on the sly during conversations about the other person's manner of speaking (this happens when the connection between people and a place is tenuous and weak). "It is in part because he is nothing like a native that Humbert can mimic the natives so well. Ramsdale, New England, is the 'gem of an eastern state,' and New England itself ('elms,' 'white church') is just what our clichés thought it was" (*Lolita,* 113).

Despite having much in common with Humbert Humbert, Nabokov adamantly asserted in interviews and elsewhere that he had none of Humbert Humbert's pedophilic urges. He was much more innocent, almost naive: he tried to hide his love affair with a language using the metaphor of pedophilia—a subtle allegory. Perhaps he thought pedophilia had much in common with his acquisition of American English. He felt self-indulgent; he felt American English had some childish phrases; and he felt clumsy, compared to all the children who could speak English fluently. Whatever the reasons, it is clear that the atmosphere of America also had a fresh influence on Nabokov's writing and creativity. Its free, radical, democratic environment allowed him to release his sense of linguistic isolation, of alternately fumbling and regaining balance in a new culture, in a radical way. Moments of lightness and ecstasy in *Lolita* reflect his joy in using English. The reader can feel that he reveled in writing English; he says rightly that he could "scale peaks" in the language.[65]

Nabokov capitalized on this sense of freedom by carrying the motif of pedophilia to its extremes. As usual, his work raises some questions about language and the pathway to mastering it. To what extent do we need to fall in love with it? Do we own it when we love it? What if we cannot own what we love? What does it mean to fall in love with a child? How close can we love someone before they become an unhealthy form of property? A hint of this wistful ambiguity lingers in Nabokov's own words below:

> It may be curious, but what charms me personally about American civilization is exactly that old-world touch, that old-fashioned something which clings to it despite the hard glitter, and hectic night-life, and up-to-date bathrooms, and lurid advertisements, and all the rest of it. Bright children, you know, are always conservative. When I come across "daring" articles in your reviews—there was one about condoms in the last *Mercury*—I seem to hear your brilliant moderns applauding themselves for being such brave naughty boys. Buster Brown has grown up. America is beautifully young and naïf, and has a magnificent intellectual future, far beyond its wildest dreams, perhaps.[66]

Humbert Humbert describes America as "the country of rosy children and great trees, where life would be such an improvement on dull dingy Paris" (*Lolita*, 27). He also mocks American intellectual life, and in a very European gesture characterizes Americans as childlike. Despite this show of disdain for America, Nabokov loved learning American English so much that he wanted to study its evolution, beginning from children's use of English. He realized that this love had its subversive aspects: the lack of English fluency opened up a space for corruption, for impersonation. In order to gain full fluency, Nabokov felt he had to pursue the children who spoke it and mimic their slang, much like Humbert Humbert, the relentless voyeur.

Amid the decadence, however, there are also some wondrous aspects to learning a language, and again we have the complex project of building a complete view of Nabokov's deep relationships to language, specifically English. Certainly he emphasizes that, in encountering the newness of a linguistic world, we are thrust into our primal instinctual world again—we have to relearn the relationship between signs and objects all over again—and we find ourselves returning to a very physical self-consciousness of how our body enunciates, pronounces, declares these signs. The writing in *Lolita* brings out the sensual qualities of language. To comprehend its richness requires more than intellectual understanding: "Lolita, light of my life, fire of my loins. My sin, my soul. Lo-lee-ta: the tip of the tongue taking a trip of three steps down the palate to tap, at three, on the teeth. Lo. Lee. Ta." (*Lolita,* 9). The affair with English starts here. This is a tribute more to the physical production of English than to the girl it describes. It is an orgy of words and alliteration. But Humbert Humbert is obsessed with literary English: "Humbert's dandyish taste for alliteration is so thoroughly indulged that he becomes almost unreadable at times. He is a prodigious stylist, capable of wonders. But he is also a fussy aesthete, capable of driving us crazy, and both aspects of his performance are important. Some of the alliteration is briskly comic, sardonically overwrought: 'garrulous, garlicky,' 'tuberculosis in the tundra,' 'hideous hieroglyphics,' 'maroon morons,' 'maudlin murals,' 'bridge and bourbon,' 'desire and dyspepsia,' and the spectacular 'connubial catch-as-catch-can.'"[67] Nabokov's use of words is verbal indul-

gence. Notice how he describes the physical action it requires
to produce the aural creation "Lolita." The words remind us
of their physicality, of their rhythm, of their association with
the body and thus their possibility to titillate. In contrast, a facility with words often signifies sexual precocity: the capacity for
wordplay reveals a capacity for sexual playfulness. For example,
Charlotte Haze is described as a "Bland American" (83) and "one
of those women whose polished words may reflect a book club
or bridge club, or any other deadly conventionality, but never her
soul; women who are completely devoid of humour; women utterly indifferent at heart to the dozen or so possible subjects of a
parlor conversation, but very particular about the rules of such
conversations" (37). She cannot find satisfaction in her sexual life
because she cannot trust words, cannot find words to create a
conversation. Nabokov equates the ability to make a conversation with the ability to inspire sexuality.

Charlotte's polished words may have nothing behind them,
but Humbert Humbert is portrayed as the Casanova of languages, with an arsenal of French, German, and English to play
with. With American English he is artful, and with his muse he
is able to play with his words even as he professes to lose control
over them: "'What's the katter with misses?' I mutter (word-con-
trol gone) into her hair. 'If you must know,' she said, 'you do it
the wrong way.' 'Show wight ray.' 'All in good time,' responded
the spoonerette" (120). Humbert Humbert's conversations with
Clare Quilty reveal that Quilty might be Nabokov's nemesis,
the man who has full control over English (as represented by
the child Lolita) and doesn't love the language but still profits
from it. Nabokov indirectly indicts America for having this gift
of English but bastardizing it with bad taste—like Quilty, who
writes plays but also indulges in sleazy pornography projects. In

one scene, sparring repartee between the two competitors can be construed as a conflict over language:

> "Where the devil did you get her?"
>
> "I beg your pardon?"
>
> "I said: the weather is getting better."
>
> "Seems so."
>
> "Who's the lassie?"
>
> "My daughter."
>
> "You lie—she's not."
>
> "I beg your pardon?"
>
> "I said: July was hot. Where's her mother?"
>
> "Dead."
>
> "I see. Sorry. By the way, why don't you two lunch with me tomorrow. That dreadful crowd will be gone by then."
>
> "We'll be gone too. Good night." (127)

If the reader chooses to view this conversation on the allegorical level that I suggest runs throughout *Lolita,* this conversation can be seen as an example of Nabokov's own sense of being a feeble conversationalist. Here, he is outwitted in a banal, puerile way by someone who has greater conversational command. Nabokov, who we have seen always attested to being awkward with English, shares this, at least, with Humbert Humbert.

Nabokov pursued English, as Humbert Humbert pursues Lolita, only to discover that its life was often derived from slang and foul language: "The Lolita whose iliac crests had not yet flared, the Lolita that today I could touch and smell and hear and see, the Lolita of the strident voice and the rich brown hair—of the bangs and the swirls at the sides and the curls at the back, and the sticky hot neck, and the vulgar vocabulary—'revolting,' 'super,' 'luscious,' 'goon,' 'drip'—that Lolita, my Lolita, poor

Catullus would lose forever" (67–68). Passages in the novel imply that Humbert Humbert is, like Nabokov, captivated by Lolita's language despite its crudity: "Humbert Humbert is infinitely moved by the little one's slangy speech, by her harsh high voice. Later heard her volley crude nonsense at Rose across the fence. Twanging through me in a rising rhythm. Pause. 'I must go now, kiddo'" (42). He calls her "Loquacious Lo" (140) and becomes nervous whenever she stops talking.

Love of language leads Humbert to place her in the literary tradition by building her with a linguistic inheritance left by Poe. "Oh, my Lolita, I have only words to play with!" (32), he utters at one point. Like Nabokov, who was teased and chided by his English muse, Lolita says to Humbert Humbert in response to his flirtations with other European languages, "Speak English!" (149), to prevent him from straying. Humbert Humbert rebels against his own Americanization by "constant dropping into fragments of French" (112). But Michael Wood questions the authenticity of this rebellion, asserting that it is "not a real retreat into a foreign language—none of these phrases expresses anything Humbert couldn't say in English, and indeed what is there that Humbert couldn't say in English?"[68] But Humbert Humbert wants to set himself apart and retreat from the harsh lines of his English muse—its swear words, its jargonistic excesses, the reality that he is not as American as his muse. The English of the "panting maniac," Humbert Humbert, is remarkable: it is so full of self-indulgence and flamboyance that it repulses, but at the same time it seduces and entrances. The reader feels disoriented by this book, by this freaky English. It seems, perhaps, always on the brink of breaking into psychobabble: "I kept repeating chance words after her—barmen, alarmin', my charmin', my carmen, ahmen, ahahamen—as one talking and laughing in his sleep while my happy hand crept up her sunny leg as far as the shadow of decency allowed" (60). A page later, we get a song: "O my Carmen, my little Carmen!" (61). The unpredictable variations that occur on every page are evidence of desire racing so quickly past thought that language can barely keep up with its pace. The reader is left following the erratic path that desire traces.

Nabokov means us to see that Humbert Humbert, being an exile, cannot communicate in a normal fashion. But the excuse is weak: Humbert's is merely an extreme form of self-deceiving rhetoric, for to some degree all of us have this type of "moral geography, infinitely reworked and rejigged and also very quirky in the first place" (119).

The novel is faithful to its allegory. The romantic scenes are rarely descriptive, but there is always a celebration of language and a fascination with its power to evoke. "I see Annabel in such general terms as: 'honey-colored skin,' 'thin arms,' 'brown bobbed hair,' 'long lashes,' 'big bright mouth'" (*Lolita*, 11). In fact, the introduction—in one of its less pretentious moments—even comments on how the language of the novel is an aphrodisiac:

> True, not a single obscene term is to be found in the whole work; indeed, the robust philistine who is conditioned by modern conventions into accepting without qualms a lavish array of four-letter words in a banal novel, will be quite shocked by their absence here. If, however, for this paradoxical prude's comfort, an editor attempted to dilute or omit scenes that a certain type of mind might call "aphrodisiac" (see in this respect the monumental decision rendered by the Honorable John M. Woolsey in regard to another, considerably more outspoken, book),

one would have to forgo the publication of *Lolita* altogether, since those very scenes that one might ineptly accuse of a sensuous existence of their own, are the most
strictly functional ones in the development of a tragic tale
tending unswervingly to nothing less than a moral apo-
theosis. (*Lolita*, 7)

Being able to allow artistic language as his aphrodisiac, Nabokov
finally feels able to transcend his previous discomforts with language, which had also translated into a discomfort with sexuality. It is hard to feel sexy when stuttering. Mastery over one's sexuality often relies on mastery over a language, for wooing and
seducing require wit and a feeling of comfort with the language
one will use for courtship.

Courageously and self-consciously, Nabokov allows us to see
his struggle with English on the most intimate level (of which
Lolita and *Pnin* are only two examples). He clearly saw his relationship to English as an emotional one, one that conflicted
with his Russian identity. Regardless, he commits to English for
life. In the words of Humbert Humbert, he writes: "I am thinking of aurochs and angels, the secret of durable pigments, prophetic sonnets, the refuge of art. And this is the only immortality you and I may share, my Lolita" (309). Humbert Humbert
may have been referring to the girl when he wrote this, but
Nabokov was alluding to the novel.

Mortal Beauty

The moral sense in mortals is the duty
We have to pay on mortal sense of beauty.

—VLADIMIR NABOKOV, *Lolita* (1955)

Nabokov realized that his love of the English language could lead to psychosis. Humbert Humbert believed that the power of art could absolve him from moral responsibility. He addresses the jury on the first page with the largeness of rhetoric, desiring us to give him absolution, forgiveness, or some acknowledgment of understanding. He does not desire acceptance into the moral community after death, but wants a certain acknowledgment that he has a moral claim to his actions. He seeks justification.

The kind of justification he desires is aesthetic. Lucy Maddox writes: "Humbert's choice of allusions already tells us a lot about his proclivities and about the kind of literary tradition in which he would like to place himself. Appropriately, the writer he appeals to most often is Edgar Allan Poe." Maddox suggests that he intends to call upon the power of writers like Poe ("Annabel Lee") to service our view of him as a benignly obsessive, even poetically obsessive individual: "As a writer, Poe was fascinated by the nature of obsession."[69] Yet Humbert also manipulates the techniques of Proust and Keats to evoke an affiliation for the aesthetic perfection he desires, and calls upon Dante and Petrarch to bolster the idea that fornicating with children can be viewed as decent if accompanied with the proper high sentiments. Maddox includes these authors in her review of the literary tradition that Humbert Humbert evokes. But there is more to this evocation than self-defense: the placement of Humbert Humbert amid a constellation of all sorts of writers, across time and countries, makes him an even more inaccessible, mysterious, confused figure than the Euro-exile he is. He wants the reader to be lost in this constellation, and to be overwhelmed by its capacity to create dizziness and loss of judgment and loss of solid ground. If we float in the realm of fantasy and let ourselves be enchanted by his story just as we have by the literary confections of the past, then we begin to share his world, even though he makes it plain that he is happy to reside there alone because of his superior aesthetic sensibility. But the beauty in his language is at odds with the ugliness of the moral disorder that occurs. This disjunction prevents him from forming a thread of communicative trust between himself and his community, as well as between himself and the reader.

To disorient the reader even more as to where a morally reliable voice might be found, the novel's introduction is written by the rather pretentious "John Ray, Ph.D.," whose righteousness at times seems even less morally self-conscious than Humbert Humbert's periodic self-lacerating criticisms. The kind of language that each employs is representative of what their moral vision is like (one rigid, closed-minded, and dry; the other lavishly self-indulgent). But given this, we become aware of how pliable this vision is because it is partially at the mercy of the stability of language habits: the linguistic practices seem to reinforce the moral ones, and vice versa. Here, judgment is complicated because we are in a literary world, and the literary world that is most beautifully expressed is that of a child molester. Given an unwieldy, unattractively expressed moral vision, we sometimes wonder what kind of sacrifices we might make for a novel like *Lolita*. In the interest of beauty, sometimes temporarily squelching righteousness—even if it protects children—may occur if we surrender to our compassion for Humbert Humbert. We must then confess that sometimes moral visions are unattractive. But what can sustain them? Shouldn't they be beautiful? And how is it possible to combine the infinite promise of beauty with the limits that moral standards imply? The novel constantly provokes this question, with its evocation of images of fairy-tale love juxtaposed with grisly reality.

In a glorious example—when Humbert Humbert visits Lolita

as Mrs. Richard F. Schiller, the power of words to inflict moral standards opens us up to the complicated situation Nabokov presents the reader in the novel:

> "What things?"
>
> "Oh, weird, filthy, fancy things. I mean, he had two girls and two boys, and three or four men and the idea was for all of us to tangle in the nude while an old woman took movie pictures." (Sade's Justine was twelve at the start.)
>
> "What things exactly?"
>
> "Oh, things . . . Oh, I—really I"—she uttered the "I" as a subdued cry while she listened to the source of the ache, and for lack of words spread the five fingers of her angularly up-and-down-moving hand. No, she gave it up, she refused to go into particulars with that baby inside her.
>
> That made sense. (*Lolita*, 277)

The most surprising line is Humbert Humbert's unverbalized thought, "That made sense." He is a self-indulgent rapist, but still has the moral capacity to acknowledge the etiquette that Lolita is invoking. And this is deeply respectful and even altruistic. He does not, with blinkered selfishness, continue to harass her to leave with him. This is one of the first moments of enlightenment for Humbert Humbert: he sees Lolita as a separate soul with a private, untouchable will to do as she believes. He has no designs here; he waits for her consent—as if for the first time seeing her as having the right to dissent.

Here, too, Nabokov fleshes out Lolita's Americanness. The language of Lolita and her husband is sprinkled with slang:

> "Dick, this is my Dad!" (273)

> "Aw, she's a swell kid, Mr. Haze, and she's going to make a swell mother." (274)

"I think"—she went on—"oops"—the envelope skidded to
the floor—she picked it up—"I think it's oh utterly grand
of you to give us all that dough." (279)

Although Humbert describes his few minutes alone with Dick
as that which "positively welled with artificial warmth" (274), he
acknowledges that Dick's wrist was "far, far finer" than his own.
In contrast to the simple, content carpenter, Humbert is satis-
fied only with his notion of grandeur. The linguistic clash awakens us to the weak and shabby nature of Humbert's aspirations,
particularly, as Wood notes, when Humbert asks Lolita to go
away with him once more. This last request, full of horrible
selfishness and lousiness, is still pathetically framed in his aspirations to grand tragedy—he's the kind of character that, Michael Wood points out, exists in Flaubert or Joyce. Wood shows
how the conversation moves from faux romanticism to the comfortably, solidly banal:

> The shift is pictured in this chapter in a beautifully
> placed, entirely banal American word. Humbert repeats
> his request that Lolita/Carmen come away with him
> ("Carmen, voulez-vous . . .") and she says, "No, honey, no."
> Humbert reflects, "She had never called me honey before."
> She couldn't call him honey before, because she didn't
> think of him fondly enough or casually enough: banality
> was outlawed from their life, which was only romance and
> torture (for him), drudgery and quarantine (for her). For a
> moment, Humbert seems to glimpse the attraction of the
> acceptable and the familiar, of the way other people daily
> talk and live—the realm of shared feeling which inhabits
> cliché and which cliché serves.[70]

Humbert's insistence on his obsession and his deification of it keep him from sharing this world of the normal and everyday. The everyday is only cliché, from Humbert's point of view. He finds no joy in daily reality, and prefers to hide from it by indulging in self-absorbed fantasy. This is evident in his insistence on metaphorizing Lolita, comparing her to shards of history: Florentine breasts, Carmen, Botticelli's Venus, Sade's Justine (274, 270, 276). But the whole of historical and literary reference cannot patch together a makeshift story for him, something that justifies child rape. It is communal dialogue that Nabokov points to that holds reality together. The "oops," "swell," and "utterly grand" of Dolly and Dick's conversation refuses grandeur but is a communal language, while Humbert Humbert's tragedy is that fantastical conversation—*his* conversation—is finite.

Linguistic pompousness, leading to narrative unreliability, is thus just surface evidence of how complicated the creation of a moral community can be in a novel. Nabokov pushes our notion of morality even further in *Lolita* than in *Pnin,* which confronts us with the subtle and overt cruelties of different levels of xenophobia, but also the detriments of isolation. In *Lolita,* we have the horrors that can occur when the exile has no sense of agency and too much fantasy, when desire is more important than the person who desires. The poignancy of *Lolita* lies in the fact that Humbert Humbert's dreams for transcendence are inversely proportional to the reality that he barely held the attention of his "nymphet"; like Pnin, he cannot seem to be taken seriously enough so that people believe he is a vessel of passion. Instead, his English, his language, is so unworldly that he remains an exile, a relic, a figure disemboweled of reality. Finally, his death is anonymous, cementing the uncertainty about the entire affair, as well as its literary immortality. But Humbert Humbert is a destroyer: everything he has touched in the world he destroys. As if he had the alchemical touch of Midas, Humbert Humbert is a destroyer of value and life. (Note that Lolita dies in childbirth and her mother's death is connected to her involvement with Humbert Humbert.) For Humbert Humbert, there is no community in which he can express his desire (part of this is self-inflicted), so his language, like his desire, is secret: a discrete, self-absorbed entity. Like Pnin, Humbert Humbert's linguistic utopia has space for only one—himself—and even his random acts of decency fail to travel to a moral community. His language searches, unrequited, for the other.

2

Chinky Writing

This is it. Here's one you'll like. That is, likee. Guarantee.
Ah. I mean, aiya. Wokking on da Waywoad. Centing da
dollahs buck home to why-foo and biby. No booty-full
Ah-mei-li-can gal-low fo me. Aiya. Aiya.

—MAXINE HONG KINGSTON, *Tripmaster Monkey* (1987)

"Yanwai ngoh hai yat goh soft-hearted pushover, ngoh
wuih only put up leih-ge rent to seventy-cheen mun. O-
mm-o-kay?" (Translation: "Because I am one piece of
soft-hearted pushover, I will only put up your rent to seventy thousand dollars. O-not-o-kay?")

—NURY VITTACHI, "From Yinglish to Sadomastication," in
Kingsley Bolton, ed., *Hong Kong English* (2002)

Chinese American "language," known as
Chinglish, is not a recognized language, de-
spite its ubiquity. Semiological theory has not been applied to
analyzing this syncretic phenomenon, even though Chinese

American artists use it in their work as a language. It is viewed as a shameful and broken language, rather than linguistically invigorating. It has been associated with stunted psychic development and limited self-awareness.[1]

Despite all this, Chinglish represents an aspect of Chinese American life.[2] It is the language of the Chinese American diasporic moment.[3] This chapter will interrogate the view that Chinglish is a parody of English, and will revalue its experimental features as signs of linguistic courage and independence. I will examine passages from Maxine Hong Kingston's novels *The Woman Warrior* (1975), *China Men* (1977), and *Tripmaster Monkey* (1987), as sites of the evolution of Chinglish—from an "uncool" stuttering origin to a thoroughly self-conscious linguistic use.

Chinglish records a historical moment, a diasporic phenomenon that cannot be as precisely said in any other language. Its aurality and rhythm force recognition of the impact of transition on Chinese immigrants. Kingston's work should be appropriated as a linguistic record of this experience. Within her texts are countless examples of Chinglish and her authorial positioning to them. Her presentation and inclusion of Chinglish suggest her emotional investment in preserving it. Yet her absorption of available linguistic theory while she was writing her novels polluted a potentially pure presentation of Chinglish. Instead of straightforwardly recording linguistic material, she toys with wrongheaded views of theorists who lack fluency in Chinese. In her first publication, *The Woman Warrior,* she seems obsessed with the ideograph. In her later novels, she retreats from emphasizing the ideographic aspects of Chinese and focuses on the sounds, vocabulary, intonations, and grammar of Chinglish. Her three novels trace a gradual retreat from the ideographic aspect of Chinese and a gradual ascension of the aural as a locus of meaning.[4] This phenomenon underlies the syncretic formation of Chinglish as a real language.

Funky Translations

Pidgin stands for—it makes audible and visible—the incommensurability of languages.

—HAUN SAUSSY, *The Great Wall of Discourse* (2002)

We can appreciate a language without fluency in or knowledge of that language. Speakers of English can often guess the meanings of words in Romance languages. We can appreciate the music of countless languages without understanding a word, and this reception is similar to the reception we have for music. We might use a language as a gimmick[5] to communicate our liking for that language or a fetish for its look or sound. In these cases, our attitude to these languages is hopeful; we want to bridge a conceptual division between ourselves and the foreign culture. Ezra Pound, for example, liked the look of Chinese characters but did not have a fluent command of Chinese. In his poetry, criticism, and translation work, he explored his affinity for Chinese.[6] Yet, as his case shows, lack of comprehension and the failure to see bundles of letters or marks as constitutive of a language can compromise aesthetic interpretation. Appreciation is inadequate if the marks that represent a language are mere visual art; in such a situation, the reader and the work remain foreign to each other.

We must see Chinglish as a language, and attempt to deconstruct it, in order to understand the full meaning of Kingston's work. After encountering a few lines of Chinglish, readers can intuit how much they are missing without translators.[7] And it is necessary to engage in interpretive work with translation in order to gain an honest vision of the author's work.[8] With regard to Asian American texts, those who refuse participation in these acts will be excluded from the absorbing Asian American texts and from the cultural capital of such texts. Contemporary Chinese American literature demands that readers become translators, or at least recognize the need for translation and its status as a phenomenon. The text itself, in Chinese American language, reveals the performance of cultural invention, and the re-formation of culture. It shows us the growing union of two cultures but also points out their sustained differences. It also complicates what we classify as cross-cultural.[9]

Do we remain hesitant to affirm Chinese American language aesthetically because we cannot understand it? What does it mean that *The Woman Warrior,* which contains the least Chinglish, is by far the most widely read and most popular of all Kingston's novels? Using her work as a variable, American consumers of her novels have favored less Chinglish rather than more. *The Woman Warrior*—with its sparse Chinglish—has been more successful than *China Men* (some Chinglish) or *Tripmaster Monkey* (abundant examples of Chinglish). Sales rankings by Amazon.com on April 15, 2002, showed *The Woman Warrior* positioned at 7,760.[10] *China Men* had a ranking of 62,822, while *Tripmaster Monkey* stood at 104,764. Critics (such as David Leiwei Li and Yunte Huang) have written about the popularity of *The Woman Warrior* and about its canonical status. It is often said to be the most widely taught novel in American universities.[11]

The success of *The Woman Warrior*—and the less prominent success of *China Men* and *Tripmaster Monkey*—suggest that *The Woman Warrior* has translated emotionally[12] to the mainstream to a greater extent than *China Men* and *Tripmaster Monkey,* even though *China Men* contains a riveting narrative of the Vietnam War and *Tripmaster Monkey* evokes the nostalgia of the beatnik era. Some critics engage in ethnographic analyses of Kingston's work, suggesting that *The Woman Warrior* is appropriable because its ethnic representations are culturally palatable to American readers.[13] Others suggest Kingston exoticizes Asian culture in this book through her use of Chinese myths, thus attracting Sinophilic reactions. In a new wave of critique, Kingston's successful appeal is due to the flagrant American nature of her Chinese cultural translations. Yunte Huang writes that she consciously pursues Americanizing in her books, while David Leiwei Li asserts that "what is truly a marvel is the way in which the author of *The Woman Warrior* prophetically enshrines her work in the 'Masterpiece Theater' of American literature.... Kingston strategically revises yet another Chinese legend, the capture of the second-century Chinese woman poet T'sai Yen by the barbarians, and transforms it into a superb meta-narrative for entry into the canon."[14] Yunte Huang echoes Li's description of Kingston, focusing on how she packages *The Woman Warrior:*[15] "What is most profoundly 'American' about Kingston's work are the ways in which stories like 'Mulan' are transformed and the ways in which this transformation is interpreted by literary scholars. Both the transformation and its interpretation exemplify a linguistic positivism shared by canonical American literature and Asian American literature in its current formation. It is this shared conception of language that brings Kingston closer to the American literary canon and makes her work truly 'American.'"[16]

Notably, neither critic cites the other in their parallel arguments about Kingston's self-inscription into the canon. Both of their extended critiques on transnational Asian literature illuminate the qualities of this literature with the exception of Kingston's work. Huang's precise, insightful critique of John Yau's countermockery of Chinglish is juxtaposed with a chapter on the American standard English of Kingston. His sense of Chinglish suggests that it is (1) a ventriloquized language, (2) a pidgin that might be creative if parodied, (3) a gaggle of bad or ill-informed efforts at translation by nonnative and nonfluent speakers, or (4) possibly even a strategically racist transcription or interpretation of dialogue: "A case in point is the second writer I discuss, who has participated in the cacophonic ensemble of representing the Chinese language—the contemporary Asian American poet John Yau. Whereas Imagists ventriloquize Chinese without parody and Biggers parodies its speakers through pidginization, John Yau follows the ventriloquism by further ventriloquizing it and parodies pidginization by further pidginizing it."[17] Huang's characterization of the "cacophonic ensemble" is humorously accurate, but his presentation of Chinglish as parody in this passage confines his interpretive scope. There are several examples of pidginization of minority discourses that have been transformed and appropriated—in a less dark spirit than Yau's—by minorities themselves; in fact it is precisely at these moments of appropriation that we see the possibility for a language that refuses ventriloquism and becomes a voice of self-affirmation. Kingston's work possesses this reformative possibility for Chinglish. In fact, in later passages, Huang begins to conceive of Chinglish as a language that goes beyond lack of fluency, that requires ingenuity in its very creation, in his analysis of Lin Yutang's work.[18] He ultimately judges Chinglish, however, as ventriloquism: "We should bear in mind that all these pidgin expressions are literal translations from Chinese. Put in a different context—in Charlie Chan's mouth, for instance—these Chinglish expressions would, to be sure, become examples of a debased tongue spoken by a debased race. But it is also interesting to see how closely these expressions resemble the version of Chinese as promulgated by the Imagists and the related ethnographers, using either Pound/Fenollosa's ideogrammic method or Lowell/Ayscough's analytic method."[19] Huang's comparison of Changlish to Pound's translations of Chinese suggests that both are forms of automatic writing. These writers are all translating fragments of Chinese without fluent command of the language, reducing them to occasionally accurate ciphers. This differs from Kingston's work, which documents the formation and use of Chinglish as she has experienced it firsthand. It is not Changlish, a purposeful parodying of Chinese speakers using English, nor is it an Imagist's attempt at uninformed translation. Kingston's Chinglish is linguistically empowering, a language that is actually used in communities rather than imagined or appropriated. Furthermore, Kingston, unlike Pound, Fenollosa, or Gertrude Stein, is an Asian American writer who has had close experience of Chinglish.

Huang's criticisms of Kingston extend to the effects he imagines her writing to have. He accuses her of writing in standardized American English, even though there is ample evidence of Chinglish in Kingston's work. Later he argues that such linear writing results in the formation of American identity:

> Despite her alleged "political correctness," Kingston's work becomes literarily problematic in that it is a positivistic approach to an American identity, which in turn may be reclaimed positivistically by means of standardized American-English writing. In contrast, Stein writes in "Identity a Poem": "I am I because my little dog knows me. The fig-

ure wanders on alone. . . . I say two dogs but say a dog and
a dog." My identity is only a label by which my little dog
knows me. But does even the little dog have an identity? I
can say "two dogs," and if you think "two dogs" is a common identity attached to the two dogs, I can simply call
them "a dog and a dog," thus separating the same but different "a dog." The indeterminacy of identity results from
the impossibility of pinning down which one "a dog" refers to.[20]

These accusations deny the complexity of Kingston's work, and
they also expose a bias that underlies Huang's critiques. He contrasts Kingston, *a novelist*, with Gertrude Stein, *a poet*. This is
significant to note because it illuminates a difference of intention between the two authors about what constitutes literary
achievement. Furthermore, if literary language reflects identity
formation, then poetry (where linguistic fragmentation is an accepted form) and novels (where narrative form is crucial) do not
have comparable approaches in the constant construction of
identity formation. Huang does not look for fragmentation on
the level of sentence in narrative. At a distance, he remarks on
the prevalence of standard English in Kingston's novel without
referencing Kingston's other writings, which I believe exhibit
identity-in-construction in a fragmented form in the language
of Chinglish. Is Kingston's project to claim an American identity
in the way that Huang suggests? If he asserts an argument of
positivism through language, as he does here, it is necessary for
him to compare one of Kingston's Chinglish passages to Stein's
poetic lines. Ironically, Kingston has asserted that she aspires to
emulate Stein's linguistic goals: "When I was writing 'No Name
Woman,' I was thinking about Nathaniel Hawthorne and *The*

Scarlet Letter as a discussion of the Puritan part of America, and of China, and a woman's place. I use the title, 'The Making of More Americans,' from Gertrude Stein, because when I read *The Making of Americans,* I thought, 'Yes, she is creating a language that is the American language; and she is doing it sentence by sentence. I am trying to write an American language that has Chinese accents; I will write the American language as I speak it.'"[21] Although Kingston later characterizes her linguistic project as generating "Say Yup with an American accent," the trajectory of her mission is clearly a deviation from standard American English. And she goes beyond mere linguistic experimentation by recording the emotional register of language in her Chinglish. She says of her own efforts: "When I compare our work to some of the mainstream work, it seems as if many of them are only playing with the words. . . . Toni's and Leslie's and my aliveness must come from our sense of a connection with people who have a community and a tribe."[22]

Kingston's effort to import the heaviness of anthropological history and past community into her Chinglish signifies that she is not ignorant of the stakes of reconstruction or playing around with an existing language. To do this is to also play around with history and the history of language, as well as the way people are comfortable in their language. In comparison with the Charliechanchinglish that Huang presents—a counter-mocking pidgin—Kingston's Chinglish contains, produces, and generates pain, including aesthetic pain, because her writ-ing-do-es-n'-tflow-the-wa-ywe'-re-use-dto. It makes us live the inconvenience of inarticulateness. It makes us experience the problem of an awkward rhythm, and this uncomfortable experience can lead us to mock the object that discomfits us—hence racist writing appears. The hardness of difference and *différance* makes human beings disrespect the object of their pain, and if this object is linguistic, linguistic mockery is viewed as appropriate.[23] In order to save readers for themselves in a psychologically uncomfortable zone, Kingston places Chinese American history next to her new language. Her Chinglish is interspersed within a heavy history—to indicate that the roughness of the language corresponds to the roughness of an unappreciated, difficult history and existence: "The Japanese and Chinese Americans warned one another what would happen if they got captured: the Vietnamese would flay Asian Americans alive. Unless you die of shock, you're still alive after being skinned. You had to die fighting. Imagine the eyes looking out of a skinless body."[24] In "The Making of More Americans," Kingston composes more painful imagery:

> The next morning, she found her husband. He said that the Communists had assigned them a place to live— the leper house. "That's where you belong," said the Communists. Lepers, the "growing yin" people, who have too much cold wind in them, died in there. The rest of the family had disappeared; his mother had run away alone with the gold and jade. They never saw her again. The Communists kept an eye on them in the leper house, waited for them to make a false move. One day her husband caught a pair of doves and hid them to feed the family. "And do you know how the Communists killed him?"
>
> "I think my mother said they stoned him in the tree where the birds were."
>
> "They pressed him between millstones," she said.
>
> Of course. In stories, stones fall crash bang crash bang like pile drivers.[25]

In contrast, Huang's Charlie Changlish is a racist script of pidgin-speak designed to get cheap laughs. Chan's Chinglish is embedded in phrases sillier than fortune-cookie prophecies and empty of suffering or anguish:

> Always harder to keep secret than for egg to bounce on sidewalk.

> Some heads, like hard nuts, much better if cracked.

> Mind like parachute—only function when open.[26]

It's not merely the Chinglish that Kingston wants us to understand.

Responding to Huang's arguments inevitably leads one to the texts of Kingston. Instead of being read as a writer experimenting with fluency, she should be read more as a writer in conflict with English. Her work is a testament to this linguistic belligerence, and should be read as a record of the linguistic history of Chinese American assimilation. Her politics are incidental, and focusing on them blocks interpretation. The value of her work—even regarding issues of canonization—lies in her insistence on using Chinese American enunciation, pronunciation, rhythm, and grammar in her linguistic landscape. In her books, I am concerned with the moments of marginalization that exist between the paragraphs of straightforward English. Although I will criticize much of her discussion of linguistic issues as "dated" (which redescribes but does not criticize Kingston, since the books were written decades ago), I will show how her employment of Chinese American English provides linguistic data, and thus subjective matter revealing the psyche of immigrant Chinese life. In her imagined classroom, a Chinese American is teaching a class of remedial students that think he's "gookish" and write *"fuck* and *chink* on the blackboards."[27] In response, Kingston asks that readers slow down and *read,* and confront their own remedial status as readers of multilingual texts. In her books, moments of syncretic cultural formation are the ones that require more interpretive effort. They force interest in new communities *on the part of the reader.*

Brave New Words

"I am fucking the world." He said. The world's vagina was big, big as the sky, big as a valley.

—MAXINE HONG KINGSTON, *China Men* (1977)

We made up our own English, which I wrote down and now looks like "eeeeeeeee."

—MAXINE HONG KINGSTON, *The Woman Warrior* (1975)

Chinese American English can seem as offensive as expletive-laden language. It is wrongly associated with lack of culture. Europeans without fluency in English do not carry the same stigma as Chinese Americans with broken English. But why should standard English be preferred as the literary language conveying the bicultural experience of Chinese Americans?[28] The psychoanalytic repercussions of immigration convey that Chinglish most accurately represents the formation of Chinese American identity.

Constructing an interpretive self thus means first constructing a linguistic self, a self cognizable in language. In *China Men,* Chinglish utterances exist in immigrant life; in *The Woman Warrior,* the Chinglish belongs both to immigrants and to settled immigrants with diasporic mentalities; and in *Tripmaster Mon-*

key, Chinglish is used by fully assimilated Asian Americans to analyze their bifurcated culture. In *Tripmaster Monkey* the use of Chinglish is accompanied by self-awareness and a well-defined subjectivity. In this novel, Chinglish is awkward and uncool. Its speakers unconsciously give "body" to the English language, but don't harness it the way African American rappers might.[29]

Thus, Chinglish is *not* the language of a personality, until later. It is only the language of the disenfranchised, until it becomes reappropriated later by a hippie, cool, collegiate character, Wittman Ah Sing. Until then, it is the language for those who don't have the privilege of having a personality, whose life conditions don't allow for it. Kingston's story—and despite the fact that her material is labeled "nonfiction," it is still story—is that of the development of Chinglish into a semiofficial, recognized tongue. The book *Tripmaster Monkey* becomes possible because the character Wittman Ah Sing becomes possible, and interpretation for that character becomes possible.

In Kingston's works, Chinglish becomes a language through which ideas can be transported and one through which identities can be made. Patricia Chu writes: "To belong in the city of words, Asian American writers must call for themselves 'the difficult names of who we are,' must make a place in the American national literature where their stories belong. Because culture—specifically the *Bildungsroman*—is a site for imaginatively transforming readers and protagonists into national subjects by erasing or containing their particular differences, Asian American literature reinscribes those differences in an alternative version of the genre, one in which authorship signifies not only the capacity to speak but the belief that speech—or literary representation—is also a claiming of political and social agency."[30] Chu perceptively conceptualizes the role of fiction in designing subjectivities, as well as the social and political existence for readers, characters, and authors. This recognition of the lack of Asian American linguistic selves does not, however, make reference to the actual words themselves. The words are the concrete evidence of politicized, socialized material. Chinglish is slowly becoming a linguistic entity through which communities can negotiate political, social, and personal identities.

In Kingston's work, these linguistic selves surface. Kingston approaches the issue of representing a distant culture by documenting the occurrence of Chinese fusing with English, as well as by demonstrating how the medium of talk-story charts this fusion both in content and form. Chinglish comes in many different varieties, and Kingston provides several of them; it is at times awkward, sometimes aphasic, sometimes rhythmically strange, but never purely English or Chinese. English takes on uncanny qualities as a body altered by a foreign language. In using Chinese rhythms and cadences while speaking English, immigrants create a language half-alive with the remnants of their former culture. Wittman will impose, mimic, choreograph Chinglish in comic routines that show a practiced retention of Chinglish.

The first construction of a linguistic self that Kingston engages in is herself. She first constructs herself as a subject of words. Later she constructs characters, performers, and by implication the readers or audience of these performances. On the level of words, Kingston represents in language her own project of unraveling a patchwork cultural history; her name is two-thirds American, one-third Chinese.[31] That Kingston spoke a different language, Say Yup, without knowledge of English until she was eight years of age, isolated her from the mainstream community.[32] When describing her writing style, she claims to be documenting the sounds of a hybrid language: *Say Yup with an American accent*. She invents a romanization system for a dialect that is, according to her, spoken by largely illiterate people. She distinguishes Say Yup, the dialect, from other dialects like Mandarin or Cantonese which already have elaborate and official Pinyin or other romanization systems. Say Yup does not; and thus, in order to gesture at romanizing the dialect, she must experiment: "Working in that dialect has posed some problems for me, especially in the area of orthography. The romanized spelling in Cantonese words has been worked out to some degree, but that is not true of Say Yup. And even if it were, it would not reflect the way that it is spoken: with an American accent. I'm specifically interested in how the Chinese American dialect is spoken in the California Valley. For proper names, I have made my own orthography. When I write dialogue for people who are speaking Chinese, I say the words to myself and then write them in English, hoping to capture some of the sounds and rhythms and power of Say Yup."[33]

This language inhabits new Americans whose Chinese culture has been influenced by their geographic relocation. Just as relocation to a new community may require some sartorial changes, their Chinese language needs to be readorned with Americanness. To convey this process of readornment with integrity is Kingston's aspiration.

Kingston says that "at about seven years old" she had already begun to acquire an acute awareness of the questions of language because her first language was Chinese and she "only knew people who were Chinese."[34] A year later, Kingston discovered that the English language could make her feel more invested with agency and creativity:[35] "I talked story and I invented poems and made up songs and heard stories, but when I began to know English and somewhere around eight years old, I started to write, and the English language was so . . . bright, full of freedom. . . . I thought, I can notate Chinese. I can write Chinese in English. I can write English in English. And I never had that power when I spoke only Chinese."[36] The different languages thus have different sensibilities and expressive functions for their communities.

For Kingston, learning English gave her a "present-day" language. English was a language she associated with America, a new world which opened up her sense of linguistic adventure. She writes of her first two books, "I thought, oh! There's more language in me, this other kind of language, this very slangy, American, present-day language."[37] She equates English with the present and Chinese with the past, and says her special version of English modernizes Chinese: "When I finished those two books [*China Men* and *The Woman Warrior*], I really had more language in me, and that's this modern language I speak that I wanted to play with. So I wrote this really new American language, and it really surprised me how free it is—how much room there is for other languages."[38] Kingston seems to feel that bilingualism provides meaning unattached to a specific language, or even to particular words; we can get meanings from phatic communication or communication that transcends the words or code form that packages a message. For her, Chinese and English "develop both sides of your brain." They provide not just a vocabulary but an attitude.[39]

Her knowledge of bilingualism thus helps her to see language as an open system, one that invites modification as well as translation: "That word 'Chinese-American'—that's brand-new."[40] Kingston believes that words can exert changes on the world by working on perception. Through language, she wants to reposition the Chinese American figure in culture:

I think that I change and the world changes as I work. . . . I also see myself changing the language out there. Just as one example, when I went about publicizing *China Men,* so many people would say "chinamen." They'd read the cover and see "chinamen." And I would have to correct them and explain that I made it two separate words because that's the way Chinese language is: it's all these monosyllabic single words.[41] And how the capital C and capital M add dignity and it doesn't slur. I'd have to explain all that to people. And now nine years later I find that when people introduce my titles, they say "China . . . Men," and I see that I've changed the way their mouths work. So I've straightened up the language a little bit. You know, maybe writers have to do that one word at a time. I feel a lot of triumph in just that one word.[42]

Kingston's writing makes the reader feel the weight of her authorial mission: to evolve English.

Ideographs and the Maintenance of the Cultural Divide

I married Brave Orchid.

—MAXINE HONG KINGSTON, *Conversations with Maxine Hong Kingston* (1998)

After constructing herself as a linguistic subject and creator, Kingston began to construct *others,* at times stumbling and creating, instead, *otherness,* and more obviously in her later novels, *différance.*[43] Jacques Derrida, with his introduction of *différance,* released linguistics from a dyadic system that separated, artificially, the phenomena of speech and writing.[44] In this section and the following one, I will suggest how Kingston, by recording Chinglish, reanimates English as a written form and grants it the kind of presence Derrida accords both speech and language.

In *The Woman Warrior,* Kingston relies on the idea of the ideograph, but later abandons it. How is her action reflective of a change in linguistic opinion? Certainly, Kingston is writing contemporaneously with Derrida, who is challenging the fixed nature of signs. Derrida's direct influence on Kingston is speculative, but both certainly destabilize the rigid conception of signs and signifieds in their work. Both are operating as linguistic tricksters whose relationship to language is often ironic.

Critics do not tend to analyze Chinese in Derridean terms. Today, critics are still hesitant to jettison conceptions of pictograph or ideograph in linguistic discussion that were used by structuralist theory. Kingston, at first, seems appropriable by structuralists,[45] particularly in *The Woman Warrior,* but in her later works she is much more attentive to eroding the ideograph as the epicenter of meaning in the Chinese language. This is a pioneering effort that still resonates today, since the notion of the ideograph remains popular and is still widely circulated. Kingston's increasing focus on the aural shifts attention from the ideograph to the tonal quality of Chinese that is imported into English. Her later works are more Derridean/Peircean in spirit: they complicate the enterprise of representation and signification in language, rather than assume a concept of the fixed meaning of the written. The most dramatic demonstration of Kingston's loss of faith in the written is her abandonment of the ideograph after committing to it in her first novel.

The striking differences between Chinese and English are contrasted constantly by scholars. Articles and books suggest that the ideographic foundation of Asian languages determines these cultures' capacity for abstract thought. Yet the concept of the ideograph is, as scholars like Haun Saussy and Ming Gu suggest, completely outdated.[46] Ming Gu writes, "The difference of the written sign has, since medieval times, often been viewed as a conceptual divide that separates the Chinese and Western languages. This view seems to find support in linguistic science. In his *Course in General Linguistics,* Ferdinand de Saussure divided [the] world's languages into two large writing systems: the ideographic system in which 'each language is represented by a single sign that is unrelated to the sounds of the word itself' and the phonetic system which 'tries to reproduce the succession of sounds that make up a word.'"[47] Gu is critical of this division, specifically because it mischaracterizes the complexity of Chinese and its level of abstraction. There are scholars who are waging a war against the conception of Chinese as an ideographic language (they might, in fact, not be waging a war against the ideograph so much as challenging the limited conception of how the ideograph functions in Chinese). Gu writes:

> The rejecters of the ideographic view set to their task of demolition out of an implicitly motivated reaction against a well-known linguistic "theory" in the West. According to this "theory," there were three stages in the development of writing: (1) pictographic or iconographic writing; (2) ideographic or hieroglyphic writing; (3) phonetic writing. This theory entails a prejudice explicitly expressed in Rousseau's words: "These three ways of writing correspond almost exactly to three different stages according to which one can consider men gathered into a nation. The depicting of objects is appropriate to a savage people; signs of words and of propositions, to a barbaric people;

and the alphabet to civilized people." Since Chinese writing consists of ideographs, it was considered to belong to the second stage and hence inferior.[48]

The ideograph suggests that characters are images of the world that have one-to-one correspondences with objects in the world, when in fact characters correspond to tonal linguistic units that are connected to meanings: "Even if we treat sound as an acoustic image, we have to admit that the image is auditory and hence invisible. It can never appear on paper or in other visual representation. Secondly, post-Saussurean theorists have argued that Saussure was wrong to equate the signified with the thing or concept which the signifier is meant to represent."[49] Thus, the suggestion that ideographic languages are pictographic is misguided. Gu's article expands on the way in which signs can be classified to convey a range of linguistic uses. The notion of the ideograph is only one function of the character. He refers to Xu Shen's graph-making principles, which illuminate the variety of ways in which signs can be indexed: "Xu Shen describes the six graph-making principles in the order of *zhishi* (indicate-condition), *xiangxing* (imitate-shape), *xingsheng* (shape-and-sound), *huiyi* (grasp-meaning), *zhuanzhu* (interchangeable notation), *jiajie* (loan-borrowing)." Gu unfolds each principle, demonstrating the complexity in the presentation of a single character and later mapping relations between characters to show how diverse positioning between them can impact overall meaning. His essay affirms that describing characters as ideographs is a very limited way to convey their range of functions in the Chinese language.[50]

Kingston's work documents the decline narrative of the ideograph as the foundation for Chinese from a personal standpoint; she begins as a die-hard fan of the ideograph, only to wilt later. In *The Woman Warrior*, Kingston refers to characters as "ideographs" several times, and many more times than in *China Men* and *Tripmaster Monkey* (versus, say, "logographs").[51] In *The Woman Warrior* Kingston's descriptions of the ideograph are almost naive, and later seem almost contrived: "I learned to move my fingers, hands, feet, head, and entire body in circles. I walked putting heel down first, toes pointing outward thirty to forty degrees, making the ideograph 'eight,' making the ideograph 'human.'"[52] Here, the body becomes ideograph. The body enacts the creation of an ideograph like bad performance art: descriptions of interaction with language that are crude, geometric-sounding, and wrong-headed. Later, she evokes a naturalistic ideograph: the ideograph as naturally occurring in the environment. "The call would come from a bird that flew over our roof. In the brush drawings it looks like the ideograph for 'human': two black wings. The bird would cross the sun and lift into the mountains (which look like the ideograph 'mountain'), there parting the mist briefly that swirled opaque again."[53] Within her narrative, Kingston intersperses the presence of ideographs: "The white horse pawed the ground for me to go. On the hooves of its near forefoot and hindfoot was the ideograph 'to fly.'"[54] The presence of the ideograph in the narrative is an incidental detail, but mythologizes the horse as marked out for the heroine. The ideograph reconfigures the horse into a sign. Even in the simplest design patterns, ideographs appear: "On the tube are gold circles crossed with seven red lines each—'joy' ideographs in abstract."[55] Ideographs are fragmented into parts, the way sentences are decomposed into words, as in the example above. Or they are imagined next to their romanized equivalents: "Simultaneously they heard a baby's cry come from the dumpling, the *dim sum,* the little heart."[56] This example reveals a straightforward, one-to-one function between Cantonese and English. "*Sweetheart* is an English word that emigrants readily learn."[57] The pictorial quality of the ideograph thus secures its status as something naturally occurring in the world: the Chinese simply discovered ideographs—they didn't create a language. This implication is unavoidable, especially when the authoritative voice of the novels is authorial, not derived from any of the characters. The constitution of the Chinese language is premised on the constitution of object(s), not subject(s), thus underscoring the limitations inherent in Chinese culture—and conveying the idea that Chinese culture does not engage the construction of the subjective.

Kingston writes: "How do you write *clear* and *bright?* At last, one of the boys was getting down to work, though he had forgotten two of the simplest and most commonly used ideographs in the language. . . . 'How do you write *wood?*' the boy asked. Baba wrapped his hand around the boy's and wrote the tree-like word. 'See?' Baba said. 'It looks like a tree.'"[58] Undoubtedly the word for "wood" *does* look like a tree as a Chinese character, but one could find countless examples of characters that don't perform their meaning by their design.[59] The suggestion of automatic connection is simplistic; such a system couldn't possibly be reliable, especially in more abstract discussions. Kingston persists, nevertheless, in emphasizing the centrality of the ideograph: "Anyway, a translation, Think Virtue, is nothing like his name; the English words are like fiction, that is, their sounds are dissimilar from Chinese sounds. Nobody would call anyone else by a translation, Think Virtue, his written name anyway. He is still disguised. Think Virtue—*think* is an ideograph combining the radicals for field and heart, and *virtue* also has the root heart in it; his name looks like two valentines and is not as cerebral as it appears in English."[60] This insistence is misleading in understanding the form of Chinese, although this passage takes on more complex aspects of character formation, such as the radical or root that can be a detachable common denominator among many characters. Nevertheless, the ideograph/natural object relation still threatens the formation of a cohesive subjectivity.

If the subjective faculties become endangered by such implications, the capacities involved in creating language are sold short as well. Kingston's appreciation of Chinese may extend as far as "seeing characters in the world," in the way that John Nash sees codes in the world,[61] but it is not a Chinese trait to engage in these ideograph-world-as-ideograph equations consistently. There is evidence that many characters were derived from pictographs—in fact, Ron Harbaugh's *Etymological Dictionary* had some appeal to Taipei's citizens—but this derivation did not provide the foundation. Furthermore, there is compelling evidence suggesting that sounds were circulated with more avidity and did not often correspond to a particular pictograph—so that pictographs began to represent sounds more than objects in the world. The language evolved with a combination of sound-representation and image-representation. Thus, referring to characters as "ideographs" is insufficient to describe their role in the language.

As Ming Gu writes, limiting the conception of Chinese as an ideograph-based language actually limits the capacities of speakers to cognize a more abstract notion of language. Kingston's emphasis on ideographs leads to the unfortunate conclusion that the habit of looking for the ideograph inside language persists even in nonideographic languages such as English. For example, she writes about one aspect of difficulty for a Chinese speaker learning English (an example that seems really contrived to me, as I have not encountered Chinese speakers who have this particular problem learning English—and they shouldn't, since Chinese is not, as I have mentioned, simplistic on this level): "The h's looked like chairs, the e's like lidded eyes, but those words were not *chair* and *eye*."[62] This sentence implies that the speaker is looking for the ideograph in written English.

Yet another instance in *China Men*[63] demonstrates the exotic aesthetic Kingston relies on in explaining her positioning to Chinese:

> We put away our brooms, and I followed him to the wall where sheaves of paper hung by their corners, diamond shaped. "Pigeon lottery," he called them. "Pigeon lottery tickets." Yes, in the wind of the paddle fan the soft thick sheaves ruffled like feathers and wings. He gave me some used sheets. Gamblers had circled green and blue words in pink ink. They had bet on those words. You had to be a poet to win, finding lucky ways words go together. My father showed me the winning words from last night's games: "white jade that grows in water," "red jade that grows in earth," or—not so many words in Chinese— "white waterjade," "redearthjade," "firedragon," "water-dragon." He gave me pen and ink, and I linked words of my own: "rivercloud," "riverfire," the many combinations with horse, cloud, and bird. The lines and loops connect-ing the words, which were in squares, a word to a square, made designs too. So this was where my father worked and what he did for a living, keeping track of the gam-blers' schemes of words.[64]

This is particularly self-indulgent, because it doesn't clearly enunciate the way in which the characters are connected. Rather it obscures the process of writing which would do this.

The practical problem of emphasizing the ideograph creates other interpretive problems as well. Kingston has limited her narrative possibilities by suggesting the pivotal, primary status of the ideograph. Because she lingers in a world of image-as-thought rather than words-as-thought, her narrative imagination often limits the characters to imagize rather than theorize, or even narrativize. Sometimes Kingston's characters seem to lack narrative richness—while the author's fictive and mythical narratives are substantive and rich, the characters are emptied of potential narrative. Thus, the primacy of the ideograph as the building block of the Chinese language for Kingston leads to speechlessness, inarticulateness, and hence unarticulated narratives. For example, there's very little speaking in the narrative of Fa Mu Lan; the narrative voice is so clearly the author's that the editor (no doubt not the most conscious) believed that the categorization "autobiography" could apply.[65]

Kingston, despite reiterating the centrality of the ideograph, nevertheless feels its lack of power in a context that is constructed from words. The pressure she feels is to capture the essence of ideographs in words, and she conveys her sense of being overwhelmed by the task in *The Woman Warrior*: "The swordswoman and I are not so dissimilar. May my people understand the resemblance soon so that I can return to them. What we have in common are the words at our backs. The idioms for revenge are 'report a crime' and 'report to five families.' The reporting is the vengeance—not the beheading, not the gutting, but the words. And I have so many words—'chink' words and 'gook' words too—that they do not fit on my skin."[66] If Kingston had dispensed with the idea of the ideograph, the translation of her culture from characters to words might have been less of an act of literary contortion.

The Essence of Uncool: Stuttering Speech

"No tickee no washee."

—MAXINE HONG KINGSTON, *The Woman Warrior* (1975)

Style becomes nonstyle, and one's language lets an unknown foreign language escape from it, so that one can
reach the limits of language itself and become something
other than a writer, conquering fragmented visions that
pass through the words of a poet, the colors of a painter,
or the sounds of a musician.

—GILLES DELEUZE, *Essays Critical and Clinical* (1997)

Maxine Hong Kingston's critics often discuss the concept of
voicelessness in her books, but ambiguously.[67] They do not describe the presence of stuttering or grammar misuse that the author herself employs—either consciously or unconsciously.[68] In
The Woman Warrior, a young Maxine says: "When I went to kin-
dergarten and had to speak English for the first time, I became
silent."[69] In *The Woman Warrior*, silence is muteness, but in *China
Men* it is more interesting.[70] In *China Men*, stuttering is a language practice, and gaps of silence make up part of a new language. Kingston strives to record and transcribe a language derived from Chinese and English rules. Her work is pioneering,
because even as late as 1979 scholars were still deciding on the
most effective romanization for Chinese.[71] Characters stutter deliberately, with momentum and strength. Both male and female
characters speak Chinese American English, and the linguistic
aspects of the novel are treated with subtlety. But Kingston writes
with the stutter of a new, unpracticed language: Chinglish. Stuttering is not simply the physical acts of hesitation while speak-

ing, but also the mental acts of dissociation from language; it is the form of uncertainty of imagination and in the imagination, not merely its physical manifestation. As readers, we even imagine stuttering when it is not necessarily written into the text with hyphens or punctuation. By writing stuttering into her language, Kingston materializes the oral. The reader must *hear* the stuttering to engage her work. She moves written narrative into the aural realm on the level of sentences, not simply within a greater narrative structure. Readers must move from being eye people to ear people to comprehend her sentences. In *China Men,* Chinglish signifies the resistance to unfettered, self-satisfied ennui. Within Chinglish we find a culture that feels contorted in the process of assimilation.

When judging the skill of writers, Gilles Deleuze views stuttering as a sign of literary talent. He explores the idea that authorial stuttering creates new features for speech—it is not merely an incompetent use of language:

> It is no longer the character who stutters in speech; it is the writer who becomes *a stutterer in language.* He makes the language as such stutter: an affective and intensive language, and no longer an affectation of the one who speaks. A poetic operation such as this seems to be very distant from the previous cases; but it is perhaps less distant from the second case than we might think. For when an author is content with an external marker that leaves the *form of expression* intact ("he stuttered . . ."), its efficacy will be poorly understood unless there is a corresponding form of content—an atmospheric quality, a milieu that acts as the conductor of words—that brings together within itself the quiver, the murmur, the stutter,

the tremolo, or the vibrato, and makes the indicated effect reverberate through the words.[72]

Kingston's way of preventing the enfeeblement of Asian American presence is to claim Chinglish as an American language: "I felt that I was building, creating, myself and these people as American people, to make everyone realize that these are American people. Even though they have strange Chinese memories, they are American people."[73] More explicitly, she expresses her work as a conscious effort to capture the peculiar in-between world in her work: "When I wrote *The Woman Warrior* and *China Men*, as I look back on it, I was trying to find an American language that would translate the speech of the people who are living their lives with the Chinese language. They carry on their adventures and their emotional life and everything in Chinese. I had to find a way to translate all that into a graceful American language. Which is my language."[74] Although Kingston calls her translation of Chinese American experience into English "graceful," her prose and dialogue indicate otherwise. As fluid as some of the passages are, there are traces of implied awkwardness, in which one imagines the physical act of pronunciation as difficult. The vibrato of Kingston's stuttering derives from the fierce grapple with language, of squeezing emotion from a language that resists the speaker: "'Kill your Romany mother's cunt,' you said between your clenched teeth. 'Kill your Romany demoness mother's cunt dead.' There is a Cantonese word that sounds almost like 'grandmother,' *po*, and means a female monster that looms and sags. In the storeroom were a black bag and a white bag, which we never opened. They were big enough for us children to climb like hills and we called them Black

Bag Po and White Bag Po. You called the gypsies those names too. 'Old bags,' you muttered. 'Gypsy bag. Smelly pig bag. Sow. Stink pig. Bag cunt.'"[75] This collection of words seems to be out of the speaker's control, just as stuttering often indicates the way language resists human control. Her form of swearing also strays from standard English; "Kill your Romany demoness mother's cunt dead" uses nouns as adjectives and word combinations improperly (Kill—dead). She often plays off the differences between Chinese and English to produce the "look" of the stutter visually: "When the demon beat his horse and dust rose from its brown flanks, he coughed from his very depths. All Chinese words conveniently a syllable each, he said, 'Get-that-horse-dust-away-from-me-you-dead-white-demon. Don't-stare-at-me-with-those-glass-eyes. I-can't-take-this-life'" (*China Men,* 104). The hyphens suggest a Chinese way of speaking English; the sentence is designed as if each word had its own tone. Kingston encourages the reader to look at English the way a Chinese person might pronounce English, over-enunciating each word to indicate a tone that English doesn't need. Kingston uses the English her readers would recognize while conveying an idea about language. In other situations stuttering or grammatical flaws have the aesthetic of uncool: "'You like come my table after you dance with me?' he invited. 'Of course,' she said. 'You speak English very well,' she said. 'Thank you,' he said. 'You be very beautiful. Pretty. You be pretty. I like you'" (*China Men,* 65). Stuttering's gracelessness reveals itself in acts of flirtation. The dancer tells the stutterer that he speaks English well—although she is merely flirting with him to get a tip. Goaded, he stumbles over grammar like an awkward Tarzan.[76] The same grammar is later appropriated for cooler contexts, like rap, but in this particular scene the character is supposed to be seen as uncool, as too self-conscious. Readers "read" the stuttering into the conversation, thus rendering it uncool.

The stutterers require interested listeners. When a young Chinese American girl is talking to her Auntie *(aiyee)*, the Chinese American language evolves as they try to hold a dialogue:

> "Are you working?" I asked because it was odd that she was having her hair done in the middle of a workday. "Is it your day offu?"
>
> "No. I'm not working anymore."
>
> "What happened to your hotel job? Didn't you have a hotel job? As a maid?" I said *maid* in English, not knowing the Chinese word except for *slave*. If she didn't know the word, she wouldn't hear it anyway. Languages are like that. (*China Men,* 205)

Sometimes the result is broken English, English which does not mimic American English but which seeks to mold English according to Chinese rules. "The new couple, young and modern *(mo-dang)*, bought a ranch house and car, wore fashionable clothes, spoke English, and seemed more American than us" (171). Kingston's statement "Languages are like that" conveys the ambiguity of language when spoken out of context. But the in-between status of the Chinese American provides a place where translation of the truly hybrid language can take place: "'Cake?' asked my aunt. 'Pie? Chuck-who-luck? Le-mun?'" The young girl tries not to patronize her aunt by correcting her; also, she understands her aunt, no matter how broken her English is. The girl's interpreting and listening skills are instinctive. In this short exchange, Kingston offers insight into the hybrid linguistic world of the Chinese American and the importance of *hearing:* "The grandfathers could understand demon talk; they told us how the demonesses praised the tomatoes all the same size. 'Allee sem,' said the demonesses" (167).

In another example, she shows how the aural component affects listening comprehension: "'Wheat germ is full of vitamins (why-huh-ming), and it is very cheap. A, C, thiamine, riboflavin, niacin, calcium, carbohydrates, fats, iron (eye-yun).' He was a scientific and up-to-date man who used English scientific terms. In two weighty syllables, both equally accented, a spondee, he said 'Wheat Germ'" (*China Men,* 190). Her reference to a spondee demonstrates poetic caution with regard to pronunciation, despite physical difficulty in enunciating certain letters (commonly, *l*'s and *r*'s are difficult). Later she continues to emphasize Chinese pronunciation:

> "You're in trouble at the cannery if the forelady is Chinese," my mother agreed. "She'll make trouble for you to impress the boss." (*Fo-laydee, chup-bo—trouble—bossu, day offu,* Chinese American words) (193).

> I stood by the kitchen door and watched my aunt cut cake. A corner of the floor was stacked with shiny gallon cans without labels. "My husband baked these cakes," she said. *Hus-u-bun,* she called him, a clever solution; some wives get so embarrassed about what to call their husbands, their names and husband such intimate words (like rooster—or cock). That they call him So-and-so's Father. (204)

Again the rhythmic nature of the word arrangement and rhyme is obvious, but so burdened by the unaesthetic associations that they cannot be fully apparent as art or artfulness. Yet they add a dimension of the guttural rhythms so characteristic of Cantonese or Say Yup, Kingston's first language: "We children became so wild that we broke Baba loose from his chair. We goaded him, irked him—gikked him—and the gravity suddenly let him go" (253). "Gik" is certainly not a standard English word.

Spoken English seems assaulted by Kingston's Chinese immigrants. The language is torn apart and restructured, not stylistically but phonetically. Kingston emphasizes speech, since she has already surrendered writing to the idea of the ideograph. As a result, the speech that is incorporated into her narratives is precisely annotated and recorded: "'Easu Bu-odd-way Su-ta-son,' she repeated. 'That's good,' he said. 'Remember that, and you can't get lost'" (China Men, 69). Ed's wife reshapes English pronunciation into Chinese—with each syllable distinct to allow the hearer to absorb the tone for each character. In another conversation that they have with each other, she tries to squeeze Chinese meaning out of English words: "After the movie, Ed explained to his wife that this cunning, resourceful, successful inventor, Edison, was who he had named himself after. 'I see,' she said. 'Eh-Da-Son. Son as in sage or immortal or saint'" (71).

In an act of will, Ed's wife hears Chinese meaning when he speaks English words. Later, it is this couple's Chineseness that removes them from the discursive zone with his partners, and he loses his laundry business: "Bak Goong counted it in front of him in Chinese and in business ('pidgin') English. He came out short. 'Too little,' he complained, holding up his fingers. 'Too little bit money. Are you trying to catch a pig?' he asked, which means to cheat, to take advantage of a greedy person" (102). Here, Kingston attempts to translate the pidgin by explaining what the soon-to-be-understood-by-a-demon Bak Goong is trying to say. This is also the only moment in China Men where

Kingston actually refers to her English as pidgin, thus demonstrating that she is not fully conscious of her use of Chinglish as a *language,* rather than simply a broken English.

On their "day offu," the China Men went into Honolulu to spend their pay (106). Kingston finds it necessary to record the lingo of vacation here. We know she is referencing a particular community by her language. In the following passage, Kingston demonstrates how the Chinglish is misunderstood by the "demons" in Hawaii: "Bak Goong saw a young countryman across the street, someone who could help him. 'Sook-ah,' he called out. 'Sook-ah,' that is, 'Hey, father's Younger Brother.' 'Sook-ah.' 'Sugar?' said the police demon. 'Sugar plantation? You better hurry. The wagon is leaving soon'" (111). This exchange shows the way in which two people presumably speaking the same language are really not speaking the same language. The community divide is also a linguistic divide. In some cases, the linguistic creativity includes poetic tropes such as onomatopoeia: "The bang—*bahng* in Chinese—when it came, always startled" (136). In foreign languages, learners often note how animal sounds are portrayed differently, as well as a host of other noises. In the case of Chinglish such anomalies also surface, in this example as well as the following: "'Look. Look,' said Say Goong, Fourth Grandfather, my railroad grandfather's youngest brother. 'A field chicken.' It was not a chicken at all but a toad with alert round eyes that looked out from under the white cabbage leaves . . . 'A field chicken?' I repeated. 'Field chicken,' he said. 'Sky chicken. Sky toad. Heavenly toad. Field toad.' It was a pun and the words the same except for the low tone of field and the high tone of heaven or sky" (166). In minorizing language, Kingston suggests that there is something lyrical, or at least formally valuable, about the minor key. "It's a Hit-lah" (13).

A force outside Kingston seems to be propelling her to record Chinglish rather than retranslate or reshape language into standard received English. The creation of Chinglish is inspired, and it is at this moment that the subjective faculties connected to language reveal themselves—and confirm that language-making in Chinese and language-making in English are both subjectivity-affirming: the subjectivity that allows her to transcribe Chinglish into written form. Deleuze reads this linguistic movement as an urge to minorize a major language, like a composer minorizing several bars in a major key. According to Deleuze,

> Great authors do not mix two languages together, not even a minor language and a major language, though many of them are linked to minorities as a sign of their vocation. What they do, rather, is invent a minor use of the major language within which they express themselves entirely; they minorize this language, much as in music, where the minor mode refers to dynamic combinations in perpetual disequilibrium. They are great writers by virtue of this minorization: they make the language take flight, they send it racing along a witch's line, ceaselessly placing it in a state of disequilibrium, making it bifurcate and vary in each of its terms, following an incessant modulation. This exceeds the possibilities of speech and attains the power of the language, or even of language in its entirety. This means that a great writer is always like a foreigner in the language in which he expresses himself, even if this is his native tongue.[77]

Deleuze's analogy to music is refreshing because we are accustomed to comprehend "major" as "majority" and "minor" as "minority"—that is, in a political sense.

Kingston's importation of Chinese combinations of words shows the possibility of the creation of a new language. Her Chinglish is inventive, unexpected, and alive. It *is* a new language.

Cool Wordtrips

No ching-chong chinaman for me.

—MAXINE HONG KINGSTON, *Tripmaster Monkey* (1983)

I wanted to sing the Chinese American self. This book actually does literally celebrate a Chinese American man from top to toe. I write his skin, his eyes, the teeth, ears, penis, the chest, hair, toes. I try to find new words to describe the kind of skin that we have, the kind of hair. I sing the Chinese American from top to toe.

—MAXINE HONG KINGSTON, *Tripmaster Monkey* (1983)

For a long time, K, a Chinese American, would listen to his father, a Shanghai-born Chinese American, quote the wisdom of "Erista Tow." K figured that his father, an extremely well-read physicist who spoke fluent English and Chinglish, was referring to one of the more esoteric figures in his panoply of reading. One day, his father pulled open the *Nicomachean Ethics* to get the exact wording of a quote by Aristotle.

We are far from the origins of Chinglish, but it still pervades America and will continue to do so as long as the phenomenon of diaspora exists. It is now a language spoken by people who are fluent in English and Chinglish and who use both in order to blend. Some artists are reappropriating terms like "coolie" and "chink" (as in Bert Wang's hit "Superchink" on the CD *Yellow*

Peril) for rap art, investing these terms with tough *kool*. Lisa Yun, speaking about coolie culture, has commented on Coolie Ranx, a rapper:

> In Brooklyn, Coolie Ranx, a popular Jamaican American artist of ska and raga music, had this to say in a recent interview: "When this name was given to me it was just a nickname. Nicknames in my hood just served as I guess a way to rebel from the system that gave names and titles to DOS's [descendants of slaves]. They're for creatin and controlin our own identity. It has since taken on an identity of its own that has helped to define me at times . . . I believe at one time with trade between Asia and Africa there was a respect for one another. But since comin to the New World, we have been put against one another. That's the only way we could be conquered and ruled."[78]

Comparative studies of African Americanglish and Chinglish have intrigued a few scholars. Michael North's book *The Dialect of Modernism* argues that racial mimicry revitalized the movement, even made it happen.[79]

As Chinglish becomes the representation of a site of struggle for many speakers, as opposed to the immediate expression of such speakers, it may have a different feel—it is more whimsical and playful by default.[80] Chinglish experiences a rite of passage—from gritty immigrant origins to a burgeoning multicultural America. Kingston's precursor, Louis Chu, writing with Sze Yup (different transliteration) and English, includes phrases like *lao yair, gimshunhock,* and *da dair* without translation.[81] In *Eat a Bowl of Tea,* his use of pidgin occurs notably in a passage about Indian boy-pimps. Ben Loy, the protagonist, is daydreaming about a vacation he spent in Calcutta:

On a street corner a youngster came up and accosted them. "Hey Joe, you like Chini goil?"

Ben Loy was delighted at the mention of Chinese girls. He had had them all. All different colors and shapes. "Chinese girls? Are you sure?"

"Sure, Chini goil. You come with me. You come." He was a mere boy, about ten or eleven.[82]

Chu uses the strategy of pidgin to divide aesthetically the communities of Ben Loy and street prostitution in Calcutta. Different pidgins are associated with each community; the Indian pidgin is transcribed by a Chinese American writer and therefore looks as silly as Chinglish transcribed by someone outside the community. For example, Chinglish was used in Charlie Chan stories by someone *outside the community*—it was not simply Chinglish but a twisted version of Chinglish. Chu's transcription of the Indian boy-pimp's language is politically charged because he is outside this community. Yet the Chinglish spoken by Chu's Chinatown community is his personal interpretation of Chinese dialogue and therefore an individual and personal effort at writing Chinglish: "'Go sell your ass, you stinky dead snake,' Chong Loo tore into the barber furiously. 'Don't say anything like that! If you want to make laughs, talk about something else, you troublemaker. You many-mouthed bird. You want to get me into trouble?'"[83] Here, the English resembles Kingston's Chinglish, with the transliterations serving to transform English into Chinglish.

The passage of time and history also influences the spoken delivery of Chinglish. It has an appropriate context, Chinatown, and the rampant stuttering is choreographed, not involuntary. In the America of Berkeley in the sixties, the speakers of Chinglish do not stutter but "sing," or rather "rap," in Chinglish, with odd rhythms.

Kingston's protagonist, Wittman Ah Sing (Kingston's electric embodiment of Walt Whitman), speaks both Chinglish and Berkeley English-major English. In the spirit of choreography, *Tripmaster Monkey* concludes with the staging of an Asian American play written by Wittman. The entire book is linguistically performative. It reenacts the genesis of Chinese American English. Wittman's poetic job is to move Chinese American English into an aesthetic context, to a language of life and spirit rather than marginalized noises. Kingston is quite deliberate about the creation of this language as a form of trickery:

> When I started to write the book, I wanted to do '60s slang because I thought that period had such wonderful words. People were inventing new words to describe psychedelic states, new visions. There were even new words for new ways of social protest such as the sit-in, the love-in, the be-in, the teach-in. There were all these words such as "tripmaster," and I wanted to use that language.
>
> Another reason is that, in my first two books, the English that I was inventing was a way to translate the dialogues of the characters who spoke Chinese. When I finished those two books, I really had more language in me, and that's this really modern language I speak that I wanted to play with. So I wrote this really new American language, and it really surprised me how free it is—how much room there is for other languages.[84]

This conception of Chinglish resonates with the Changlish that Huang discusses, but we are allowed to have Wittman's valuable subjectivity. In one scene, Wittman participates in mimicking

Chan—in the style of John Yau's countermockery: "A set of teeth were smiling on the floor, clackety-clack Hallowe'en choppers. Who choo laffin' at, boy? The cat disappeared, his smile remained. Trick or treat. Is that a mask or is it your face? Ha ha. Whose hand is that? Doing what to whom? 'Suspicious, Mr. Chan?'"[85] The language is imagined in Wittman's mind. He is its composer, and willfully hears Chinglish into being. Wittman cannot resist absorbing, dissecting, and analyzing Chinese immigrant language: "The mom had on a nylon or rayon pantsuit. ('Ny-lon ge. Mm lon doc.' 'Nylon-made. Last forever.')" (*Tripmaster Monkey,* 5). This observation includes the tonal qualities of Cantonese, as well as its English translation—fragmented pieces of English.

Later, Wittman practices Chinglish for the purpose of "cultural retention," as Kingston implies. The language that he uses is temporary because it is a pre-assimilation language, one that will lose its poetry as the community loses its tones and the past that the tones musically capture: "'Fu-li-sah-kah Soo.' He said 'Fleishhacker Zoo' to himself in Chinatown language, just to keep a hand in, so to speak, to remember and so to keep awhile longer words spoken by the people of his brief and dying culture" (6). Wittman's attempts at linguistic preservation make him singular, and this is apparent in his interactions with other characters in the book. For example, in contrast to Wittman, the Chinese American girl Nanci requires translation of phrases that Chinglish speakers are familiar with, such as FOB, ABC, and others: "'Conservative like F.O.B.? Like Fresh Off the Boat?' He insulted her with translation; she was so banana, she needed a translation" (19). Wittman's relationship with Chinglish is comfortable; he navigates the world with an English-Chinglish dictionary evolving in his head. For example, he envisions a key that remakes / re-mak-u-si standard English into Chinglish: "Stockton = Soo-dock-dun. Gilroy = Gi-loy. Vallejo = Wah-lay-ho. Lodi = Lo-di. Fresno = Feh-see-no" (19). Like someone immersed in learning a language, Wittman hears Chinglish and celebrates puns in English and Chinglish. His psycholinguistic relationship with the world is characterized by Kingston as the state of possessing "Chinese ears." In other words, despite himself, Wittman hears Chinglish even when it may not be the actual language being spoken. Kingston describes this situation by presenting actual statements adjacent to what Wittman hears: "'The Dow for the week up six good points.' He heard: 'The Tao is up,' 'Friday's Tao up 2.53 points . . .' Wittman felt pleased with himself, that he hadn't lost his Chinese ears. He had kept a religious Chinese way of hearing while living within the military-industrial-educational complex. . . . Oh, god, the cosmic nature of puns. To show that he had gotten the joke, and could run with it and maybe cap it, Wittman said, 'Osaka Stock Exchange, yeah. Sell GM. Buy Kawasaki. Sell my sole for sashimi futures'" (85). Wittman's mental activity, his experience of language as a diasporic subject, is enhanced. Kingston shows that there is valid aesthetic capital in Chinglish, that word-agility and word-love can arise out of such a rich experience of language. She is aware that such activity is bicultural, and in interviews cites Vladimir Nabokov's use of bilingual puns with Russian and English as inspiration. In the passage above, the puns obviously play on the homophonic relationships between words—"Tao" for "Dow," "sole" for "soul," "Osaka" for "stock-a," and other homonymic entities. For Kingston, being able to make such associations is the retention of the poetic or artful skill that undergirds Chinese literary culture. Wittman's predisposition to engage in wordplay is his inheritance.

For Wittman, not only linguistic tradition but ancestral etiquette influences his behavior. For example, when Wittman and Nanci are at a social gathering they feel mildly compelled to behave in a way socially acceptable to their ancestors: "He and she gave each other the old once-over. They both looked away; why should they greet each other? (Because your parents and grandparents would have run up yelling to one another and shouted genealogies of relatives and friends and hometowns until they connected up)" (59). This social intuition, a kind of phatic communication, is absent from those unfamiliar with Chinese culture. For Kingston's Chinese Americans, diasporic existence possesses its own peculiar references that illustrate a particular form of life. For example, at one party there are Chinese Americans, Asian Americans, and others: "They were white people, and didn't know what she was talking about. They do not have those phrases, 'double lid' and 'single lid' Yoshi. Those are our words. No, not ours, they are Japanese-American idioms, and just because they're English words, you think white people can understand them. A.J.A. words. Chinese are not that subtle to have a thing about a fold in the eyelid" (107). Kingston's mission, to reclaim English for Asian Americans (she conveys this mission several times in different interviews), is complicated by the clash of languages. How can she claim English if it does not capture the form of life for Chinese Americans? Why would she want to?

Talk-Story in *China Men* and *The Woman Warrior*

There is a Chinese word for the female I—which is "slave."
Break the women with their own tongues.

—MAXINE HONG KINGSTON, *The Woman Warrior* (1975)

"You act like a piece of liver. Who do you think you are?
A piece of liver?" She did not understand how some of us
run down and stop. Some of us use up all our life force
getting out of bed in the morning, and it's a wonder we
get to a chair and sit in it. "You piece of liver. You poet.
You scholar. What's the use of a poet and a scholar on
the Gold Mountain? You're so skinny. You're not supposed to be skinny in this country. You have to be tough.
You lost the New York laundry. You lost the house with
the upstairs. You lost the house with the back porch."
She summarized, "No loyal friends or brothers. Savings
draining away like time. Can't speak English. Now you've
lost the gambling job and the land in China."

—MAXINE HONG KINGSTON, *China Men* (1977)

The larger linguistic phenomenon of talk-story permeates
Kingston's novels, and though it seems like a self-indulgent form
of "talk-therapy" or cheap counsel, it influences, strongly,
Kingston's narrative style. Talk-story is the key to Maxine Hong
Kingston's narrative technique but also antedates Kingston as a
free-standing linguistic phenomenon. It is a hybrid of Chinese
and English; it is a Chinese concept but uses English words. It
reflects her view of language and history as interactive and symbiotic. Talk-story not only fashions past events and makes them
examples for the community (thereby providing rules for
communal behavior); it is also susceptible to historical changes.
"Talk-story" is a compound verb, and means what it compounds.
Talk. Story. It is not telling stories, but conversing with others
through a story.

Kingston describes talk-story as a mode of being: it can be one
of several Chinese linguistic structures for conversation. Often

the stories are a polite way of telling somebody something important without being openly critical, without making the person lose face.[86] Talk-story also reminds individuals to observe rituals in order to avoid curses. Talk-stories thus serve a homiletic function: "Husbands and wives exchanged stories to frighten one another. The men told about a husband who smeared his cheating wife with honey and tied her naked on an anthill. The women told how there was once a queen, who, jealous of the king's next wife, had this other woman's arms and legs cut off and her eyes, tongue, and ears cut out. She shoved her through the hole of the outhouse, then showed her to the king, who looked down and said, 'What's that?' 'It's the human pig,' said the queen" (*China Men,* 47). These stories are comparable to anecdotes: "Avoid turning a fish over in its plate during a meal if the future held travel by boat; wrap sticky rice during the spring months";[87] eat every grain of rice served or a future husband will be pockmarked with the number of remaining grains. Talk-story, roughly, is a combination of superstition, history, and anecdotes. But it can reinforce behaviors that bind communities.[88]

The difference between talk-story and fiction is that fiction is simply an author's imagined terrain, whereas talk-story might have happened. Each degree of retelling may be a degree further from the reality, but reality is behind the story. So in Kingston's work, what the reader might take as an imaginative flight of fancy might actually be latent truth. Kingston emphasizes this: "In our culture the mythic is real. There are people who are people, and there are people that are ghosts doing real things, like selling newspapers and bringing milk and driving taxicabs. So I am describing an actual cultural phenomenon. These books have the artistic problem of how to write the true biographies of real people who have very imaginative minds. And there is always the exciting possibility that I will break through into another world that's about to happen."[89] In fact, Kingston believes that what might count for imaginative creations in one culture may be the bedrock of tradition in another. In the case of Chinese American culture, what seems to be an approximation of truth in one culture is actual truth for another. For example, in *China Men* the conversations about America are—from the Western point of view—energetic, excited, and somewhat contorted versions of the truth. But to the Chinese Americans the stories convey the heart of their experience: "He heard voices, his family talking about gems, gold, cobbles, food" (*China Men*, 50). The voices continue, "They'll invent robots to do all the work, even answer the door." Later he admits, "The villagers had to make up words for the wonders" (51). Kingston's subject may be the past, but her narrative is not history. Her narrative is the record of an ever-evolving voice. Her appropriation of talk-story is a tribute to an oral tradition that provides history, but also a way of exposing the cultural medium of talk-story as a weapon, not simply a way of passing down stories. It *does* matter who is talking-story in her book; their personal history gives meaning to their stories (and may be the reason for their stories). Kingston's project is thus more complex than she at first blush implies; she is actually rewriting oral history, but it is refracted through several speakers whose sense of truth may be culturally different from that of their audience. Do the horror-filled images document actual events passed down to warn future generations? Or are they concoctions of talk-story? If so, this kind of talk-story seems too saturated with pain to enable its audience. But what is the proper dose of truth, and what written account can be considered a trustworthy, fair judge of history that will do what talk-story is meant to do—set standards for behavior and remind the conscience to take responsibility for the past? Kingston says that she wants to make a better vision of society, so that we can achieve it;[90] but it is unclear whether her recipe is the foundation upon which a new vision of Asian America can be built. If there is too much trauma written into the history, we may feel so saturated with it that we are paralyzed instead of transformed for the better. Talk-story is a medium, and it is a direct transference of horror between people, but it might also create disabling trauma.

Kingston persists in suggesting that talk-story is history. Furthermore, this kind of history is always in progress; her work reads like a history-in-progress. To some extent, other writers like Toni Morrison and Chinua Achebe also emphasize the ambiguity that oral history provides. Kingston describes her writing in more detail in a later interview:

> Part of the tension in my writing is that the oral tradition is very different from the written, and I see the oral tradition as being very alive, very immediate. It has the impact of command; it has the changes from telling to telling. It changes according to the needs of the listener, according to the needs of the day, according to the interest of the time, and the story can be different from day to day. So what happens when you write it down? Writing is so static. The story will remain as printed for the next two hundred years and it's not going to change. That really bothers me, because what would really be neat would be for the words to change on the page every time, but they can't. *So the way I tried to solve this problem was to keep ambiguity in the writing all the time.*[91]

For Kingston, the rewriting of history is literary and personal, rather than accurate and factual in method. We are awakened to the contrast between these two methods when we encounter in *China Men* (51) a timeline of legal history that lists—unaccompanied by any commentary—influential legal decisions that affected immigrants' lives. Kingston's talk-story accounts seem more real than these legal statements. The contrast makes the reader wonder what constitutes the reliable narration of reality.

Although converting the past into talk-story has normalizing, harmonizing, and idealizing proclivities, it also creates reality. Kingston wanted to find a way of converting traumatic knowledge into practical knowledge; story, after all, teaches us what we need to avoid, change, or suppress. But then we realize that Kingston needs our communal decision making to complete the mission of talk-story; she cannot talk-story alone. Perhaps the best way for us to participate is to see her talk-story as a version of events that is not meant to be history record, but still contains a kind of approximate truth. As a writer, Kingston manages to use her multiple voices to communicate Chinese and American cultures as well as past and present. She demonstrates how societies which value all of these elements can come to terms with unrelenting history:

> I guess as a minority person in America, and with a lot of perceptions that English is not my language, there is a lot of leaving me out of this culture. So a lot of my work is appropriation. I'm going to appropriate this job and these books and this language—the American language. I'm going to appropriate this country. . . . With *Tripmaster,* I said I'm just going to play with all the books that I read and it felt to me like an outpouring of things that I had been holding back and denying. I felt some really exciting things were happening with the language in the Sixties because people were finding that vocabulary for psyche-

delic states or visions or social action. But as I was working with that language, I saw too how it had its roots a
hundred years ago in Whitman. . . . Walt Whitman said,
"Look to the East, that's also your motherland." He also
had the idea that our myths are not just from Europe, but
from Asia. So I'm saying, "Look at Asia," because we already know that we come from Europe. For a long time
when we say classical, we meant Greek and Roman. And
I'm saying, "Look, there's more classics, more."[92]

In Kingston's view, these myths can belong to anyone, and she
advocates a shared history, or communal sense of history. But
this history is continually subject to revision. She views the development of this history not so much as a stabilizing force but
an entity that undergoes perpetual reincarnation. As a bilingual,
she also recognizes that language can stretch to accommodate
this continual revision process and describe both cultural worlds
that she explores: "The women who sat on him turned to direct
their attention to his feet. They bent his toes so far backward
that his arched foot cracked. The old ladies squeezed each foot
and broke many tiny bones along the sides. They gathered his
toes, toes over and under one another like a knot of ginger root.
Tang Ao wept with pain. As they wound the bandages tight and
tighter around his feet, the women sang footbinding songs to
distract him: 'Use aloe for binding feet and not for scholars'"
(*China Men,* 4). By embedding the consciousness of the exile in
narrative, she makes it a public issue. She externalizes "internal"
exile. The result is that exile becomes a shared state rather than a
purely psychological condition. And thus it becomes a collective
or communal problem.

In this way, Kingston expands the scope of exile to include

the exilic sensibility of a community, and it is through her community that she can cope with the impalpability of her original homeland. She echoes Wittgensteinian ideas about language and community: "My aliveness must come from our sense of a connection with people who have a community and a tribe. We are living life in a more dangerous place. We do not live in new subdivisions without ceremony and memory; and if those other writers have to draw from that non-magical imagination, then of course their writing will be gray and black and white."[93] Thus, her reliance on a community to produce a solid sense of identity is a way of recapturing the feeling that her memories are authentic and therefore trustworthy. Wide community boundaries encourage and even enable the search for authenticity.

Driven by the desire to widen these boundaries, Kingston constantly searches for the most seamless language, the language that will break down boundaries and pave the way for the expansion of communities. When she discusses her work, she is very conscious of its being connected to the work of others across time and space. She considers herself to be on a mission very similar to those of Virginia Woolf and William Carlos Williams,[94] asserting that her work is an extension of Williams' *In the American Grain*:

> Williams retold the American myth, which I think is exactly the right way to write American history. His book starts with Leif Ericsson and ends with Abraham Lincoln, but his Lincoln is a woman, a feminine force in American history. He's like an old nurse, tending to his soldiers; it's as if he were the mother of our country. Williams has told American history poetically and, it seems to me, truly. In a way, I feel that I have continued that book. The dates are

even right. The earliest episode in my book is about 1850,
which is roughly where Williams left off.[95]

She says that she wants to reclaim history for Chinese Americans, whose exile has been protracted because of voicelessness
and invisibility in American history. She says, "We're not outsiders, we belong here, this is our country, this is our history, and
we are a part of America. We are a part of American history. If it
weren't for us, America would be a different place."[96] Kingston
wants to reclaim the historical legacy of Asian Americans that
has been excluded or badly represented in the American historical canon. She adds, "When I write, I also claim America in a literary way, in an artistic way. When people claim countries, it's
usually thought of as conquering them in war. I'm claiming
America in a pacifist way, in an artistic way."[97]

Does Kingston really appropriate America? Or just borrow it?
She says, "In a sense, when I wrote these books, I was claiming
the English language and the literature to tell our story as Americans. That is why the forms of the two books are not like other
writers', and yet, it's American English. I guess my thought is: If
I can use this language and literature in a really beautiful, strong
way then I have claimed it for all of us."[98] The strength of her
claim can be evaluated by examining different kinds of
Chinglish—spoken and written—in her novels. If we recognize
Chinglish as a language, she has accomplished more than claiming English. She has allowed it to take part in the imaginative
construction of another language.

3

The Politics of Design

ARUNDHATI ROY

There's a sort of political vision, a way of seeing, which is just expressed in different ways. Sometimes it's a film, sometimes an architectural thesis, sometimes a novel, sometimes non-fiction, sometimes it's just walking down the street and the way you look. Fundamentally, running through all these things is a way of examining the relationship between power and powerlessness. I'm very interested in that relentless circular fight.

—ARUNDHATI ROY, quoted in *The Independent* (November 30, 2002)

Rule One for a writer, as far as I'm concerned, is "There Are No Rules." And Rule Two (since Rule One was made to be broken) is "There Are No Excuses for Bad Art."

—ARUNDHATI ROY, *Power Politics* (2001)

Arundhati Roy compares her new image as "writer-activist" to "sofa-bed."[1] It is an ironic term for Roy, for whom writing itself is a form of anarchy. Roy is anti–nuclear war, anti–dam construction, anti-empire, anti-corporatization, and anti-globalization. In *The God of Small Things,* her political vision is anti-BIG and pro-small. In Roy's work, small is not merely a reference to size, but connotes harmlessness and powerlessness; it suggests images of children, small animals, unnoticed gestures. Smallness is a form of life, and its representation in language is one of Roy's main concerns. The way in which Roy's advocacy for small things emerges in her linguistic style and political rhetoric is the central subject of this chapter.

"Smallness" and "vision" are two terms Roy employs in her discussions about goodness.[2] Seeing is an important part of Roy's notion of politics; this is evident not only in the epigraph above, but also in her essay "The Greater Common Good."[3] As noted earlier, Iris Murdoch, in *The Sovereignty of Good,* also emphasizes vision as vital to moral judgment. Murdoch says that we "grow by looking," and the idea of vision recurs thematically in her moral universe: "Human beings are obscure to each other . . . in certain respects which are particularly relevant to morality, unless they are mutual objects of attention or have common objects of attention, since this affects the degree of elaboration of a common vocabulary. We develop language in the context of looking: the metaphor of vision again."[4] For Murdoch, the idea of vision encourages thinking about morality as a sensory capacity; morality is not simply gauged by the level of someone's talent for logical decision making. Likewise, for Arundhati Roy, acute vision is—as Murdoch says—vital for morality: "Painters, writers, singers, actors, dancers, filmmakers, musicians are meant to fly, to push at the frontiers, to worry the edges of the human imagination, to conjure beauty from the most unexpected things, to find magic in places where others never thought to look. If you limit the trajectory of their flight, if you weight their wings with society's existing notions of morality and responsibility, if you truss them up with preconceived values, you subvert their endeavor."[5]

For Roy, the ability to include certain things in one's field of vision is a moral capacity. Her language is a tool that guides us to the magic in places and people that are often excluded from our field of vision. In the sing-song fragments of her narrative in *The God of Small Things*, Roy encourages us to see the sense in what seems to be nonsensical uses of language in her book: "a rushing, rolling fishswimming sense"; "No Locusts Stand I"; and "dinner-smelling sea."[6]

Roy champions weird English as the antidote to the dominance of bigness. In her essays, big words are often used to shore up big values, values that scare the small into submission: words like "globalization," "corporate," and "nuclear," which can lead to the commission of evil against the powerless. The form of her writing encourages allowing small, often visually dismissed, marginalized entities into our field of vision. We may have the urge to deflect attention from errors in writing or strange spellings, yet Roy does not allow us to avert our gaze but celebrates off-the-cuff writing, smallness of writing, and thoroughly whimsical prose. What is political about her literature? It is not simply the content of her work, which is openly anti-caste, but the form of her writing, which forces us to notice the details and read closely.

Roy's novel illuminates the complexities of linguistic formation in formerly colonized Indian communities. The political situation affects the individual psyche, as well as the development of language and semiotics. To return to a conception of goodness through language, Roy has to chop English up and start over, afresh, without the stains and staleness of colonial English marking her language.

The Origin of a Political Anarchist

India's redemption lies in the inherent anarchy and factiousness of its people, and in the legendary inefficiency of the Indian state. Even our heel-clicking, boot-stamping Hindu fascists are undisciplined to the point of being chaotic. They can't bring themselves to agree with each other for more than five minutes at a time. Corporatizing India is like trying to impose an iron grid on a heaving ocean and forcing it to behave.

—ARUNDHATI ROY, *Power Politics* (2001)

So when I say that Kerala, a state of twenty-nine million people in southern India, is unsettling and bizarre, I am making a strong claim. In certain ways it may be the oddest place on earth.

—BILL MCKIBBEN, "The Enigma of Kerala," *Doubletake* (1995)

In the early twenty-first century, Roy is garnering attention as an activist. She has been threatened with lawsuits for her public support of coalitions fighting government plans backing the construction of the Sardar Sarovar Dam on the Narmada River,[7] adding to her already long history of activism as an Indian woman.[8] Her book, she asserts, is an extension of this activism:

"True, *The God of Small Things* is a work of fiction, but it's no less political than any of my essays."[9]

On the surface, Roy's politics might look like liberal politics from an American viewpoint, but they are in fact more anarchic in her own country than American leftism is in the United States. Her political goals aim to unseat traditions that still pervade Indian culture (while leftism is but one branch of politicking in the United States), and at the same time withdraw from the larger trend of globalization—or corporatization—that is seizing the world. She writes about love for the Dalit ("Oppressed") and the environment, and alludes in interviews to a hippie-ish upbringing that encouraged free-thinking and self-reliance: "My mother was divorced. I lived on the edge of the community in a very vulnerable fashion. Then, when I was sixteen, I left home and lived on my own, sort of. . . . You know it wasn't awful, it was just sort of precarious, . . . living in a squatters' colony in Delhi."[10] Within the walls of Delhi's Ferozshah Kotla, she sold empty beer bottles to survive. Her love for the Dalit communities and their natural world is apparent in *The God of Small Things*. In this novel, she celebrates the courage of the hero, Velutha—the "god" of the title.

Roy experienced exile as a young woman, an outcast status that generated self-reliance: "When I think back on all the things I have done from a very early age, I was determined to negotiate with the world on my own. There were no parents, no uncles, no aunt; I was completely responsible for myself."[11] Most apparent, however, is her defiance against the oppression of establishments: official languages, histories, industries, and countries. Roy reveals her modus operandi: "I don't believe in rules."[12] Roy's anarchic writing repositions English from "colonialist" origins to nativist self-expression.

Where does all this love of anarchy come from? Roy's home state, Kerala, has been described by writer Bill McKibben as a pocket of social welfare enlightenment where "all the disputation can be overwhelming." McKibben's writing uses vocabulary that might be ascribed to liberal America. His ability to remake Kerala into a "Civil Liberties Union as state" makes us wonder whether we are reading a well-choreographed and carefully arranged text that aestheticizes a global version of liberalism. Whether or not this is entirely accurate and not simply beautiful wish fulfillment, McKibben's political fervor—and Roy's own political persona—resonate with the contemporary debates about whether or not the world can be a uniformly interpretable place. How do we interpret anywhere without some level of appropriation?

McKibben's article exhibits a mixture of appropriation and transaction. He interviews several Kerala natives, one of whom offers a long analysis of Keralan political life.

> In a long account of his home village, Thulavady, K. E. Verghese says that "politics are much in the air and it is difficult to escape from them. Even elderly women who are not interested are dragged into politics." After several fights, he reports, a barbershop posted a sign on the wall: "No political discussions, please." But for the most part the various campaigns and protests seem a sign of self-confidence and political vitality, a vast improvement over the apathy, powerlessness, ignorance, and tribalism that govern many Third World communities.[13]

McKibben's assessment and conclusion that "political vitality" is a "vast improvement" over "apathy, powerlessness, ignorance, and tribalism" asserts that politics is a good (which seems orthogonal to Roy's conception of the good).

But McKibben's values of politics are also derived from what he assumes can be associated with the rise of politics: positive demographics. According to McKibben, the demographic features of Kerala are concrete indications that this state—though still agrarian and poor—is progressive compared to the rest of India, and even compared to developed nations. McKibben provides a cascade of demographics that is revealing about Kerala. For instance, the life expectancy for males in North America is seventy-two years, while in Kerala it is seventy.

The latest in literary campaigns by the United Nations certified Kerala as 100 percent literate. Kerala's birthrate is around eighteen per thousand, compared with sixteen per thousand in the United States. And Kerala's birthrate is falling faster. The norm for number of children per family is two. And the average age at which women marry is twenty-two, whereas it is eighteen in the rest of India. "Whatever the historical reasons," writes McKibben, "this quartet of emancipations—from caste distinction, religious hatred, the powerlessness of illiteracy, and the worst forms of gender discrimination—has left the state with a distinctive feel, a flavor of place that influences every aspect of its life." McKibben goes on to describe a typical day in Kerala:

> Strikes, agitations, and "stirs," a sort of wildcat job action, are so common as to be almost unnoticeable. One morning while I was there, the *Indian Express* ran stories on a bus strike, a planned strike of medical students over "unreasonable exam schedules," and a call from a leftist leader for the government to take over a coat factory where striking workers had been locked out. By the next

day's paper the bus strike had ended, but a bank strike had begun. Worse, the men who perform the traditional and much beloved kathakali dance—a stylized ballet that can last all night—were threatening to strike; they were planning a march in full costume and makeup through the streets of the capital. . . . Although the activists' constant flurry occupies much of Kerala's space and time, there is also a move to cure the budget deficits that all the politicking has racked up—either because it disrupts the economy or drives factories away to other degraded parts of India where unions weren't as strong and therefore labor was cheaper. Keralites have begun to "ruralize": they have started to examine the soil, topography, and amount of water in their environment and grow crops and become a self-sustaining community. This has created jobs and preserved the environment, a goal that developing countries have strived for but at seventy times the expense of Kerala.[14]

It is expected that such an atmosphere would produce several versions of Arundhati Roy.

Furthermore, in Kerala, the caste system is less influential than in other parts of India, and progressive thinking seems to dominate that society. Roy says, "I grew up with people like Velutha. They were my closest, dearest friends. They were much more my family than my family: they were who I fished with, swam with, dug up earthworms with. I had a sense of what would come down on someone's head. Syrian Christians think they're the salt of the earth. Even within the Church, there are sub-sects. They don't even marry between themselves."[15] Roy's closeness with the Untouchable community still remains. Recently, she offered her book to the Kerala Dalit Sahitya Akademi to be translated into Malayalam; the royalties would be used to promote Dalit literature. She said, "This is not a gift. It is an invitation to enter into a working contract with me. I hope you will publish it, sell it and use the royalties from the Malayalam book to help Dalit writers to tell their stories to the world."[16]

A Sign, Not a Wonder

I was the worst thing a girl could be: thin, black, and clever.

—ARUNDHATI ROY, quoted in *The Progressive* (2002)

Love Laws dictating who should be loved, and how. And how much.

—ARUNDHATI ROY, *The God of Small Things* (1997)

In her fictional world, Roy exhibits a powerful anarchist spirit to match her politicized persona. Her appropriation of English on a personal level destabilizes it; her linguistic anarchy defies orthodox English. In her language, fragmented words, unusual word usage, words as design, meaningful nonsense, a sensual use of sound are the physical traces of her literary anarchy. In *The God of Small Things,* Roy breaks apart the language and puts it together on her terms. Words like "later" are written as "lay. Ter"; "an owl" becomes "a nowl." In metaphysical terms, she communicates the dilemma of the postcolonial exile, who is fated to barter and converse in this language, to *be* in this language, but who is also unable to accept all the rules (especially colonialist rules) that seemed at one time in history—in the early twentieth century—to be embedded in this language. Roy makes an art of rule breaking; her novel is a grammatical affront to orthodox English.

By being defiant of the rules that made English English, she directly defies English as a language whose rules require following. By playing with language she dismantles the rules that undergird correct English:

> Rejoice in the Lo-Ord Or-Orlways
> And again I say re-jOice.
> Their prer NUN sea ayshun was perfect. (*God of Small Things*, 147)

The children purposely sing off-spelling; and despite the misspelling of pronunciation, the logic of the spelling of "prer NUN sea ayshun" seems more loyal to the sound of the word than the correct spelling.[17]

The idiosyncratic, anarchic linguistic design makes us conscious of being part of the experiment of comprehension, of being a case study: it awakens us to our own psychological role, the way in which a broken, fragmented English represents, causes, or sets into motion the conception of a broken world. We realize that the ability to conceive of unbroken worlds, of space as meaningful, is possible only if language seems unbroken—if language can still serve as sign and referent. The ability to conceive of a world, of space that is meaningfully organized, is dependent on our ability also to conceive of the author and ourselves as signs, referents, and interpreters. Roy's fragmented linguistic world shows that we are all, contrary to this, fragmented psychical creatures when it comes to comprehending the world she sets before us; her world is defiant of meaning and what is required to make that meaning.[18] She rebels against the sign "author," the sign of authorship, the sign of herself that we as interpreters might attempt to construe as Arundhati Roy, author.

In terms of content, design sensibility in the novel not only functions on the level of fragmented sentences and words but also reveals itself in the overall structure of the novel. The superstructure of the novel is circular: the first page of the novel is not the beginning, but an arbitrary point on the circle of the narrative. Although as readers our relationship with the book starts on page one, Roy makes it clear that our process of getting to know the novel is not equivalent to our familiarity with the narrative, because that narrative exceeds the novel (we have a sense that there is a reality outside the book, that there are occasional elisions between fiction and reality). The beginning of our relationship with her book is only that; we do not enter into the reality of the world the characters inhabit. Their time is outside ours; it is circular. The design of the novel thus keeps out the reader and contains the narrative. Furthermore, the book is constructed by weaving memories and fragmented narrative moments which do not have meaning until the very end, when the fragmented images connect together into a narrative. Specters or ghosts. Role of dreams. Ammu dreams of the god, the god who can do only one thing at a time. "If he held her, he couldn't kiss her. If he kissed her, he couldn't see her. If he saw her, he couldn't feel her" (God of Small Things, 205). The narrative is suggestive of vulnerability, of Velutha's handicap as an Untouchable. His body, lacking one arm, thematically connects to the fragmentation of the book.

Roy emphasizes structure in her comments about The God of Small Things. It is her way of owning a memory. She starts at the base with some history, and goes backward with a series of memory images to fill in the story:

> People keep asking me why I don't practice architecture and I think, what do you think this is? This is exactly that. It's really like designing a book for me.
>
> The only way I can explain how I wrote it was the way an architect designs a building. You know, it wasn't as if I started at the beginning and ended at the end. I would start somewhere and I'd color in a bit and then I would deeply stretch back and then stretch forward.
>
> It was like designing an intricately balanced structure, and when it was finished it was finished. There were no drafts. But that doesn't mean I just sat and spouted it out. It took a long time.[19]

We comprehend in a sustained but constantly moving gaze the network of components that create the building. Similarly, Roy shows how the society of Ayemenem is constructed out of rules that eventually conspire to destroy Velutha. She repeats continually throughout her book certain phrases of foreboding that accrete meaning throughout the text: "It really began in the days when the Love Laws were made. The laws that lay down who should be loved, and how" (*God of Small Things*, 33). These phrases achieve their full sense when disaster happens. And as disaster unfolds, the term "structure" is the skeleton in the closet that emerges, the ghost within the text that becomes full-blooded as Velutha is beaten and killed: "What Esthappen and Rahel witnessed that morning, though they didn't know it then, was a clinical demonstration in controlled conditions (this was not war after all, or genocide) of human nature's pursuit of ascendancy. Structure. Order. Complete monopoly. It was human history, masquerading as God's Purpose, revealing herself to an under-age audience" (293). Structure lingers underneath the text as an organizing function, but does not have any power until there is a purpose for it. Actions seem unguided and random until the narrative weaves them into relationships. There is a form of life behind each action, and the existence of words presupposes the existence of community. Wittgenstein emphasizes that words are customs and forms of life—they are the structure of life: "It is not possible that there should have been only one occasion on which a report was made, an order given or understood, and so on.—To obey a rule, to make a report, to give an order, to play a game of chess, are customs (uses, institutions)."[20] The redesign of the structure of the world is intrinsic to Roy's writing. She is changing not just how we read, but also the world that we read.

The Art of Letters

In Roy's work, the images created by letters can be more revealing than any letters linked to form words, especially about the characters using language in this manner. Thus, to fully comprehend the characters of the book, we have to engage with the authorial presence—to engage with the effort of understanding the design as the book's meaning, its ontology. We cannot rely upon the rules of written English to guide us, so the comprehension of her work may mean that other senses are engaged more than usual.[21] In meaning accretion, we think about certain words that rely on narrative, on the evolution of meaning, on having a kind of evolution to have meaning. We think of certain words as requiring introduction, a relationship, a working-over of signifier-signified until the meaning is satisfactory to the individual. We think of signs as prerequisites for a relationship to happen—whether the relationship is professional and requires jargon or technical words, or whether it is intimate and personal.

Wittgenstein remarks that all words have a use—their existence presupposes this; the use is frequently the origin. Some words or phrases have obvious histories; some have mysterious ones. Wittgenstein mentions the gesture of pointing upward as indicating up. We might think of its origin as derived from the gesture of pointing at the sky, but the connection is not obvious when we think about the gesture of pointing in other directions. Pointing itself as an expression of direction reminds us of the use value within expression, but also of the difficulty in confirming linguistic purpose.

Roy's experimentation with language seems to play in this gray area of language evolution and development, seems akin to the games that develop in the learning of a language:

> Language games are the forms of language with which a child begins to make use of words. The study of language games is the study of primitive forms of language or primitive languages. If we want to study the problems of truth and falsehood, of the agreement and disagreement of propositions with reality, of the nature of assertion, assumption, and question, we shall with great advantage look at primitive forms of language in which these forms of thinking appear without the confusing background of highly complicated processes of thought. When we look at such simple forms of language, the mental mist which seems to enshroud our ordinary use of language disappears. We see activities, reactions, which are clear-cut and transparent. On the other hand we recognize in these simple processes forms of language not separated by a break from our more complicated ones. We see that we can build up complicated forms from the primitive ones by gradually adding new forms.[22]

By giving the narrative voice to children, Roy allows for the accumulation of forms of language both as a biological event and as a political event: for the weird-English writer, getting to the bottom of the original language is parallel to getting to the bottom of the power structure located in the use of words, of discourse.

Roy's narrative plays out Wittgenstein's description of language games. She writes as if she doesn't know the rules. Kind of innocence. Like children. Or like a bad artist. Who likes small things, words that aren't long, words of miniature size. Who writes in half-sentences, communicative bits still in formation:

> Later in the light of all that happened, "twinkle" seemed completely the wrong word to describe the expression in the Earth Woman's eye.
>
> *Twinkle* was a word with crinkled, happy edges. Blue-grayblue eyes snapped open.
>
> A Wake
>
> A Live
>
> A Lert. (*God of Small Things*, 226)

Roy's work at times lacks, in effect, a standard of seriousness. When we speak language, we want to appeal to a kind of seriousness. We want to create a standard of mood when we speak. Roy doesn't see herself as responsible to this standard, which makes us ask about our own responsibility to it: "When he was in this sort of mood, Chacko used his Reading Aloud voice. His room had a church-feeling. He didn't care whether anyone was listening to him or not. And if they were, he didn't care whether or not they had understood what he was saying. Ammu called them his Oxford Moods" (*God of Small Things*, 53).

In some places words are given a life of their own: "Estha sat up and watched. His stomach heaved. He had a green-wavy, thick-watery, lumpy, seaweedy, floaty, bottomless-bottomful feeling. 'Ammu?' he asked. 'Now WHAT?' The WHAT snapped, barked, spat out" (102). Or: "All right. Later. And Later became a horrible, menacing, goose-bumpy word" (139). These descriptions eschew traditional adjectives—for example, the "Reading Aloud" voice and the word combination of "bottomless-bottomful." There is a meticulous honesty, an assertion of individuality in each of these weird grammatical moments, and Roy relishes them: "I love English. But I want to write in my English," she has said. So much so, that sometimes her English prose seems unnatural or concocted: "She used her windows for specific purposes. For a breath of Fresh Air. To Pay for the Milk. To Let Out a Trapped Wasp (which Kochu Maria was made to chase around the house with a towel)" (29). Roy is calling attention to her English, with its quirky unpredictableness. It is not an excuse to write ungrammatically but aims to provoke an inquiry about how we organize language for different purposes. We make lists; we think in nonsentences. And a lot of our language isn't diagrammable.

The Politics of Design and the Design of Politics

Aristotle's text has the detached and sober diction that exhibits the classical architectonic structure in which language, as speaking, remains secure. The letters show the sounds. The sounds show the passions in the soul, and the passions in the soul show the matters that arouse them. . . . Showing is what forms and upholds the intertwining braces of the architectonic structure.

—MARTIN HEIDEGGER, *On the Way to Language* (1971)

Roy's spirit of anarchy and her sense of design—that of a former architecture student—are mutually strengthening: her anarchist spirit generates rebellion against the rules of English, and her design sense helps perform the anarchy by making patterns with English.[23] At times, design sensibility seems to take priority over the narrative sensibility; words have the status of design pieces and are not simply linked together to create meaning. Roy shows how our interaction with language reveals our social tendencies; we can take it as art, law, or property. On the other hand, the design of language is revelatory on several levels. Language designs: we design it, it designs communities, and it designs interpretation. Roy is aware that her language accretes meaning and interpretation. She writes: "Little events, ordinary things, smashed and reconstituted. Imbued with new meaning. Suddenly they become the bleached bones of a story" (*God of Small Things,* 32).

Roy calls attention to the way letters look, emphasizing the importance of perception to meaning in a verbal version of Wittgenstein's duck-rabbit. The meaning of Wittgenstein's picture is determined by the observer, and how the observer is trained; one cannot insist on the rightness of one's interpretation. The sense is related to complicated cultural factors that control interpretation. Wittgenstein uses this picture of the duck-rabbit to draw a distinction between "seeing" and "seeing as": "We might see the picture as a duck or a rabbit, but either way we are seeing it *as* duck or rabbit. In order to justify what we were seeing the object as, we would have to refer to all sorts of experiences of perception of rabbits that we'd had before: 'Rabbits have ears like this!' we might say. The upshot of this is that we are thinking about what we see. If you are looking at an object, you need not think of it; but if you are having the visual experience expressed by the exclamation ['A rabbit!'], you are also thinking of what you see."[24] Implicit in the terms "big" and "small" are political meanings. "Big" seems allied with the establishment or the imperialist mindset; "small" is vulnerable, childlike, Untouchable. In *The God of Small Things* there is a constant shift between the languages of the "small" and the "big." We can put the vocabularies into groups with ease—for example, "small" is Love-in-Tokyo, Chinese Bangle (135), Puff, Ambassador E. Pelvis, S. Insect, and backward-reading; "big" is Written Complaint (97), Police, History, Jolly Well Behave, Touchable, Untouchable, Work Is Struggle, and Fear. And these categories almost overlap with "children and nature" versus "bullies and bureaucracy." But Roy juggles both kinds of vocabularies within the consciousnesses of children, and the resulting narration is conflicted, with no evidently victorious language. Yet the children's made-up language is not incoherent, while sometimes the language of characters like Pillai or Chacko seems to defy rather than provide expression:

> Comrade Pillai disliked being addressed as My Dear Fellow. It sounded to him like an insult couched in good English, which, of course, made it a double-insult—the insult itself, and the fact that Chacko thought he wouldn't understand it. It spoiled his mood completely.
>
> "That may be," he said caustically. "But Rome was not built in a day. Keep it in mind, comrade, that this is not your Oxford College. For you what is nonsense, for Masses it is something different." (264)

For Pillai, reappropriating power comes at the price of badly emulating his colonizers. Predictably, it results in a poorly articulated sense of the world.

Roy's characters play with letters and sound patterns in a way that suggests evolution and conveys the effort of making language. Not only do we witness scenes that resonate with the idea of language making, we also witness the consequences of language making as an all-consuming creative act. Heidegger describes our relationship to language as something constitutive of world making, in a way that resonates with Elaine Scarry's conception in *The Body in Pain*. Heidegger's view in *On the Way to Language* suggests that language should be examined as a thing in itself: "Instead of explaining language in terms of one thing or another, and thus running away from it, the way to language intends to let language be experienced as language. In the nature of language, to be sure, language itself is conceptually grasped—but grasped in the grasp of something other than itself. If we attend to language exclusively as language, however, then language requires of us that we first of all put forward everything that belongs to language."[25] Roy encourages the appreciation of language as a design, as an art, and simply that: "I like the way it looks on the page," she says. This willful effort to simplify readers' reaction to her use of a language is a way of denying the reader the liberty to overinterpret and potentially appropriate her narrative.

Her demand for a simple reaction subordinates not only signification but also the practice of concocting meaning. To read *The God of Small Things* is to witness anarchy against the mechanism of meaning concoction, since this mechanism also generates meanings that create oppressive practices. Roy thus subverts colonial English as a diseased practice. As an outsider whose history is simultaneously outside and inside the language, who does not inscribe her personal history or ancestry in English, Roy can perform new practices with the language that do not evoke colonialist practices. Her appropriation of the words and letters cannot, by virtue of her position to the language, be an appropriation of history simultaneously, since her history is located in languages other than English.

To some extent, Roy is a postcolonialist writer because she is writing against the colonization of India. Furthermore, the term "postcolonialism" is vague enough to accommodate her. But Roy is not a postcolonialist, in that her colonialist enemy exists now and in the future: the worst is not past for Roy. Gayatri Spivak, in her essay "The Burden of English," notes that teaching literature and teaching the English language are *now* different practices.[26] In the emerging Bollywood film industry, films combine spontaneous bursts of song and dance with spells of acting (the most recent being Aamir Khan's blockbuster *Lagaan*, which was an Oscar nominee for Best Foreign Film). These depictions of Indian experiences under colonialism contrast with those in Rushdie's *Midnight's Children*, Anita Desai's *Clear Light of Day*, and other novels.[27] Roy's interpretive energy and attitudes are directed at past postcolonial writers—energies and attitudes with taxonomic pursuits that may result in confining her rather than positioning her. Ever conscious of this, Roy defies these energies and attitudes. She refuses the notion of grouping, the urge to taxonomize. Such urges lead to exclusion and oppression.

In *The God of Small Things*, she actively rejects the reinforcement of hierarchy and writes about the evils of taxonomy, not only on the political level but even in the small world of children:

> Rahel's list was an attempt to order chaos. She revised·it constantly, torn forever between love and duty. It was by no means a true gauge of her feelings.

"First Ammu and Chacko," Rahel said. "Then Mammachi—"

"Our grandmother," Estha clarified.

"More than your brother?" Sophie Mol asked.

"We don't count," Rahel said. "And anyway he might change. Ammu says . . ."

"Anyway, after Mammachi, Velutha, and then—"

"Who's Velutha?" Sophie Mol wanted to know.

"A man we love," Rahel said. "And after Velutha, you," Rahel said.

"Me? What d'you love me for?" Sophie Mol said.

"Because we're first cousins. So I have to," Rahel said piously. (*God of Small Things,* 144)

Rahel's internalization of social rules is followed by a moment of uncertainty about her own unstable classification. Both Estha and Rahel argue about whether Rahel is a "dwarf." Sophie Mol offers a solution: "Maybe you'll be a midget. . . . That's taller than a dwarf and shorter than a . . . Human Being" (145). Their grappling with external categories points to both the absurdity and the influence of taxonomies in designing lives, worlds, and social relations.

The internal grammar of language contains this same combination of absurdity and power: any system, or ordering, inherently implies hierarchy and value. Thus, disorderliness and chaos must be imposed on a system to provide new energy. Roy wants to revive English by destroying its ruliness. She enjoys the English language while recognizing its role in damaging India. She tears words apart with the mission of linguistic revival, and imposes graphic form on words that makes them seem mere line drawings rather than receptacles of meaning:

    Nictitating

     ictitiating

      titating

       itating

        tating

         ating

          ting

           ing (180)

Here the word's disappearance into fragments of itself constitutes a devolution of language, a reversal of its construction. None of the successive letter formations are w O r D s, aside from "ting," which is less a word than onomatopoetic gesturing. The lack of meaning of each of the successive fragments reveals the children's relationship to English and how unadulterated by history and culture this relationship is. The children are absorbed in the sensual qualities of language, the sounds and the look of *nictitating* in italics. We can understand appreciating the language in this way: even if we couldn't read the words or extract meaning, the word would still be visually interesting. This consciousness of language as visual art—that is, simply lines and curves, as opposed to bundles of meaning—is an interesting position to have with respect to English. Usually it is Korean, Chinese, Sanskrit, Arabic, or Ancient Greek that is contextualized as "ideograph" or "art." But Roy shows us that English can be contextualized as art as well. Roy can systematically construct English as an exotic language, just as other languages have been constructed, contextualized, and characterized. Her politically literary performance does this to English, and thus in *The God of Small Things* she levels the linguistic playing field. English is not presented as having more meaning than other languages, as having automatic interpretive priority or interpretability. Rather, it develops translatableness only because of ubiquity. Its virtue of being "translatable" is gained through the power of its speaking population. But it can be exoticized or reconceptualized as visual art like any other language.

On a positive note, English, like other languages, can be redeemed by artistic possibility. Roy opens us to the humanness of all language. As sophisticated as language can become, and as reflective of theoretical complexity as it can be, ultimately all of it is a human attempt at expression and no more.

Clean White Children

For Indian writers, the historical life of English is inevitably political. For John Hollander or e. e. cummings, abandoning the traditional grammatical or syntactical rules of English or using words to design New York steaks or swans constitute an experimental aesthetic expression which could be achieved in a political vacuum. Though their experiments constitute a form of anarchy against grammar, these are not as politically loaded as Roy's, since her work is a combinative anarchy of the linguistic, literary, and political. Her subject is an English of soiled origin. Roy asserts an aesthetic drive and pursuit. She said in an interview: "For me, the way words and paragraphs fall on the page matters as well—the graphic design of the language. That was why the words and thoughts of Estha and Rahel were so playful on the page. . . . Words were broken apart, and then sometimes fused together: 'Sour metal smell' became 'sourmetalsmell.'" Fused words such as "furrywhirring" and "sariflapping" (*God of Small Things*, 8) are sprinkled throughout. But she also realizes the inevitability of the political in the practice of writing: "To be a writer—a supposedly 'famous' writer—in a country where three hundred million people are illiterate is a dubious honor. To be a writer in a country that gave the world Mahatma Gandhi, that invented the concept of nonviolent resistance and then, half a century later, followed that up with nuclear tests is a ferocious burden."[28] Roy's ethical position is not hard to decipher: Writing and reading can't be a community practice with a hugely illiterate population. The burdens of poverty and powerlessness that are implied by illiteracy require the work of writers to unearth them and provide a narrative for them. One tactic for a writer is to realize, in a material way, the way in which language is an artistic practice, and to indulge the art in it. Roy's approach to artistic delight in language refuses the weight of politicization, and that brings a reckless, even irresponsible mood to the novel.

Political residue is oppressive. We taste this when the children, Estha and Rahel, watch and internalize the power of whiteness in *The Sound of Music* at a local cinema called Abilash Talkies. Roy's observations remind us of the incredible caution required to resist the propaganda that infects language.

> Baron von Trapp had some questions of his own.
>
> (a) *Are they clean white children?*
>
> No. (*But Sophie Mol is.*)
>
> (b) *Do they blow spit-bubbles?*
>
> Yes. (*But Sophie Mol doesn't.*)
>
> (c) *Do they shiver their legs? Like clerks?*
>
> Yes. (*But Sophie Mol doesn't.*)
>
> (d) *Have they, either or both, ever held strangers' soo-soos?*
>
> N . . . Nyes. (*But Sophie Mol hasn't.*) (*God of Small Things,* 101)

By positioning the children at odds with English, Roy demonstrates how—most transparently in postcolonial countries like India—the act of learning a language can be a psychologically problematic pursuit. She shows how the production of language is the production of a psychology that is disseminated through a community. But this psychology is not stable, because language is flexible (like human beings). With individual oddities, children—such as Estha or Rahel—can trigger the mutation of language and thus a new psychological orientation toward the use of language. Despite being born into a postcolonialist practice of language, the children in the novel are able to use language without being entrenched in the postcolonialist psyche. Their English is a generation away from the historical moment of colonialism; their English is the material manifestation of psychic development in a new community; their interpretive communities are already lagging in the practice of finding meaning in their language.

There are other obstacles more harmful and burdensome that the children confront. Estha, in particular, is molested at Abilash Talkies by a man the children call the Orangedrink Lemondrink Man. This encounter with corruption happens simultaneously with the children's exposure to *The Sound of Music*. They are awakened to their own vulnerable status—their Indianness and their smallness. Just as these events are conflated at Abilash Talkies, so we conflate minority and the small linguistically, conceptually, actually, and practically.

In order to protect the small with words, Roy uses words with political intent and at times anger. There is rage in the use of English, as well as aesthetic carefulness: like Ammu, described as having the "infinite tenderness of motherhood and the rage of a suicide bomber" (44), Roy will display an infinite talent to play with letters but also a rage that makes her defy the rules that construct meaning in English. In another situation the twins become fascinated by the logic of the word "cuff-links": "When the twins asked what cuff-links were for—'To link cuffs together,' Ammu told them—they were thrilled by this morsel of logic in what had so far seemed an illogical language. Cuff + link = cuff-link. This, to them, rivaled the precision and logic of mathematics. Cuff-links gave them an inordinate (if exaggerated) satisfaction, and a real affection for the English language" (50). The twins' enjoyment of English is pure; they have not been cultivated in the correctness of spelling in English. The natural delight they take in English communicates their innocence to it as a postcolonial signifier, their lack of comprehension about speaking a colonized language. Their language is not intentionally transgressive but untrained. Roy implicitly argues—through the innocent playfulness of the children's language—that what seems transgressive is really just unbrainwashed behavior. Their natural behavior cannot be received as such, because the environment in which they exist is traumatized.

The context of transgression distracts from a view of Roy's language as delightful. The novel is certainly tonally serious but packed with moments of linguistic delight—a delight of the small. Roy locates the small in children, in nonhuman animals, in the world of nature. Are the children the most well-constructed selves because they can manipulate and play with the signs of the world, interacting with the world as signs the way human beings without baggage can? The children constantly delight in reading things backward and playing with letters and words (57). They are interpreters of signs; they have a linguistic health which points to a kind of psychic health. Their language is an outgrowth of their trust in the world.

They are also unpoliticized, like Chacko—innocent to the cultural belonging that certain languages provide, and thus left to a pure enjoyment of the English language. Their position with regard to English contrasts with that of Chacko, who constantly strives for correctness and propriety: "Chacko said: You don't *go* to Oxford. You *read* at Oxford. After *reading* at Oxford you *come down*" (55). By contrasting the positions of the children and Chacko, Roy continually suggests that the effort to exert a correct spelling may be a form of cultural corruption, may equal an effort to oppress. Utterances exhibit a political form; words are evidence of cultural belonging. A lack of facility with words is evidence of cultural exile. Thus, Roy actively presents the versatility of English by transgressing its rules of use. And she is able to convey this more effectively as a multicultural migrant. She shows how English is malleable enough to describe environments that its words were not meant for. Certain passages in the novel remind us that there is play with languages throughout:

> "See, you're smiling!" Rahel said. "That means it was you. Smiling means 'It was you.'"
>
> "That's only in English!" Velutha said. "In Malayalam my teacher always said that 'Smiling means it wasn't me.'"
>
> (19)

In the novel, English conveys meaning only to later distort it. Roy shows how it can often betray its speaker but also itself. For example, her most inventive linguistic anarchists are children. In fact, the twins Estha and Rahel are also foreign to English. They do not understand the rules of English and create their own version continually. In one encounter with a born-again Christian, Miss Mitten, they read a storybook, *Susie Squirrel*, both backward and forward. The whims of the children are taken as signs of evil by a culturally ignorant and limited adult:

> They showed Miss Mitten how it was possible to read both *Malayalam* and *Madam I'm Adam* backwards as well as forwards. She wasn't amused and it turned out that she didn't even know what Malayalam was. They told her it was the language everyone spoke in Kerala. She said she had been under the impression that it was called Keralese. Estha, who had by then taken an active dislike to Miss Mitten, told her that as far as he was concerned it was a Highly Stupid Impression.
>
> Miss Mitten complained to Baby Kochamma about Estha's rudeness, and about their reading backwards. She told Baby Kochamma that she had seen Satan in their eyes. *NataS ni rieht seye.*
>
> They were made to write—In future we will not read backwards. In future we will not read backwards. A hundred times. Forwards.
>
> A few months later Miss Mitten was killed by a milk van in Hobart, across the road from a cricket oval. To the twins there was hidden justice in the fact that the milk van had been *reversing*. (58)

Here language becomes an area of religious contestation when it is simply a native-nonnative misunderstanding. For the children, English is not an institution. It is not the language and the meaning derived from it that create or install order in the world, as is the case for Miss Mitten. When English is used in an unorthodox way, she takes it to be used evilly rather than with cultural difference. Estha and Rahel sense that the world has rules but have not concluded what these are. They must be trained in the rules, but they refuse.

The redeeming beauty of the novel resides in the capacity of the children and Ammu to resist this training that the Anglophilic Chacko so strongly embraces. Velutha cognizes this untrainableness when he allies himself with the children and sees them as kindred spirits. The status of English is unstable for the children. They learn that learning English is an unsteady process; the language is pliable and vulnerable to change. They spell what they hear, unconditioned to the rules of spelling orthodoxly: "Lemontoolemon, too cold" (100) or "Porketmunny" (102). In rearranging the English language, Roy gives us a sense of English in formation (a postcolonial country in formation). She describes India's way of life in contrast to that of the "developed" West: "We have less money, less food and smaller bombs [than the West]. However, we have, or had, all kinds of other wealth. Delightful, unquantifiable."[29] Gradually, she creates a new language by training us to understand how she is using it. Thus, while certain words and phrases will make no sense at the beginning of her book, they accrete meaning toward the end. The same word repeated later is given meaning with each repetition. Thus, the language is a way of understanding Roy's most vital self. Her political writing does not make design-oriented or architectural demands on her, but her fiction wrings patterns out of letters with a relentlessness that conveys the urgency of her project: to change the way we read and see English, and what it stands for.

Her English is still searching for the best way to transcribe sound. It challenges the rules and design plan that have already been laid down by colonial guardians of English. But this is not to say she is *not* "doing" language or that her language isn't fully formulated. It only looks so because of the lack of alternatives to an already established system of English. The children in Roy's book, for instance, see violence done to their language—a discounting of their own versions of English as evil.[30] Their language practice, in the eyes of others, contorts language; but to them it makes English familiar, informal, even friendly. English is not kept at arm's length. There's no reason why it must be formal. They are not subalterns. They are still unaware of the subaltern complex. Yet they are learning about the ways in which language can be injurious, and their narrative will gain its momentum from the development of their relationship to language. They will learn to injure in language, which is what Estha does by saying "yes." As he watches Velutha die in jail, Estha tells the police that Velutha is guilty, after being pressured to save Ammu. With one word, he absolves the police from committing murder.

The language instinct, Steven Pinker asserts, is a tool of survival.[31] Language is an extension of our other instincts, and so is interpretation—the instinct that we employ to establish and build communities. The cessation of interpretation, words, and signing is the cessation of ourselves, our communities, and our lives. But in the meantime, humans form identities with as much surging passion as they can. We make meaning—and in creating new meanings, we endure moments of being untranslatable to or by those around us. In *The God of Small Things,* this phenomenon is acutely present: meaning accretes and things don't make sense until later. Later we discover the meaning and significance of the Orangedrink Lemondrink Man, or the lucky leaf. Meanwhile, the children and the world are described with delicate, precious language—language that someone would choose to create beauty. The language of the novel is not the language of the real world. It remakes space into a world and existence into a life through language.

Linguistic Injury

The novel, in many ways, points to the construction and destruction of the self and the association of language with this destruction and construction. It affirms the constitution of self and psyche through language by showing linguistic and psychic health to be connected: our language is embedded in psychic existence. The children play in their linguistic world. Their vernacular of silliness, such as the Love-in-Tokyo, the Elvis puff, "jams jams and jellies jellies"—all of these phrases contribute to a play that is rebellious, that has much in common with the larger political anarchy. Words, phrases, or sentences are not always translated, and we're often left uncomprehending. But we couldn't imagine a glossary to this book, since the lack of understanding is beyond the words. We understand the tone, even if we can't translate or understand the sentences. Literary cousins to Roy use equally vernacularized prose with different political agendas. We need to see her writing as a strategy of anarchy, as natural as it reads.

In *Excitable Speech,* Judith Butler writes about the relationship of violence and language by asking: "How do we account for the specific kind of injury that language performs?"[32] For Elaine Scarry, the presence of pain causes us to "resist language," and places us in a dangerous space where we could forfeit our trust in the world and language: "This dissolution of the boundary between inside and outside gives rise to a fourth aspect of the felt experience of pain, an almost obscure conflation of private and public. It brings with it all the solitude of absolute privacy with none of its safety, all the self-exposure of the utterly public with none of its possibility for camaraderie or shared experience."[33]

Judith Butler's arguments about language connect language and being with equal vehemence: "Could language injure us if we were not, in some sense, linguistic beings, beings who require language in order to be? Is our vulnerability to language a consequence of our being constituted in its terms?"[34] Her assertion—that we are constitutive of language and that this constitution makes injury possible—is suggestive when we are interpreting Roy's positioning to language. For Roy, language constitutes human beings in multiple ways. It can subordinate us such that self-constitution through language may be the worst option we have. Butler realizes that how we choose to constitute ourselves and others through language is an ethical move. Without the security of constituting language independently, however, we lose our humanness. In much of his work, Stanley Cavell comments on the same phenomenon: that our relationships begin with "words for a conversation," that words between people create acts of humanness and civility that provide the foundation for social protection, love, affirmation—beautiful creations between human beings. In contrast, Lenin Mon (Comrade Pillai's son, who is made to give speeches for guests in English, which he is able to reproduce though clearly not think in) becomes a puppet, a creature barely signified as human.

Butler recognizes the ethical nature of the linguistic. She writes:

> The question of how best to use speech is an explicit ethical question that can emerge only later. It presupposes a prior set of questions: Who are "we" such that without

language we cannot be, and what does it mean "to be"
within language? How is it that injurious language strikes
at this very condition of possibility, of linguistic persistence and survival? If the subject who speaks is also constituted by the language he or she speaks, then language
is the condition of possibility for the speaking subject and
not merely its instrument of oppression. This means that
the subject has its own "existence" implicated in a language that precedes and exceeds the subject, a language
whose historicity includes a past and a future that exceeds
that of the subject who speaks. And yet this "excess" is
what makes possible the speech of the subject.[35]

Butler's questions about language apply to the postcolonialist
linguistic situation. Especially resonant is her question, "How
is it that injurious language strikes at this very condition of
possibility, of linguistic persistence and survival?" It is resonant
because injury comes to mean a very different thing for a postcolonial product like Lenin Mon, whose self-constitution is going to be injured by a language that he isn't able to inhabit. He
will be trained so that language does not affirm his being or constitution, and thus he may find that his deconstruction of English will promote a sense of being far greater than his being a
carrier for a language that wants to survive.

Linguistic injury in *The God of Small Things* becomes something
else when interpreted as postcolonial linguistic injury, exceeding
the space of the novel. The novel chronicles the osmosis of environmental linguistic pollution by individuals, and what their
psyche looks like after repeated acts of injury. We begin to see
this as real historical documentation; the novel begins to perform its own deconstruction and reconstruction as not simply

fiction but reality. As mentioned before, Roy herself stipulates that the novel is "no less activist than anything else, . . . even though it is a work of fiction." Her mental elision of reality and fiction causes readers to feel the activist impact of the book, to take it as epic rather than local.

We witness the text perform its transformation from novel to colonialist narrative in a scene where Comrade Pillai persuades Chacko that Velutha is a dangerous Communist Party member. During this scene, in which Pillai mouths jargon at Chacko, Pillai's children emerge and "perform" English without understanding it, providing a direct contrast to the acutely sensitive Estha and Rahel, who cannot perform English (they refuse to greet Sophie Mol with standard English phrases) but who understand its ambiguous ethical presence in their lives. Pillai's son Lenin (the humor of this name is not lost on the reader, and neither is Pillai's soi-disant "Comrade" reference) reiterates Antony's speech from Shakespeare: "I cometoberry Caesar, not to praise him. / Theevil that mendoo lives after them, / The goodisoft interred with their bones." Roy continues, "He shouted it fluently, without faltering once. Remarkable, considering he was only six and didn't understand a word of what he was saying" (*God of Small Things*, 261). Roy interprets this performance as a form of subordination through language, and her rephrasing of the speech illustrates how language can make our presence absent, subordinate, erased. This performance is a sign for an actual historical event, a linguistic phenomenon that illustrates the ultimate subordination of the subaltern. Roy's self-consciousness of this phenomenon and her interpretation of it place her at a distance from the subaltern, but simultaneously we know her—as sign—to have inhabited a subaltern community.

Another brand of noise is a kind of neuroticism in language

brought about by a sense of powerlessness. Estha designs mantras to prepare for death: "(a) Anything can happen to Anyone. (b) It's best to be prepared" (186). In *The God of Small Things*, Roy invokes the same questions that Butler does, but with a curious twist. She may ask: Do we deal with forms of language that break rules of language, are violent in their own way, but are instrumental in leading to a remedy for oppression? Heidegger describes language as "making a way."[36] Indeed, language like Roy's is making a way. In the case of writers like her, we want to hear these languages, allow them to grow, because they are the languages of negotiation that authentically represent people looking for a way, a psychological zone, or some form of not feeling the weight of history and of colonization. Language not only makes a way; it makes a way out. Simultaneously, such a way out requires that other ways surrender space: in this case, orthodox language is thrown into question as a communicative tool for those populations who have been colonized. Inevitably, anarchic English not only is transgressive on the level of language but also interrogates the conditions of existence, since the interrogation of the design of language is also an interrogation of its designers.

Language Makes the Untouchable Body Touchable

In the novel, the Untouchable becomes touchable; the Untouchable's invisible footprints become tracks the police use to trace him; the Untouchable's body becomes, in its pain at the hands of a brutal beating, the most vivid material experience of the entire novel. Roy harnesses the crescendo to ensure that words provide a material experience, to show us the power of language as a physical experience. When Velutha gains a voice, he becomes the most material, most tactile figure in the novel. His metaphor is the "untouchable" postcolonial language that becomes translatable and sensible as the narrative progresses.

Throughout, Roy inundates the senses with word-pictures and word-images, with the artistic urge to make words be as concrete as their pictures. She wants to make concrete the coming-into-being of a word, the solidification of thought into language. For example, she systematically reproduces Velutha's subjectivity when he is awakened to the fact that he is alone in the world, that he will be condemned for his relationship with Ammu, and that he will not be helped by Pillai:

> As he walked away from the house, he felt his senses had been honed and heightened. As though everything around him had been flattened into a neat illustration. A machine drawing with an instruction manual that told him what to do. His mind, desperately craving some kind of mooring, clung to details. It labeled each thing it encountered. *Gate.* He thought as he walked out of the gate. *Gate. Road. Stones. Sky. Rain.*
>
> *Gate.*
> *Road.*
> *Stones.*
> *Sky.*
> *Rain.* (269)

Velutha's thoughts become objects in the world: stones, gates, and rain. His sense of self is allied with these objects. His fear and sense of aloneness give rise to an instinct for language: he starts to name things in the world.

Velutha's sensual experience of fear is expressed in this basic attempt at survival, this reaction to survive. The capacity to name the world provides a way of mooring, a way of supporting oneself, or perhaps a way of sheltering the self metaphorically. We could imagine that this happened to the first human being. Rousseau in fact locates the origin of language in the origin of fear.[37]

National Linguistic Anarchy

There are more people in India that speak English than there are in England. And the only common language that we have throughout India is English. And it's odd that English is a language that, for somebody like me, is a choice that is made for me before I'm old enough to choose. It is the only language that you can speak if you want to get a good job or if you want to go to a university. All the big newspapers are in English. And then every one of us will speak at least two or three—I speak three—languages. And when we communicate—let's say I'm with a group of friends—our conversation is completely anarchic because it's in any language that you choose.

—ARUNDHATI ROY, quoted at website.lineone.net/
~jon.simmons/roy/tgost4.htm

For Roy when she was growing up, English was simply another language, another mode of expression rather than a representative form of the establishment. Roy commonly used English along with other dialects, just like most other Indian citizens in her environment, which encourages simultaneous use of English and Indian dialects.

The English-language edition of an Indian newspaper, for example, might refer routinely to "roti, kapra, and makan (bread, clothing, and dwelling), a rail roko (a railway strike), and to such quantities as a crore (10 million) or lakh (100,000)."[38] South Asian English incorporates regional features into its version of English. Some writers are developing this regional dialect into a standard. The author Raja Rao says, "Our method of expression has to be a dialect which will some day prove to be as distinctive and colourful as the Irish or the American. . . . The tempo of Indian life must be infused into our English expression."[39] From the reverse end, many Indian words have made their way into standard English. Consider the sentence, "The pundit with the cheroot—a sahib—saw the cheetah in nirvana." All the nouns in this sentence are Indian, but are often taken to be English words.

Despite the casual mixture of English and other Indian dialects, the rhythm of English distinctly changes when influenced by Indian grammar. Braj Kachru painstakingly cites some aspects of South Asian English that deviate from the standard. Some of these are tag questions, such as "He isn't going there, is it?"[40] and reduplications, such as "hot, hot coffee" (for "very hot coffee"), "small, small things" (for "many small things"), "to give crying crying" (for "incessantly crying"), "who and who came to the party" (for "who came to the party").[41]

Roy says she uses repetition because it is comforting, revealing her comfort zone with South Asian English: "Repetition I love, and used because it made me feel safe. Repeated words and phrases have a rocking feeling, like a lullaby. They help take away the shock of the plot."[42] The rhythm of South Asian English is thus distinct from that of standard English, but this rhythm cannot be achieved without altering the grammar of English to fit the tempo of the indigenous languages. The conversion of English to South Asian English is further accomplished by the addition of Indian words, and is perhaps why Roy includes Indian names to communicate the different linguistic feel of Indian utterances: "Velutha," "pappychachen," "Peter Mon" (*God of Small Things,* 203). Or the revolutionists' cry "Inquilab Zindabad!" Or this song that Kuttppen sings to pass the day: "Pa pera-pera-pera-perakka / Ende parambil thooralley / chetende parambil thoorikko. / Pa pera-pera-pera-perakka" (196). These are phrases that lovers of sounds and rhythms dream of (although the content of the song, which permits someone to "shit" in his brother's compound, is obscene). It is no wonder that Indian linguists and writers want to retain their linguistic tempo.

Criticizing Roy's Critics

Critics of Roy have described *The God of Small Things* as "a banquet for the senses" and "lush." Some of this criticism has an almost inappropriate, naive tone. These adjectives seem more appropriate to describing a vacation spot than a novel, which prompts the question of whether we are thinking about these books as novels. If we are not thinking these are novels, are they then exotic, *National Geographic* accounts of people's lives? What does it mean for our interpretation of character, for example, to echo Ammu: "Must we behave like some damn godforsaken tribe that's just been discovered?" (171).

The assumption that these books are meant to be authoritative on their culture can lead to a formation of criteria stipulating that properly regionalized prose is prose that is not too Westernized. The prose is authentic if there are sprinklings of foreign phrases or words and if English grammar is at times abandoned completely, or if there is some implication that a culture is untranslatable by English and full of linguistic secrets. We envision, perhaps, a group of dark people uttering some foreign tribal language while cooking food over a fire in a small yurt. This is an extreme example, but the point I am trying to make is that there is a gap between the image that the literary critic holds in the mind and the writer who writes in a foreign culture. And although writing in English helps foreign authors convey their world without the risk of having it translated poorly, it doesn't do more than this.

Whether these foreign utterances are the easiest expressions at hand or whether they are unconscious slips of the author's tongue is unanswerable. But whatever the reason, it is evident that a description of their world is not complete without a complex mosaic of different sets of vocabularies they have grown up with. Furthermore, in India, although English might have stood for imperialism, colonialism, labor exploitation in the past, it now connects India to the globe. The assimilation of English language into the linguistic life of the people may have been difficult because of its association with the British Empire, but in recent years Indians have been creating their own brand of "South Asian English" to add to the dialects that already exist globally, including Welsh English, Australian English, and others. There's no question that Roy has refined the South Asian English in *The God of Small Things*.

A Small Frame of Mind

Before the Booker Prize dinner at Guildhall in London I asked Roy, mistakenly described as a magical realist, about this aspect of her work. She spoke with passion about her continuing dialogue with Rushdie, and of her disappointment at his disregard for Indian writers work-

ing in the vernacular languages. She said: "When I was in
America I went on a couple of TV shows with Rushdie.
And he said [she borrowed the voice of an officious
schoolmaster], 'The trouble with Arundhati is that she
insists that India is an ordinary place.' Well, I ask, Why
the hell not? It is my ordinary life. The difference between me and Rushdie begins there."

—Interview with ARUNDHATI ROY, *India-Today*

Why the emphasis on having India ordinary? It certainly seems
provincial of Rushdie—the cosmopolitan urbanite—to insist that
Roy call India exotic. But this bespeaks perhaps the difference between the Indias that each knows: Roy is a small-town
Kottayam girl, whereas Rushdie is a traveled urbanite. By conde-
scending to Roy, Rushdie risks missing the radicalness of writing with which Roy portrays her views. Her writing contains a
sarcasm and sense of irony that have inflamed Indian natives.
One of them wanted to have her censored: "In June 1997 a lawyer,
Sabu Thomas, filed a public interest petition alleging that the
novel was obscene and likely to corrupt or deprave the minds of
readers. He wanted the final chapter removed, in which there is a
lyrical description of a sexual act. This from a country that produced the Kama Sutra!"[43] The veteran Marxist leader E. M. S.
Namboodiripad also took offense at the way the three Communist characters are depicted in the novel. One can even imagine
that many Indians may have taken exception to the way Chacko
serves as a representative of an Indian Anglophile (though many
chuckled). But this is because they were feeling the effect of
Roy's wicked sarcasm and ability to caricature:

In the old house on the hill, Baby Kochamma sat at the
dining table rubbing the thick, frothy bitterness out of

an elderly cucumber. She was wearing a limp, checked seersucker nightgown with puffed sleeves and yellow turmeric stains. Under the table she swung her tiny, manicured feet, like a small child on a high chair. They were puffy with edema, like little foot-shaped air cushions. In the old days, whenever anybody visited Ayemenem, Baby Kochamma made it a point to call attention to their large feet. She would ask to try on their slippers and say, "Look how big for me they are!" Then she would walk around the house in them, lifting her sari a little so that everybody could marvel at her tiny feet. (*God of Small Things*, 21)

Roy later writes with frank observation: "Comrade Pillai himself came out in the mornings in a graying Aertex vest, his balls silhouetted against his soft white mundu" (15). She continues her openly critical characterizations: "Estha watched as they walked along the railing, pushing through the crowds that moved aside, intimidated by Chacko's suit and sideways tie and his generally bursty demeanor. Because of the size of his stomach, Chacko carried himself in a way that made him appear to be walking uphill all the time" (140). There is oftentimes a surprising insert of profanity: "He was a naked stranger met in a chance encounter. He was the one that she had known before Life began. The one who had once led her (swimming) through their lovely mother's cunt" (89). This boldness is encapsulated by Rahel's behavior toward Comrade Pillai: she is both provocative and (for the reader who is aware of Pillai's corrupted nature) satisfyingly rude: "'So!' Comrade Pillai said. 'I think you are in Amayrica now?' 'No,' Rahel said. 'I'm here'" (123). This tone of rebelliousness fits the themes of the story: there is anger at the way history and biology have conspired to give some people unhappy lives.

Ammu expresses feelings that might be Roy's: "Suddenly Ammu hoped that it had been him that Rahel saw in the march. She hoped it had been him that had raised his flag and knotted arm in anger. She hoped that under his careful cloak of cheerfulness he housed a living, breathing anger against the smug, ordered world that she so raged against" (167). This connects to Roy's comments about herself; she herself proclaims that "transgression" is a major theme of her work, and this is apparent in both the plot of the book and its language: "Perhaps Ammu, Estha and she were the worst transgressors. But it wasn't just them. It was the others too. They all broke the rules. They all crossed into forbidden territory. They all tampered with the laws that lay down who should be loved and how. And how much. The laws that make grandmothers grandmothers, uncles uncles, mothers mothers, cousins cousins, jam jam, and jelly jelly" (31). Implicit, thus, in establishing an *individual* existence is the necessity of anarchy.

A Small World

He [Estha] longed for the river. Because water always helps.

—ARUNDHATI ROY, *The God of Small Things* (1997)

Smallness is ubiquitous in *The God of Small Things*. The children are small people who feel the restrictions of their size in the novel. It requires the gentleness of Velutha to bring reality to the children, who are so vulnerable to the performance of language. The word "yes" haunts Estha forever, while Rahel sees words as having the dimensions of moths: "A cold moth with unusually dense dorsal tufts landed lightly on Rahel's heart" (107). The children—Estha, Rahel, and Sophie Mol—dress up as society ladies in order to inhabit the reality of the adult universe. Roy is able to cultivate the significance of the small by choosing—intermittently—the viewpoint of the children, and by examining what they value. It's important to recognize that Roy is cultivating this small point of view. It is a well-crafted notion of the point of view of children that influences the conditions of space and time in which the novel is located.

The Keralite world often seems suspended in time, or at least free of being defined by any specific time period. This is exemplified by Rahel's child watch, which is always set at ten to two. The cultivation of small things is a slow, careful process that stretches the novel's temporal structure. Roy lingers on the little things, delivering the minute details of the village of Ayemenem to the reader with a slow pace. Examining the natural beauty of Kerala, she brings us a new lens with which to examine her world, one which allows us to be very close to the natural objects that force us to travel at their speed, with their tiny coverage of geography. There is also a love of nature's little things—insects, leaves, water—that grows between Ammu and Velutha. They adopt a spider:

> *Chappu Thamburan,* Velutha called him. Lord Rubbish. One night they contributed to his wardrobe—a flake of garlic skin—and were deeply offended when he rejected it along with the rest of his armor from which he emerged—disgruntled, naked, snot-colored. As though he deplored their taste in clothes. For a few days he remained in this suicidal state of disdainful undress. The rejected shell of garbage stayed standing, like an outmoded world-view. An antiquated philosophy. Then it crumbled. Gradually

Chappu Thamburan acquired a new ensemble. Without admitting it to each other or themselves, they linked their fates, their futures (their love, their Madness, their Hope, their Infinnate Joy), to his. They checked on him every night (with growing panic as time went by) to see if he had survived the day. They fretted over his frailty. His smallness. (321).

Roy's ability to write about nature in such detail grew out of living in the countryside as a child. She writes:

I think the kind of landscape that you grew up in, it lives in you. I don't think it's true of people who've grown up in cities so much, you may love a building but I don't think you can love it in the way that you love a tree or a river or the color of the earth—it's a different kind of love. I'm not a very well-read person but I don't imagine that that kind of gut love for the earth can be replaced by the open landscape. It's a much cleverer person who grows up in the city, savvy and much smarter in many ways. If you spent your very early childhood catching fish and just learning to be quiet, the landscape just seeps into you. Even now I go back to Kerala and it makes me want to cry if something happens to that place.[44]

The phrase "learning to be quiet" resonates with the tone of much of what is beautiful in *The God of Small Things:* "A white boat-spider floated up with the river in the boat, struggled briefly and drowned. Her white egg sac ruptured prematurely, and a hundred baby spiders (too light to drown, too small to swim), stippled the smooth surface of the green water, before being swept out to sea. To Madagascar, to start a new phylum of Malayali Swimming Spiders" (195). Roy's love for the natural world pervades her novel. But her myriad natural details are expressed anthropomorphically, or at least compared to manmade objects: "It was raining when Rahel came back to Ayemenem. Slanting silver ropes slammed into loose earth, plowing it up like gunfire. The old house on the hill wore its steep, gabled roof pulled over its ears like a low hat. The walls, streaked with moss, had grown soft, and bulged a little with dampness that seeped up from the ground. The wild, overgrown garden was full of the whisper and scurry of small lives. In the undergrowth a rat snake rubbed itself against a glistening stone. Hopeful yellow bullfrogs cruised the scummy pond for mates. A drenched mongoose flashed across the leaf-strewn driveway" (4). The liveliness and vibrancy of this world is one which the children often see—but often adults don't, unless they are in love.

> Even later, on the thirteen nights that followed this one, instinctively they stuck to the Small Things. The Big Things ever lurked inside. They knew that there was nowhere for them to go. . . .
>
> They laughed at the ant-bites on each other's bottoms. At clumsy caterpillars sliding off the ends of leaves, at overturned beetles that couldn't right themselves. At the pair of small fish that always sought Velutha out in the river and bit him. At a particularly devout praying mantis. At the minute spider who lived in a crack in the wall of the back verandah of the History House and camouflaged himself by covering his body with bits of rubbish—a sliver of wasp wing. Part of a cobweb. Dust. Leaf rot. The empty thorax of a dead bee. (320)

The awareness of this world provides a landscape in which Roy configures the rest of the plot. The laws of nature set into motion the carrying out of human laws. Sophie Mol is killed in the

river, and Velutha, more a part of nature than any other character, is sacrificed in a move of frightening vengeance against nature. There is no doubt that nature is participating in this novel:

> Three children on the riverbank. A pair of twins and an-
> other, whose mauve corduroy pinafore said *Holiday!* in a
> tilting, happy font.
>
> Wet leaves in the trees shimmered like beaten metal.
> Dense clumps of yellow bamboo drooped into the river as
> though grieving in advance for what they knew was going
> to happen. The river itself was dark and quiet. An absence
> rather than a presence, betraying no sign of how high and
> strong it really was. . . .
>
> There was no storm-music. No whirlpool spun up from
> the inky depths of the Meenachal. No shark supervised
> the tragedy. Just a quiet handing-over ceremony. A boat
> spilling its cargo. A river accepting the offering. One small
> life. A brief sunbeam. With a silver thimble clenched for
> luck in its little fist. (275, 277)

For Roy, the acoustics of nature, the phonetic hearing of children, and the possibility of linguistic death at the hands of
larger human forces illuminate the place of instinct in language.
The vernacular of Roy is the vernacular of self-assertion.

4

"The Shit That's Other"

Unintelligible Languages

What I always felt from learning English and my language acquisition experience was that unintelligibility is an absolute bedrock component of language. I always felt intimately, I was always comfortable with it—that there was always going to be a part of language that I wouldn't understand. You always get these fucking critics talking about it, but I always felt it, I always knew there was part of language I would never understand. And there was going to be a part of my speech act that someone wasn't going to understand. There was never this myth of perfect communication.

—Junot Díaz, quoted in *Gulf Coast* (2002)

Weird English illuminates our potential unintelligibility to one another. When other languages are mixed with English, the weirding of English could be sustained infinitely. Narratives contain this potential for linguistic unintelligibility and illuminate the social impenetrability between communities, illustrated by garbled, jargon-laden, or hybrid languages. Junot Díaz explores the possibilities for linguistic disjuncture and compatibility in his work by including a variety of communities in his fictive universes. To read their interactions is to experience the ways in which communities grow proximate to and distant from one another through language. He shows us linguistic utopias of heterogeneous discourses where no group has more dominance than any other in terms of linguistic power:

> When I wrote *Drown* most people only noticed—whether it was reviewers or readers—what attracts the average person is the otherness of the language—the Spanish. They weren't being drawn to the intellectual language. I just felt there were a number of registers in there—there was Dominican Spanish, general Spanish which is like a Spanish drawn from growing up with a bunch of Latinos, so it's not specific to Dominican-ness, then there's the various Englishes. I just found it really weird that the other language everyone kept focusing on was the homogenized Spanish. . . . I always thought I have a number of readers, I knew that I would have that from the beginning. I was going to have a black readership because one of the people who was reading my work and who I was writing to was AfAm [African American], and I knew I was going to have a Latino readership, and I knew there was going to be a readership that only read English. So it was good that there was going to be unintelligibility for each group. A lot of my Dominican friends always flip out because they get the book and they get the stuff, but they're always like, yo, the shit that's other for them is the intellectual lan-

guage. It was really fun to have these different registers going on and to force communities—it's not to say that the
intellectual language is exclusively for a certain group, but
I knew a lot of the Dominican kids I grew up with weren't
going to know who the fuck Foucault was—but I thought
it was real nice to put all these people together in one
room and to see if they could speak to each other.[1]

Díaz eschews the position of interpreter or translator for that of
producer of diverse linguistic registers.[2] His fiction allows for the
convergence of diverse linguistic worlds, each populated by a different language: (1) homogeneous or standard Spanish; (2) Dominican Spanish; (3) street-speak English; (4) Spanglish; (5) nerd-
speak. These linguistic registers reflect Díaz's own mixed heri-
tage. Díaz says, "One thing I have: I know the Dominican world
as a Dominican man, but I also know it as an outsider, as someone who is not Dominican."[3] His internal hybridism materializes as this space of heterogeneous unintelligibility. Each section
in this chapter will explore some of the aspects above that exist
in Díaz's writing.

Spagnol Americano

What remains *untranslatable* is at bottom the only thing *to
translate*, the only thing *translatable*. What must be translated of that which is translatable can only be the untranslatable.

—JACQUES DERRIDA, *Acts of Literature* (1992)

English might be the official language in the United States, but
standard received English is only one form of English in America. Immigrant communities have their own coded forms of

English with various levels of unintelligibility. Díaz reforms the idea of what constitutes American language by asserting that his Dominican and homogenized Spanish is American. In his view, to embrace Spanish as an American language is to resist the urge to translate or appropriate it. Díaz asserts by performance that *Spanish is an American language* (or he performs the Americanization of Spanish): "For me, allowing the Spanish to exist in my text without the benefit of italics or quotations marks a very important political move. Spanish is not a minority language. Not in this hemisphere, not in the United States, not in the world inside my head. So why treat it like one? Why 'other' it? Why de-normalize it? By keeping the Spanish as normative in a predominantly English text, I wanted to remind readers of the fluidity of languages, the mutability of languages. And to mark how steadily English is transforming Spanish and Spanish is transforming English."[4] Díaz claims that Spanish words can be considered part of American English just as many other non-English words have been appropriated and become part of the English language:

> Look for instance at dictionaries and their way of adopt-ing foreign words. When does a loan word become an English word? Is "hacienda" a word in Spanish or English? You know what I'm saying? The point is, I'm pushing the dates on a lot of these words. I decided I don't need a hun-dred years for the *Oxford English Dictionary* to tell me that it's okay to adopt this or that word as part of our normal vocabulary. I feel that's what we always should do. We should be pushing the dates on words. It's like being a saint. You have to wait five hundred years to be canonized. I'm saying, "Let's not wait. Let's get there now."[5]

Díaz exhibits this philosophy in all of his work—in the collection *Drown* and his short stories "The Sun, the Moon and the Stars" and "The Brief Wondrous Life of Oscar Wao."[6] In each of the excerpts below, all from "Oscar Wao," Spanish is an assumed American language:

> Oscar was a carajito who was into girls mad young. (99)

> He was our little Porfirio Rubirosa. (99)

> Look at that little macho, his mother's friends said. Qué hombre. (99)

> He got uncomfortable with himself and no longer went anywhere near the girls, because they always shrieked and called him gordo asqueroso. (100)

> She had a habit of screaming NATAS! In the middle of homeroom. Sorry, loca, home instruction for you. (99)

> We wouldn't want you to turn into one of those Greenwich Village maricones, Tío Rodolfo muttered ominously. You have to grab a muchacha, broder, y metéselo. That will take care of everything. Start with a fea. Coge that fea y metéselo! Rodolfo had four kids with three different women, so the nigger was without doubt the family's resident metiéndolo expert. (100)

> At Rutgers, she'd shaved her head down to the bone, Sinead style, and now everybody, including their mother, was convinced she was a jota. (103)

> Standing in his foyer, in full-length leather, her trigueña skin blood-charged from the cold . . . (103)

Tío Rodolfo had got the clap from a puta (Man, his tío cracked, what a pisser! Har-har!), after he'd seen his first Haitians kicked off a guagua because niggers claimed they "smelled," after he'd nearly gone nuts over all the bellezas he saw. (109)

She didn't have the Mirador Norte wanna-be American look. (109)

His mother met him at the door and couldn't believe his sinvergüencería. (110)

His tío seemed thrilled that he no longer had a pájaro for a nephew. I can't believe it, he said proudly. The palomo is finally a man. (119)

Poor Oscar. At night he dreamed that his rocket ship, the Hijo de Sacrificio, was up and off but that it was heading for the Ana Acuña Barrier at the speed of light. (119)

A skinny forty-something-year-old jabato standing near his spotless red Jeep . . . (118)

Oscar was lucky; if he had looked like my pana Pedro, the Dominican Superman, he probably would have got shot right there. (118)

Se acabó. Oscar refused to look at the ocean as they drove to the airport. (120)

In addition to writing in Spanish words on the level of sentences, Díaz also creates rules for including Spanish in his narratives. Although in his early works he italicized Spanish words, he has decided to leave Spanish romanized in later texts. Díaz wrote *Drown* first (1996), then "The Sun, the Moon and the Stars"

(1999), then "The Brief Wondrous Life of Oscar Wao" (2000), which he refers to as a novella. In "The Sun, the Moon and the Stars," Díaz italicized Spanish in order to concede to the wishes of his editor. "The *New Yorker* forced me to put italics in, but after that I stipulated as part of my contract that if they didn't accept the stories' nonitalics that's that—they can't publish it. . . . What I should have done is stand my ground and said they couldn't publish it."[7] But in *Drown* and "Wao," Díaz left the Spanish romanized.

Díaz's language-mixing technique varies in degree, depending on the story. The variety of interaction between English and Spanish individualizes each story. In some stories the presence of Spanish signifies the barrio, while in others the presence of Spanish adds to the landscape of Santo Domingo. Spanish and English collide or commune, depending on the configuration. Díaz recognizes different levels of interaction between the languages of English and Spanish. He has spoken of their peaceful coexistence and "mutability": "Back home in the Capital, Rafa had his own friends, a bunch of tigueres who liked to knock down our neighbors and who scrawled *chocha* and *toto* on walls and curbs.[8] Back in the Capital he rarely said anything to me except Shut up, pendejo. Unless, of course, he was mad and then he had about five hundred routines he liked to lay on me. Most of them had to do with my complexion, my hair, the size of my lips. It's the Haitian, he'd say to his buddies. Hey Señor Haitian, Mami found you on the border and only took you in because she felt sorry for you" (*Drown*, 5). Rafa's tone is audible—it jumps off the page—and anyone who can remember back to childhood can feel the intonations of a bullying brother here. Childhood anxieties erupt in his description of Ysrael, a boy with a mutilated face: "He was something to talk about, a name that set the kids to screaming, worse than el Cuco or la Vieja Calusa" (7). Or "*La chica de la novela* was still on the charts. Can you believe that? the man next to me said. They play that vaina a hundred times a day" (11). And in many places, casual Spanish pervades Díaz's work as transcription: "Coño, compa'i, ¿cómo va todo?" (31). In "The Sun, the Moon and the Stars," Díaz associates Spanish with intimacy and implies that using it has to be earned: "Her father, who used to treat me like his *hijo,* calls me an asshole on the phone, sounds like he's strangling himself with the cord. 'You no deserve I speak to you in Spanish,' he says. I see one of Magda's girlfriends at the Woodbridge Mall—Claribel, the *ecuatoriana* with the biology degree and the *chinita* eyes—and she treats me like I ate somebody's kid" (98).

For Díaz, the presence of Spanish signifies explosive agency and lack of self-consciousness simultaneously—a combination concretely manifested in the use of English and Spanish. Spanish is both an expression outside the American majority and the language that brings him into a psychological comfort zone.

His use of Spanish possesses a political as well as personal and linguistic thrust: Spanish rescues Latinos from invisibility to the white world or occlusion from African American activists. Díaz states: "The Black community loves Dominicans and Puerto Ricans only as long as we support them and erase ourselves."[9] Cultural translation is automatically anti-assimilative and anti-harmonizing, unless it includes elements of the culture being translated. Allied with this reasoning, Lawrence Venuti says that "good translation is minoritizing" and creating a "heterogeneous discourse."[10] Díaz could appropriate Venuti's words to argue that complete translation of his culture into English results in "inauthenticity, distortion and contamination."[11] In hybridizing his English, and in asserting the integrity of heterogeneous discourse, Díaz dirties the reputation of translation, demotes it to a mistaken, impossible, and potentially damaging ideal. The concept of translation is crafted by a dominant culture; in practice, *translation is erasure*. He implicitly argues for the coexistence of cultures. The representation of another culture in another language should be hybrid, so as to avoid assimilation or erasure. For Latinos and Latinas, this means, principally, erasure by the black or white communities.

In contrast to Jhumpa Lahiri, who describes her own writing as continual translation ("I translate, therefore I am"), Díaz *is* when he doesn't translate.[12] A political, not purely aesthetic agenda defines Díaz's use of language. He says: "History is changing. Now a formerly colonial language [Spanish] is the site of struggle to maintain space."[13] Díaz incorporates the cadence of words such as "jaivas" and "jurones" (*Drown,* 4), "pastelito" (11), "chicharrón" (10), and "cobrador" (11), to offset the rhythms of English. These words disrupt English's familiar patterns of stressed and unstressed syllables; they transform the natural beat of English sentences—for example, "I got the cojones to ask her up for café, which was mighty manipulative of me" (*Drown,* 115), or "the aroma of lechón" (170), or "his lips were greasy from Nilda's pollo guisado" (185). For Díaz, the reading experience is physical, not simply mental gymnastics. Díaz engages in the art of assertive nontranslation, placing Spanish words side by side with English words without calling attention to them, without contextualizing them or grammatically indicating that Spanish is other. By infusing English with new rhythms, he rejuvenates it, while also suggesting the power of Spanish sounds and inflections.[14] In other passages, he shows Spanish enacting retaliatory violence against English when embedded in it: "When I learned English in the States, this was a violent enterprise. And by forcing Spanish back on English, forcing it to deal with the language it tried to exterminate in me, I've tried to represent a mirror-image of that violence on the page. Call it my revenge on English."[15]

Spanish is also just as originally hybrid as English. Díaz views his language as a result of accumulated cultures, not simply the Spanish immigrant tradition: "I have multiple traditions, like anyone else. I'm part of the mainstream 'American' literary tradition. I'm a part of the Latino literary tradition. I'm a part of the African diasporic tradition as well as the Dominican literary tradition. But there's also the oral tradition and the rhythmic tradition of the musics I grew up with, which deeply influence how I write a sentence and how my work sounds."[16]

The oral component in his work is emphasized in striking concordance with Kingston's assertions about the rhythms of one language being incorporated into another. But Díaz acknowledges that language is also visual experience. He notes the physicality of language: "I even like the way words fall on a page.[17] Literally, the physical way words look. If a sentence looks wrong on the page, I don't care what it says, I change it. It's weird, but that's the way instinct works. Instincts don't work at any level that you can recognize. A lot of people say your subconscious is like five hundred times more powerful than the rest of you. Maybe your subconscious is signaling you when a sentence or paragraph physically looks wrong. All the words are given the same status."[18] Asked about the absence of quotation marks, he says: "There's a visual component to reading. There's this sense of democracy—I always love the way that looks, that everything is democratized."[19] He adds that the lack of marks plays with "the line between what is spoken and what is thought," while it also "mirrors the connotation in everyday life. After a day or two, you can't remember whether one person or another said something. . . . I'm doing the old cliché stereotype by purposefully putting a flaw in the work that makes it more real."[20]

Rap English

> You know what? There is no Latino Generation X. "Gen-
> eration X" is used to describe white suburban kids. You
> know, we are not Generation X, everybody knows what
> generation we are. It's funny because I feel that the term
> "Generation X" only came up because Latinos and black
> kids had such a well-defined identity. . . . And I think, in a
> way, the fact that white kids needed to come up with this
> term is more of a sign that, you know, they are the blah
> generation, and we are the generation of fucking serious
> hip-hop and the return of Salsa and Merengue, you
> know. And just fucking roqueros. Es hora, shit!
>
> —JUNOT DÍAZ, quoted in Maximo Zeledón, "Dominican Do-
> minion: An Interview with Junot Díaz," *Frontera Magazine* (1998)

For Díaz to characterize his own work as a form of "resistance
vernacular" is only half true, since it is thoroughly compelling.[21]
Like rap, his writing is unimpeachably hip, phat and cool.[22] If
anything, Díaz writes in *irresistible* vernacular. It is empowering.
He attributes the rhythm of his work to Caribbean influences,
but the hip-hop element is unquestionably constitutive of his
sentences' beats. He disrupts any of the meters that stressed and
unstressed markers provide in English by either using Spanish
or creating unusual structures. Díaz says:

> When it comes to writing sentences, for me I believe in the
> fucking music of it. I know it sounds really fucking ridicu-
> lous. I should be wearing my dashiki and banging a drum,
> but honestly each sentence for me resonates. Its rhythms
> are the most important. I feel like in all my language,
> rhythm is the key. People ask me could you describe what
> is really Caribbean about your work? I'm like, I don't have

to describe it to you, but if I really have to, if I have a gun to my head, it's rhythms. Those polyrhythms of Santo Domingo where I grew up all my life, which were in people's body language, in the music they listened to and in the words they spoke. These rhythms infiltrated all my writings. I think a really good sentence, a really good piece of work should really have a certain attention paid to its rhythm. It's not just like, "Does it look good? Is it pleasing to the eye?" I'm really interested in how it fucking sounds. Right now, that's the way I'm working, when it comes to the level of language.[23]

It's not simply the rhythms of the Caribbean or the dashiki that underlie the language of Díaz. His prose is influenced by hip-hop and rap; these American rhythms pervade his prose. Díaz's connection to rap is personal, social, political, and aesthetic. Not surprisingly, one of his childhood friends, Bert Wang, is an Asian American rap artist and activist whose own raps deal with issues of race. Here are some lines from his song "Asian for the Man":

> You seen Kung Fu with David Carradine
> Another hakujin in the scene
> Representin' Asian philosophy
> That white-washed bullshit not what we need
> Show us what they're thinkin' say we're passive and weak
> White knight savin' Asians usin' Eastern techniques
> Swine eating sucker give it a rest
> To get his black belt you just take a written test
> David Carradine you shoulda learned from the start
> You're an unskilled white boy pimpin' the arts
> Alcoholic bastard still out and about

If I met that piece of shit I'd knock his ass out

Bruce Lee wannabe grasshopper white ghost

Comes to martial arts you got nothin' to boast

Serves another purpose in society

Preachin' Asian impotence and white superiority.[24]

Implicit in the form of rap is its structural revolt and linguistic nonconformity to standard English—the performance of violence to and destabilization of standard received English. The form is just as important as the words; the rhyme is key to the performance of emotion.

Hip-hop and rap music contribute to the political and musical sense of Díaz's work. The political thrust of Díaz's work is evident all over, but mainly he writes about pain: "Most people do shit out of self-pain. We would be totally different people if we were getting happy ass and weren't raped as kids. By the time we were thirty, people wouldn't be so into genocide. . . . It's the immigrants—people who grew up as minorities among whites—that have [racial] issues. Dominicans who came here after their identities were formed don't have issues," Díaz observes. The violence of the Dominican world has a different quality from that of New Jersey barrio violence. Díaz says, "When you spend your whole life being brutalized by economic and social conditions, the things that titillate you are [forms of] brutalization."[25] It is the violence of suffering in combination with the violence of identity formation that makes Díaz's work explosive, that makes its diasporic element distinct. In America, where capitalism is successful, violence is akin to overstimulation, to sensory overload, rather than physical punishment: you have to see the third world to reconfigure the idea of suffering in the terms that Díaz sees it. Diasporic communities are familiar with violence: the violence of encounter with a new culture, the violence of living through third-world conditions. Forced unintelligibility is an act of violence; when one can't speak, this is a prelude to violence as expression. The element of the third world exists on every page. The danger of drinking water: "We can't drink the water around here. It would kill us. And he's already sick" (*Drown*, 16). Or the lack of writing utensils: "We each had one pencil and if we lost that pencil, like I did once, we had to stay home from school until Mami could borrow another one for us" (71). The details of *Drown* elaborate on what Díaz says: "The third world is a violent culture because their lives are so hard."[26] As for the violence that explodes in the language of his own work, Díaz says:

> Children, especially, you know—children are exceptionally violent. And I think especially young boys, who were brought up to value violence and male behavior. And this is not common just to Latinos. When everybody is saying machismo, I'm like, suck my dick, because this is not common to Latinos. It's common to everybody who belongs to a hyper-patriarchal society, very much like the one in the United States. What was interesting about the story, was the way older brothers trained younger brothers. I think people forget . . . see, I think people forget that older brothers spend a lot of time training younger brothers, and it's usually through violence, whether they inflicted it on other people or on them. Because older brothers know life is no fucking joke.[27]

The engagement of predisposition to violence contributes, in a clear way, to the formation of identity. Rap and hip-hop, strong language, expletives constitute the performance of, reaction to, and absorption of violence implicit in culture, and the resulting commodity is an identity that compels attention. Those on the suffering end of the world's hierarchies are riveted to violent expression because they repress it. Minorities *work* to achieve this strength of identifiable vernacular, and it's not simply about content; enunciation, volume, delivery, and beat are features that immediately accompany rap, hip-hop, and rock. Violent language—again, not simply judged as such in terms of content—creates a space, forces a language into the auditory field of languages, and simultaneously forces the presence of a community into the visual field of communities that accompanies the imaginative act of reading. Whereas language mavens in the past relied on hyperbole and expletive to reshape narrative, Henry Miller among them, Díaz's narrative precipitates out of an environment that is saturated with the form of protest, of nonconformism to standard English. Miller's mission, though obsessed more with sexual issues than racial ones, still resonates: "This is not a book. This is libel, slander, defamation of character. This is not a book, in the ordinary sense of the word. No, this is a prolonged insult, a gob of spit in the face of Art, a kick in the pants to God, Man, Destiny, Time, Love, Beauty . . . what you will. I am going to sing for you, a little off key perhaps, but I will sing. I will sing while you croak, I will dance over your dirty corpse."[28] Díaz's own presence is riveting; his book does not capture the aural drama of his speech; a conversation with him awakens you to the musical range of his voice, his precise pronunciation of Spanish, and his consciousness of the artistic aspects of speech.[29]

Barrio language without Spanish is equivalent to hip-hop without a beat: less compelling, and unquestionably without equal impact. A paragraph of Díaz is performance art. His writing can be easily converted to rap:

Prose from *Drown*	My mediocre rap interpretation
The corner's where you smoke, eat, fuck, where you play selo. Selo games like you've never seen. I know brothers who make two, three hundred a night on the dice. Always somebody losing big. But you have to be careful with that. Never know who'll lose and then come back with a 9 or a machete, looking for the rematch . . .	The corner's where you smoke, eat, fuck

Playin' selo try your luck

Brothers makin' three buck a night

But you gotta be careful to avoid a fight

Never know what loser will return with a 9 |
| We're all under the big streetlamps, everyone's the color of day-old piss. When I'm fifty this is how I'll remember my friends: tired and yellow and drunk. (*Drown*, 57) | Watch your back or it's your last time

We're under the lamps, faces the color of piss

Díaz es feliz that he didn't write this. |

This exercise in transformation exposes the strong rhythm in Díaz's prose, which is more apparent and detectable than in many forms of poetry. His beat resonates with the meter of rap or hard rock.[30] The performative aspect of Díaz's efforts lies not simply in good writing but in intuitive musicality. His art comes in the delivery of this musicality, by the exploitation and execution of the musical features of the languages he uses. The employment of Spanish, barrio speech, and English combines to form new rhythms and tones in English, a new kind of musical writing. Díaz makes us read and listen closely for the music inside his words.[31]

Urban pain and ethnic pain inform the issues under the music of *Drown,* and make it a book for the young: "It had a big impact on young writers. It's what's been said to me. It's not that great of a book; it's a good book. But because of some of my approaches, it doesn't fit into the usual ethnic pieties, and people feel much more comfortable talking about some of the issues in it."[32]

Urban space has become a confluence of different classes, cultures, and temporal zones; diverse cultures living next to each other result in a cacophony of untranslated communities. The closer in proximity the groups are, the more identity formation happens, often in the form of hybridism. In New York, the result is the celebration of Cuban-Chinese food (Flora de Mayo), Thai and Vietnamese children waving Irish flags on St. Patrick's Day, African Americans teaching aikido (Shinbudokai NYC), and Russian-vegan restaurants (Veselka on the Lower East Side). Díaz aims to explore the connection between cultures on a deeper level than appropriation: he explores its psychoanalytic repercussions and the way social structures develop from history. When this exploration occurs on the level of writing, his language becomes tense with example, loosened from theory. Not many race theorists can really talk about race issues with the concrete detail, emotion, and sensuality that writers have. The sensual aspects of cross-cultural mixing are the locations of tension, not the theory behind such mixing. In theory, "the human race is my race," but in practice, as Díaz says, "Across the axis of our self-hate flows half a capital. The challenge for us is to build totally healthy sexual identities."[33] Díaz quotes David Mura on this same topic: "We have no problems discussing who we hire; but we don't talk about who we desire." He ruminates on the beginning of writing about groups of color:

> Groups of color rarely write across to each other; they write for themselves or white people. Rarely do you see Asian American writers writing for themselves and the African American or Latino community, or African American writers writing for themselves and the Latino community. There's a lot of logical interlocutors we've had in our lives, but because we want to belong to our own community we suppress that. For me, it's easier to belong in the Dominican community if I don't talk about how many Asian people I know. It confuses things and complicates things, and in some ways it's just easier if I focus on my Dominican community; but in some ways it's dishonest. There's a second level of complexity that writers of color have to step into. The reason most of us don't do it is because we don't get rewarded for it, or when we do do it, it's really fucked up. Fucked up appropriation. Asian kids calling each other niggers and hip-hop or black kids getting Chinese-character tattoos or wearing kungfu outfits. They encounter each other at the level of appropriation but not on a deeper historical level. You encounter each other at the level of kitsch but not at the deeper historical level, where we used to encounter each other. For me it's like, it's one thing to like Japanese food, but it's another to know that in 1956 Japanese people arrived in the Dominican Republic and were enslaved and worked by Trujillo the dictator there, and no one there said anything.[34]

Unlike proliferating accounts of urban space, which provide a stiflingly detailed conception of what constitutes the urban, or a bird's-eye view that daunts as much as informs (think of the writings of Saskia Sassen), Junot Díaz provides a firsthand, empirical account of urban life in many of his stories. The energy, implicit violence, and tension that exist in the culture surface and detonate his words. Continual transactional energy with the city pervades his work. His vernacular is, in many ways, the vernacular of violence. Many of his sentences seem to have just barely entered the discursive zone, precipitated from the atmosphere of violence by chance.

These sentences erupt when describing poverty. When Henry Miller pictures himself as one large intestine in order to express the enormous visceral being that erupts in the psyche as a result of starvation, the imagery brings his situation to life.[35] Likewise, in Díaz's descriptions of government cheese, intestinal worms, physical punishments, molestation, and deformity there is no masking. The writing is concise, sharp, and unflinching. In his story "Negocios" the language is punchy and uncompromising, and contrasts sharply with later passages from "Aguantando" that exhibit a slow mythic grandeur:

> Don't get me wrong: it wasn't that he was having fun. No, he'd been robbed twice already, his ribs beaten until they were bruised. He often drank too much and went home to his room, and there he'd fume, spinning, angry at the stupidity that had brought him to this freezing hell of a country, angry that a man his age had to masturbate when he had a wife, and angry at the blinkered existence his jobs and the city imposed on him. He never had time to sleep, let alone go to a concert or the museums that filled entire sections of the newspapers. And the roaches.

> The roaches were so bold in his flat that turning on the lights did not startle them. They waved their three-inch antennas as if to say, Hey puto, turn that shit off. He spent five minutes stepping on their carapaced bodies and shaking them from his mattress before dropping into his cot and still the roaches crawled on him at night. No, he wasn't having fun. (*Drown*, 179)

The roaches provoke a mixture of the fanciful, the comic, and the disgusting. Again, their tactile element makes them real; and by virtue of this, the body of the character Ramón comes into effable relief.

"It's Not Where You're From, It's Where You're At"[36]

A South Jersey accent makes me reach for the shotgun
and tell the kids to hide under the bed.

—JUNOT DÍAZ, interview with Evelyn Ch'ien, July 26, 2002

Díaz is a product of diaspora, and his stories, with their multiple linguistic registers and geographic locales, provide pieces of his identity. Santo Domingo represents the past; America, the present. Spanish is his tradition; English, his experimental space. Díaz remains suspended over both languages, but the past materializes as a country frozen in past time: "There was this great Salman Rushdie quote: 'It can be argued that the past is the country from which we all emigrated,' and so that's the epigram of the book, that opens the book and has been the guiding principle to shape this story about my parents, about their generation."[37]

Díaz was two years old when his father went to America and became a factory worker.[38] Díaz says that five years later the family left for northern New Jersey, to a "low-income neighborhood fronting a landfill."[39] The family lived in the town of Parlin, in an apartment complex called London Terrace:

> I had a terrible fucking homelife. I was always angry and depressed. We were really poor. Other families were buying houses and cars. My father was a bitter, angry, violent person; my brother got cancer when I was thirteen; my sister ran away and became a stripper. We were on welfare, being bused into a white school system, and when you're thirteen and you're full of that adolescent self-hate . . . For me, what helped was escapism. AIDS and crack wasn't a joke to you. It's so funny—you wouldn't ever think it if you hadn't lived it. This shit had a big impact on poor communities. People were losing their minds. All this stuff was happening to me at once, and what I did was withdrew. I read fucking science fiction books, played Dungeons and Dragons, didn't go to school, hated everybody. It was nuts. I fucked up in high school, failed a bunch of classes and barely graduated. A lot of weird unhappiness. What saved my life was being a nerd, watching all these bad science fiction movies and reading cartoons. It really saved my life. I was fucking pissed off. Poverty is a motherfucker. And at my age I didn't have the language. I was like, why do I hate myself so much? Why do I feel so bad all the time? Yo, I had no language for it, and there's a lot of shame to it. Being that broke. I remember when I only had enough shirts that I'd have to recycle one in the middle of the week, and this incredible shame you could

feel how it works on you. Poor people were bad to each other, too—really bad to each other. My mother always says, if you're ugly the worst place to be ugly is around poor people. And what she means is that the people at the bottom always internalize the economy and are more deranged. We're more likely to torture an ugly person than the people who taught us that we are ugly.[40]

When he moved to America, Díaz had a speech therapist to help him conquer a stammer. He says that he became an avid reader in order to "compensate for my lack of control of spoken English."[41] But he doesn't play the sympathy card. His aim in *Drown* is "to see how much I can leave silent about the way this child, this character, went from being a child to a young man. What does that say? We never see this kid learn English, and I think that was important. I have read a thousand stories where we see the kid learn how terrible English is, how hard it is. Not to take anything away from that, but I actually wanted to leave it out because it works so much better, for me—just for me."[42] He implies that he forced his own loss of language: "I grew up with avoiding all things Latino and black. I wanted no attention paid to those things because I wanted to deny those things. And I grew up during the eighties, where Puerto Ricans . . . First of all, nobody knew what a Dominican was—Puerto Ricans didn't know what Dominicans were. They didn't know some of them were supposed to hate us—but I didn't notice anybody trying to be proud of it. The eighties was like assimilation time."[43] Díaz definitely sees assimilation time as a period of self-hatred. His reaction to the eighties is a one-eighty; now he is an activist for his community. His concerns often veer toward the publishing industry for writers of color, and how the publishing gaze corrupts and prevents the authenticity of self-representation on the part of people of color. He analyzes the relationship between writers and publishers as inherently problematic because writing has become a commodity:

> The older generation of color in some ways is a lot more interesting than the younger generation. There's just too much money in it [publishing] now. You know the phrase that the male gaze will alter the female behavior. Well, the capitalist gaze alters communities of color and the way communities of color represent themselves. When I wrote *Drown*, young people weren't in. That allowed me to write. I wasn't writing to white people. So many young writers write to white people; they talk about agents and money. I'm like, yo, you have that gaze on you. Some people have never existed without the white gaze, so they don't know what it would mean *not* to respond to it.[44]

For Díaz, regaining language, or voice, occurred with the reestablishment of familial intimacy. Díaz first began writing when his brother Rafa contracted leukemia (the speculative source for the disease being the landfill). The younger brother wrote the stories to amuse Rafa during his hospital confinement. Rafa survived, and the brothers remain close; Rafa has helped Díaz weather his recent stormy success. Díaz continued writing while at Rutgers (he transferred there after one year at Kean College). Although he says that Latinos there were "invisible," he found his writing voice in the multiple linguistic structure displayed in his work.

"A Sheet of Fire": Díaz's Nerd-Speak

Jesus Christ, he whispered. I'm a Morlock.

—JUNOT DÍAZ, "The Brief Wondrous Life of Oscar Wao" (2000)

In the distance you can see the Raritan, as shiny as an earthworm.

—JUNOT DÍAZ, *Drown* (1996)

In Díaz's latest work, weird English is Spanglish plus the linguistic register of the nerd, so that the result is a weird combination of Spanglish and sci-fi language: "A milagro! He'd finally repaired his ion drive; the evil planet Gordo was pulling him back but his fifties-style rocket, the Hijo de Sacrificio, wouldn't quit" ("Oscar Wao," 109). Díaz has said that being a nerd "saved his life," and one dimension of that was his love of words, which led to his becoming a writer. In "The Brief Wondrous Life of Oscar Wao," he demonstrates the nerdiness that brought Spanglish to written form in his works. In the novella, the mixed English-Spanish moments have the extra resonance of telling us how barrio language made it into a book. Díaz has said: "Who's writing this story? Oscar isn't the only geek, but the story is in his language, and he is in all of us but open about it."[45]

Díaz, self-described nerd, incorporates allusions to subjects ranging from poetry, to anthropological theory, to Dungeons and Dragons in his work. But "Oscar Wao" introduces, with more openness, the variety of linguistic registers that have infused Díaz's writing.

> With the new work, I'm trying to see how far I can push it, some of the new languages. ["Oscar Wao"] is the one people have no idea [about], what the fuck, because most

people don't get the weird science fiction and apocalyptic language that gets used through it. The thing with "Oscar Wao" is that there is always the sense that almost all people of color who write that I know are nerds. If you're a writer you're basically a nerd, no matter what kind of nice clothes you put on, how much you go to the gym. I think it's okay to be a nerd, but people try to hide it.

It was weird—I was on a panel with a bunch of male writers of color, and all of them were trying to be super-ghetto, and all of them had written books about being fucking drug dealers. Now, none of them—I know this for a fact because I know them—none of them had sold a fucking bag in their entire fucking lives. And I was sitting there thinking, my god, what these guys are writing is, what they're basically doing is regurgitating back to a white audience, a white mainstream, the image—the twisted warped image—they have of us. And their connection to it is so foreign that basically what they're writing is science fiction. But this is the kind of imaginative act— these guys writing about drug dealing—this kind of imaginative act gets rewarded in the publishing industry even though it's no more intimate to them than a visit to an alien planet would be.

If these motherfuckers are writing science fiction, I might as well feel free to write science fiction. And since the thing that they were all hiding—this hyper-masculinized drug dealer, this passing for masculinity in these Africanized communities, whether it was Latino or black—was that these motherfuckers were putting on this mask to try to hide the nerd. Because all of them were nerds, but the thing they were trying not to write about was the nerd. The great silence on that panel was the silence of this experience these guys lived immediately. Being nerds, loving words, being writers, going to elite graduate schools, going to elite schools—that was the huge silence. But what there was . . . was this excess of bullshit prepackaged hyper-masculinity.

So that gave me the first fucking idea that I should write, totally try to flip it, that I should write a book, a story, about a fucking nerd. And not just about a nerd, but deploy the language, to tell the story in the language of the nerd. It's not enough to write about what I would consider the losing end. If we have a masculine hierarchy in the Dominican community, the Yunior character tends to be on the winning end. He's a guy who's comfortable with girls, and even though he himself is fucked up he is always dating girls, can get girls, and would be considered a man in this economy and on the winning end. And I thought I would take it as far to the opposite end, to try to write about a nerd. There was just something about that silence that needed to be addressed.

The story is told by Yunior; he had dated Lola, the guy's sister. Oscar and Lola had a really interesting relationship. There's nothing worse. Again with this notion of a world where someone like Yunior is the pinnacle—that's what he wished he could have been, secretly; and in this world, your sister being raped on your watch is not considered a great thing. It's another one of the big silences in the book, the novella—is that Lola is raped. And in the Dominican community it has a big resonance, and it's your sister and you're supposed to be protecting her, and it's your sister who you love more than anyone. And Yunior falls in love with this girl, but he never likes her brother, because her brother represents stuff he himself doesn't want to get into.

How does Yunior tell the story so well? Why does he know all this vocabulary, all these words, all this stuff? Is it research or affinity? The whole problem with Yunior was that he was never able to show his true face to anyone—could never tell Lola who he really was, or tell anyone. Part of the story was that he gets as close as he can to admitting how much he had in common with Oscar. He couldn't come out and say it.

It's all about how these kinds of masculinities are implicated in each other—and especially in the Dominican community, where most of the boys I know are passing for boys. You hear women all the time who say, "You act totally different in public. When you're with me you are totally different." And yeah, most of the dudes I know are only passing.

So many people of color—science fiction, cartoons, all of this stuff is part of their lives. Yo, how many of these fucking MCs are rhyming and they drop rhymes about comic books and cartoons—you hear all these raps. It's such a part of our lives, what being a ghetto boy is, and it's—yet it's almost absent from this two-dimensional posturing of masculinity.

So my idea was to center it, and to have those things that are a part of it. Someone said to me I was simplifying my Dominicanness because I didn't write about Asian American stuff. She knew I was friends with Bert. We dream up communities we never belong to. When I write, because I was concentrating on my family, that complex-

ity fell away. In my next project, I am going to see if I
can bring part of that complexity back and disrupt that
circle.[46]

Díaz's observations contrast with those of Joseph Conrad's
Kurtz, who, in *Heart of Darkness,* ends his life as a rich colonialist
exploiting tribal people and sees "The horror! The horror!" Oscar dies with the exclamation, "The beauty! The beauty!": "He
wrote that he couldn't believe he'd had to wait for this so goddamn long. (Yvon was the one who suggested calling the wait
something else. Yeah, like what? Maybe, she said, you could call
it life.) He wrote: So this is what everybody's always talking
about! Diablo! If only I'd known. The beauty! The beauty!"
("Oscar Wao," 117). If critics spend time wondering about what
Kurtz meant by "The horror! The horror!" they can sigh with relief at the declarative tone of Díaz's phrase, "The beauty! The
beauty!" which, though symmetrical in structure with the former, contrasts with it by its lack of obscurity. This phrase is
infinitely clear about what it is describing: Oscar's one experience of sexual intercourse. These are the most clearly referential
words in a story where a geek is the protagonist of a narrative
without being understood. His last words grant him an intelligibility unexperienced in life. Oscar's existence is a nerd's. Nerds
are the emblems of unintelligibility, jargon-laden creatures who
roll for initiative (a term from Dungeons and Dragons) and are
caught up in the tangled essence of the suppression of desire.
The following is a catalogue of geek life:

> What little faith Oscar had in the world took an SS-M-17
> Snipe to the head. (101)

> What is it with us niggers and our bodies? Not even
> Fanon can explain it to me. (106)

Ana nodded; she smelled of a perfume, and when she pressed close the heat of her body was *vertiginous.* (103)

Wasn't it Turgenev who said, Whom you laugh at you forgive and come near to loving? (106)

Her Jedi mind tricks did not, however, work on Oscar. When it came to girls, the brother had a mind like a four-hundred-year-old yogi. (108)

Throughout high school he did the usual ghettonerd things: he collected comic books, he played role-playing games, he worked at a hardware store to save money for an outdated Apple IIe. He was an introvert who trembled with fear every time gym class rolled around. He watched nerd shows like *Doctor Who* and *Blake's 7,* could tell you the difference between a Veritech fighter and a Zentraedi battle pod, and he used a lot of huge-sounding nerd words like "indefatigable" and "ubiquitous" when talking to niggers who would barely graduate from high school. (100)

Despite swearing to be different, he went back to his nerdy ways, eating, not exercising, using flash words, and after a couple consecutive Fridays alone he joined the university's resident geek organization, R.U. Gamers. (106)

After college, Oscar moved back home. Left a virgin, returned one. Took down his childhood posters (Star Blazers, Captain Harlock) and tacked up his college ones (Akira and Terminator II). (107)

In a burst of enthusiasm, he attempted to start a science-fiction club, and for two Thursdays in a row he sat in his classroom after school, his favorite books laid out in an

attractive pattern, listening to the roar of receding foot-
steps in the halls, the occasional shout outside his door of
Beam me up! And Nanoo-Nanoo! (107)

He wasn't svelte by any stretch of the imagination, but he
wasn't Joseph Conrad's wife no more, either. (108)

This collection of nerdiness is yet another aspect of Díaz's advocacy for minority discourse.

Metaphors

Díaz's metaphors softly radiate through the tough veneer of barrio rhythms, making *Drown* have an alternative musical splen-
dor: "Let her comb her hair, the sound of it stretching like a
sheet of fire between you" (148). He speaks of an ex-girlfriend
having "tiny beautiful moles on her neck, an archipelago leading
down into her clothes" (133). Both of these metaphors represent
universes of beauty in a particular experience. In the first, the
image of a sheet of fire captures the dynamic of a first date, the
tide of emotion kept at bay by a vertical plane of fire. In the
second, the focus on the pattern of the moles inspiring a picture
of an archipelago pulls an observation into an unexpected context. Díaz repeatedly shows this skill. Leaflets dropped from a
single-prop plane fall "as slow as butterfly blossoms" (7). In the
campo, "rosebushes blazed around the yard like compass points
and the mango trees spread out deep blankets of shade where
we could rest and play dominos" (4). Díaz also employs syn-
aesthesia: "From the shack you could hear voices, as bright as
chrome" (13). The presence of an imaginary world, where shad-
ows serve as blankets, voices reflect light, and roses serve as compass points, is evidence of an enriched experience of the world.

The narrator's experience of the world happens through his mental reorganization of it. Later he says that he awakens to find the "amapolas were flushed with their flame leaves" (84). The metaphors often peer from the slang, conflating the abstract (here, it is love) and the physical (the heart): "Loretta's new boy was Italian, worked on Wall Street. When she told me about him we were still going out. We were on the Promenade and she said to me, I like him. He's a hard worker. No amount of heart leather could stop something like that from hurting" (114). The mention of "heart leather" punctured by unrequited love combines the intangible and the visceral. Díaz's similes also accomplish the materialization of the ineffable: "Me and Rafa, we didn't talk much about the Puerto Rican woman. When we ate dinner at her house, the few times Papi had taken us over there, we still acted like nothing was out of the ordinary. Pass the ketchup, man. No sweat, bro. The affair was like a hole in our living room floor, one we'd gotten so used to circumnavigating that we sometimes forgot it was there" (40). Often literary tropes are used to hyperbolize emotional states. Images emphasize the tragicomic: "Being around Papi all her life had turned her [Madai] into a major-league wuss. Anytime Papi raised his voice her lip would start trembling, like some specialized tuning fork" (27). The power of Díaz's descriptions is often in their punch, in their cruelty. His descriptions are testaments to an underlying commitment to barrio culture.

When the narrator describes his tía's household, for example, his testimony is mixed with affection and outrage simultaneously: "From what I'd seen so far, the place had been furnished in Contemporary Dominican Tacky. The less I saw, the better. I mean, I liked plastic sofa covers but damn, Tío and Tía had taken it to another level. They had a disco ball hanging in the living room and the type of stucco ceilings that looked like stalactite heaven" (*Drown*, 32). These comical images reverberate—they strive not for poeticism but for visual impact. Aesthetic moments surprise the reader throughout *Drown*. The presence of desire crystallizes in a description of a travel experience: "I was always too depressed to notice the ocean, the young boys fishing and selling cocos by the side of the road, the surf exploding into the air like a cloud of shredded silver" (75). The evocative image of the "surf exploding into the air like a cloud of shredded silver" is accompanied by countless other images that indicate an instinct for beauty in the world. The ability to form metaphors gives the narrator a sense of possibility; his capacity to find symbols in ordinary life suggests that worlds of different kinds may be accessible to him: "Most people don't realize how sophisticated pool tables are. Yes, tables have bolts and staples on the rails but these suckers hold together mostly by gravity and by the precision of their construction. If you treat a good table right it will outlast you. Believe me. Cathedrals are built like that. There are Incan roads in the Andes that even today you couldn't work a knife between two of the cobblestones. The sewers that the Romans built in Bath were so good that they weren't replaced until the 1950s. That's the sort of thing I can believe in" (128). Pool tables, cathedrals, Incan roads, and sewers built by Romans in Bath are strong, traditional, and sound objects. They are enduring aesthetic objects. Permanent and sturdy, they inspire belief. This contrasts with Díaz's ghetto existence, which is immediate and ephemeral.

Added to the qualities of strength, permanence, and solidity that the pool table possesses is height. Higher locations in space are prized as symbolizing success or conquest. Lower positions are associated with failure. Díaz writes, "One teacher, whose family had two grammar schools named after it, compared us to the [space] shuttles. A few of you are going to make it. Those are the orbiters. But the majority of you are just going to burn out. Going nowhere. He dropped his hand onto his desk. I could already see myself losing altitude, fading, the earth spread out beneath me, hard and bright" (*Drown*, 106). The tone of the lecture by the teacher is fatalistic and self-certain. Recalling this image, which was so strong to him in childhood, the narrator reels from its vivacity. The picture of a failed future is too graphically powerful and too public. The earth is not a dark plain where it is possible to fall and blend anonymously and soundlessly; it is "hard and bright." The message is rescued from the banal because of its emotional impact on Yunior, who rewrites the narrative of ghetto failure as a rocket gone wrong, falling to earth with incredible velocity and terrifying inevitability, unmercifully.

The theme of losing altitude—of drowning—figures centrally in all the stories in *Drown*. This notion of "losing altitude" is extremely important to Díaz, who associates drowning with being overwhelmed. In a pool, however, the boundaries separating water from air are permeable; so there always exists a possibility of reaching higher places. The metaphor of a swimming pool is an apt representation of this permeability. In the title story, "Drown," the narrator says of being in a pool at night that "everything above is loud and bright, everything below is whispers" (93), alluding to the Dominican community within America. Above and below the water are two separate but independent worlds. The pool is often characterized as an "underground" area for self-expression; the water is a medium that stifles authority. This atmosphere provides a sense of freedom to express oneself, including one's ethnicity. Significantly, the narrator notices that "at the bottom [of the pool] someone has scrawled in

No Whites, No Fat Chiks and someone else has provided the missing *c*" (94). The whites are outside the water, where their voices ring clearly and loudly. The ethnic world is the world below water, the environment where sounds are muffled, intelligible only if you dive underneath.

A Whirlwind, a Comet, a War: Linguistic Dis-Orientations

> Years later Nilda and I would speak, after he had left us
> for good, after her children had moved out of the house.
> ... We sat and drank and finally talked, two strangers re-
> living an event—a whirlwind, a comet, a war—we'd both
> seen but from different faraway angles. ... He left in the
> morning, she explained quietly.
>
> —JUNOT DÍAZ, *Drown* (1996)

Díaz may engage in assertive nontranslation to rebel against the majority, but his use of English is deft in terms of establishing the locations of author and reader. He manipulates the balance of slang, English, and Spanish to increase the pace of his sentences, to reflect degrees of agency in narration, and to control the reader's proximity to the text. Languages also represent the street or the domicile. Street Spanish is abrupt and hard; home Spanish is gentle and intimate. The street, or outside, requires tough language, while the family home encourages a soft, intimate tone, often invoking the presence of memory matter that is distinctly Dominican. Díaz also inhabits different points of view that contribute varied positions to each story.

Certain patterns typically unfold in his work. There are distanced voices—more English, more translated text and dialogue

(Santo Domingo). There are proximal voices—more Spanish or slang, less fluent, consisting of complete translation (the barrio in New Jersey or New York). And Díaz also tries to capture the different sentiments of generations through use of Spanish, English, and a mixture of the two.

Occasionally Díaz's voice is so distant that it might be voice-over, a narrator whose presence can be extracted and superimposed on the events in the book. Stories that are littered with literary tropes are often originating from a distanced, nostalgic position. In these stories, Spanish is translated. Translation automatically distances the reader; the added literary refinements reduce the immediate and raw feel of the text. In the story "Negocios," the language is fluent English, and often translations of Spanish into English, with only an occasional intrusion of untranslated Spanish. An example is the conversation between the narrator's father and grandfather in "Negocios" that was assuredly conducted in Spanish:

> I am here to talk to you about my life with your daughter, he said, removing his hat. I don't know what you've heard but I swear on my heart that none of it is true. All I want for your daughter and our children is to take them to the United States. I want a good life for them.
>
> Abuelo searched his pockets for the cigarette he had just put away. The neighbors were gravitating towards the front of their houses to listen to the exchange. What about this other woman? Abuelo said finally, unable to find the cigarette tucked behind his ear. (*Drown*, 165)

Thus, the images of the world are not as full-blooded and raw as those in America. Time seems to slow down. In "Aguantando," landscape is beautiful but stylized, pleasing but distant and vague: "The ocean was never far away and most of the time I was down by the beach playing with the local kids, turning black in the sun" (75). Despite the beauty of Boca Chica, the narrator says, "I never wanted to be away from the family. Intuitively, I knew how easily distances could harden and become permanent" (75). This trace of paranoia seems to be inherited from the experience of his father abandoning the family, framing his life experiences and making them seem derivative and thin. Life in Santo Domingo seems close to despair. Disasters are commonplaces that elicit surrender: "On Saturday a late hurricane passed close to the Capital and the next day folks were talking about how high the waves were down by the Malecón. Some children had been lost, swept out to sea, and Abuelo shook his head when he heard the news. You'd think the sea would be sick of us by now, he said" (85). The spareness and poverty of the Dominican Republic are ubiquitous, and the hopelessness and powerlessness that difficult living inflicts on its victims pervade the story. People are portrayed as having less agency than the forces of nature. Díaz is subject to life and its desperation and poverty, with "long gray parasites" (71), rats (72), and scarcity.

Slang increases the velocity of some of his stories, and thus creates immediacy and proximity. In "Boyfriend" and "How to Date a Browngirl, Blackgirl, Whitegirl, or Halfie," the narrative pace is fast and punchy, and often the narrator's language is so colloquial that he brings the reader into close proximity. We can hear the intimate conversations of the people next door that the narrator describes in "Boyfriend": "I should have been careful with the weed. Most people it just fucks up. Me, it makes me sleepwalk. And wouldn't you know, I woke up in the hallway of our building, feeling like I'd been stepped on by my high school marching band. My ass would have been there all night if the folks in the apartment below hadn't been having themselves a big old fight at three in the morning. I was too fried to move, at least right away. Boyfriend was trying to snake Girlfriend, saying he needed space, and she was like, Motherfucker, I'll give you all the space you need" (*Drown,* 111). "How to Date a Browngirl, Blackgirl, Whitegirl, or Halfie" also establishes the tone of no-nonsense abruptness immediately: "Wait for your brother and your mother to leave the apartment. You've already told them that you're feeling too sick to go to Union City to visit that tía who likes to squeeze your nuts. (He's gotten big, she'll say.) And even though your mom knows you ain't sick you stuck to your story until finally she said, Go ahead and stay, malcriado" (143). Later in the story Díaz includes more directions and imperatives:

> Get serious. Watch TV but stay alert. Sip some of the Bermúdez your father left in the cabinet, which nobody touches. A local girl may have hips and a thick ass but she won't be quick about letting you touch. She has to live in the same neighborhood you do, has to deal with you being all up in her business. She might just chill with you and then go home. She might kiss you and then go, or she might, if she's reckless, give it up, but that's rare. Kissing will suffice. A whitegirl might just give it up right then. Don't stop her. She'll take her gum out of her mouth, stick it to the plastic sofa covers and then will move close to you. You have nice eyes, she might say. Tell her that you love her hair, that you love her skin, her lips, because, in truth, you love them more than you love your own. (147)

Díaz's imperatives are not simply content-based; they are about attitude. They indicate a life full of rules that are absolute and nonnegotiable. The economy of the language reflects the lack of leeway and options that *you* have. And *you* are unquestionably one of the guys who share his aims. This set of quasi-paramilitary instructions indicates a form of discipline that must be adopted to get ahead in the barrio. Díaz might have added, "Do not tell her you love her more than you love herself. Do not dream."

As if to underscore the loss of agency that constitutes immigrant inheritance, Díaz demonstrates the crippling accent of Ramón, or he translates his Spanish for him. Still, the story is punchy because, as always, too many elements of Ramón's life make no sense in English. Ramón's life is much like that of the exiled Pnin, whose lack of fluency leads to an unstable and impermanent existence. In "Negocios" the immigrant is handicapped, a figure so hounded and bullied he cannot even form his own dreams. "He told himself, Think only of today and tomorrow" (*Drown*, 173). For Ramón, the act of leaving requires practice and rehearsal; he practices memorizing a new set of coordinates until they are home: "Whenever he felt weak, he'd take from under the couch the road map he bought at a gas station and trace his fingers up the coast, enunciating the city names slowly, trying to copy the awful crunch of sounds that was English. The northern coast of our island was visible at the bottom right-hand corner of the map" (173). Again, the finger traces on the map, creating a tactile connection between the person and the object—bringing the character into three dimensions. (This echoes a previous scene where Yunior's imagined father's finger traces a circle on his cheek.) The finger traveling up the coast on the map is a synecdoche, a fragment of the whole person (Ramón) who travels to New York from Miami (a startlingly similar word to "Mami": significantly, Ramón leaves both of them). The "crunch of sounds" alludes also to the sounds of the folding and unfolding of the map, but Díaz uses it to allude to English as other ("the awful crunch of sounds that was English"): it is not meaningful noise, but simply noise that is harsh to the ear. For Ramón, English has not yet become a language.

The focus on North America, with the small piece of the island peeking in at the bottom, correlates with the geography of Ramón's mind. His island exists in his mental picture, but only peripherally. Again, the voice-over, which stipulates the island as "our" island, seems to hover over both North America and the Dominican Republic, an entity that is exiled from both places, with no specific coordinates for its location.

Though the voice-over may imply this airy exile, Ramón experiences the liminal state of hovering with no specific coordinates on a concrete level: "Nueva York was the city of jobs, the city that had first called the Cubanos and their cigar industry, then the bootstrap Puerto Ricans and now him. He had trouble finding his way out of the terminal. Everyone was speaking English and the signs were no help. . . . In the darkness he could see little of Northamerica" (167). Ramón is still in the darkness of exile and experiences the disorientation of the exile in a new environment. His resulting tentativeness comes out in his voice and language: "How far are you going? the driver asked. New York, he said, carefully omitting the Nueva and the Yol" (175). Ramón, like Pnin, cannot buy real estate; he is socially disadvantaged because of his English, and he is prevented from finding permanent work. Ramón's life seems to conspire against him by placing obstacles in the way of his commitments. He is cheated by his roommates, and later he is unfaithful to his wife. In addition to this, he is severely injured at work numerous times and unable to consistently perform. He reacts to all of the disasters by becoming less and less inclined to commit to any path, shaken by the series of unexpected disasters that seem to descend upon him without hesitation, leaving him no time to recover. Early in the story, before he is seriously injured, he is the configuration of movement, never precipitating into a solid. His third child inherits his sublimated state and is "a handsome child who roamed the house restlessly, tilted forward and at full speed, as if he were a top that had been sent spinning" (204). A bundle of motion, Ramón is always traveling, walking, hitchhiking, or on an airplane. His travels become family myth after he returns. As if to acknowledge the storytelling that forms the spine of the story, the narrator writes, "He left Miami in the winter. . . . There are two stories about what happened next, one from Papi, one from Mami: either Papi left peacefully with a suitcase filled with Eulalio's best clothes or he beat the man first, and then took a bus and the suitcase to Virginia" (174). The peripatetic and elusive Ramón in "Negocios" contrasts starkly with the slow-moving, stifling feel of "Aguantando." In "Negocios," Ramón is also a working man, enduring pain that flashes and throbs in the prose: "The first year he worked nineteen-, twenty-hour days, seven days a week. Out in the cold he coughed explosively, feeling as if his lungs were tearing open from the force of his exhales and in the kitchens the heat from the ovens sent pain corkscrewing into his head" (177). This three-dimensional, multisensory entity contrasts sharply with the flat portrait of the father in "Aguantando." A series of portraits of Ramón in pain give him a palpable quality: "Papi was helping another man shove a crate into position when he felt a twinge about midway up his spine. Hey asshole, keep pushing, the other man grunted. Pulling his work shirt out of his Dickies, Papi twisted to the right, then to the left and that was it, something snapped. He fell to his knees. The pain was so intense, shooting through him like fireballs from Roman candles, that he vomited on the concrete floor of the warehouse" (200).

Díaz gives us layer upon layer of these portraits. Soon we learn that Ramón's "spine felt as if there were broken glass inside of it" (203). *This is visceral writing.* The reader is inside a spine, and it breaks. This layering creates an exile hero-type whose ineluctable narrative is pain. There is no escape for Ramón from a story and a history of pain. The narration seems to recognize its own futility in rising above the narrative of Dominican culture. In "Negocios," the narrator writes about his father deserting his second family:

> He had left in December. The company had given him a two-week vacation, which Nilda knew nothing about. He drank a cup of black café in the kitchen and left it washed and drying in the caddy. I doubt if he was crying or even anxious. He lit a cigarette, tossed the match on the kitchen table and headed out into the angular winds that were blowing long and cold from the south. He ignored the convoys of empty cabs that prowled the streets and walked down Atlantic. There were less furniture and antique shops then. He smoked cigarette after cigarette and killed his pack within the hour. He bought a carton at a stand, knowing how expensive they would be abroad.
>
> The first subway station on Bond would have taken him to the airport and I like to think that he grabbed that first train, instead of what was more likely true, that he had gone out to Chuito's first, before flying south to get us. (*Drown,* 208)

Who is the greater exile—the narrator who grows up belonging nowhere, or his father, who wanders in a disoriented state full of pain in America? Certainly the voice of *Drown* seems more exiled than its characters—at least that of Ramón, who manages to form a community and even a new family. Jürgen Habermas describes exiles as "lost in the discursive zone,"[47] and it seems that this problem afflicts the narrator in each of the stories in *Drown* more than the characters in the stories. Though the narrators in "Aguantando" and "Negocios" are not lost in the typical sense—that is, they are not grappling their way back into a discourse—there is an awareness of the potential of losing their language. Just as there is a discursive zone between, in which nothing can be said in Spanish or English, there is water between North America and the Dominican Republic. The narrating voices of *Drown*, orbiting in the space between the island and North America, are aware of the potential to fall into this watery space and be lost forever.

5

Losing Our English, Losing Our Language

THE UNINTELLIGIBILITY OF POSTCOLONIAL THEORY

Yo, lost generation, fast paced nation,
World population confront their frustration,
The principles of true hip-hop have been forsaken,
It's all contractual and about money makin',
Pretend-to-be cats don't seem to know their limitation,
Exact replication and false representation,
You wanna be a man, then stand your own,
To MC requires skills, I demand some shown . . .

> —THE ROOTS, "What They Do," *Illadelph Halflife* (Geffen
> Records, 1996)

Whoever makes that distinction [between using patois
and using English] is saying, you do not have any right to
English. Either that, or you are betraying or ignoring
your own language. This would be a very easy accusation
to point at the Caribbean, but it would also be totally
stupid, because no one is responsible for the consequence

of history. The Caribbean artist is not responsible now
for the fact that languages have been lost in the Caribbean, either lost from history, because they have been
forcibly erased from the memory of people who, for example, spoke Hindi or an African language, or lost from
the passing of time in terms of forgetting the language.

—DEREK WALCOTT, "The Antilles: Fragments of Epic
Memory," Nobel Lecture (1992)

Walcott's Darwinian sense of linguistic adaptation as a natural and unforced phenomenon contrasts with Diaz's belief in
the will-driven reformation of linguistic activity. In this chapter
I will revisit Walcott's vision of language as conveyed in his poetry, then show how his vision diverges from the movement of
postcolonial theory. Walcott's conception of language and the
appropriation of vernaculars diverges from the conception put
forth by Homi Bhabha, one of the original postcolonial theorists. Bhabha's work demonstrates that the domestication of the
postcolonial situation through academic theory refutes its aim:
postcolonialism aims to show that its theory and its brand of vocabulary transform our conception of former colonialist geographies, but its language reflects a semicolonialist outlook, one
which still begs the presence of an institutional framework in order to express itself. In contrast, voices within former colonies
that rebel against the idea of an institutional mode of expression
glimmer with the possibility of postcolonial emergence.

"No one is responsible for the consequence of history," Walcott
writes. With the absence of blame comes the shared burden of
bettering the world for all humanity rather than enabling inter-

nal strife, as well as the possibility of remaking loss into creation. Walcott writes, "Visual surprise is natural in the Caribbean; it comes with the landscape, and faced with its beauty, the sigh of History dissolves."[1] Creative language dissolves the weight of historical narrative, creating imaginary landscapes and histories and expanding notions of human possibility.

If the presence of imaginary and imagined communities generates feelings of social connections outside our own immediate communities, then writing about these communities fixes and secures the potential for immensity of consciousness. In Walcott's spirit, it is possible to conceive of English as a collective tool for encouraging community rather than contestation between classes. Theorizing about weird English requires using it.[2] In this book, the form is the content: the ventriloquy of weird English constitutes its critique. In contrast, the weird English of theory is not ventriloquy. Its weirdness is expressed through jargon, not linguistic connotation; its unintelligibility is due to its abstract or obscure word usage rather than its foreignness.

The theorist Homi Bhabha, in *The Location of Culture,* suggests that unintelligibility might characterize theory because it is beyond or outside any situation it describes. For example, our theories of post-anything (postcolonialism, postmodernism) are responses both to the past and to the immediate present: "It is the trope of our times to locate the question of culture in the realm of the beyond. At the century's edge, we are less exercised by annihilation—the death of the author—or epiphany— the birth of the 'subject.' Our existence today is marked by a tenebrous sense of survival, living on the borderlines of the 'present,' for which there seems to be no proper name other than the current and controversial shiftiness of the prefix 'post':

postmodernism, postcolonialism, postfeminism."[3] Bhabha uses the idea of the beyond—which remains an obscure term throughout his text—to suggest an unidentifiable and unspecifiable point from which theorizing should begin. By disabling the position of origin where theory starts, he automatically generates a theory of argumentative relativism. This is essentially Bhabhian theory: he doesn't disclose his position to an argument, so his ultimate arguments are elusive. This happens in both physical terms and temporal terms: we do not know where his positioning is, or how it will change over time; he invests his energy in a theory-yet-to-evolve (since we are the beyond, as he asserts), to provide a theory of postcolonial being:

> The beyond is neither a new horizon, nor a leaving behind of the past. . . . Beginnings and endings may be the sustaining myths of the middle years; but in the fin de siècle, we find ourselves in the moment of transit where space and time cross to produce complex figures of difference and identity, past and present, inside and outside, inclusion and exclusion. For there is a sense of disorientation, a disturbance of direction, in the "beyond": an exploratory, restless movement caught so well in the French rendition of the words au-delà—here and there, on all sides, fort/da, hither and thither, back and forth.[4]

Bhabha's sense of the beyond is cloudy. This definition of the "beyond," which is the foundation of his theory, celebrates ambiguity: the beyond of constantly shifting space and time. When these shifting conditions are the structure for language, the production of stable meaning becomes impossible; all words must be redefined on a continual basis because they have no stability of meaning. "Translation is the performative nature of cultural communication. It is language in actu (enunciation, positionality) rather than language in situ (énoncé, or propositionality). And the sign of translation continually tells, or 'tolls,' the different times and spaces between cultural authority and its performative practices. The 'time' of translation consists in that movement of meaning, the principle and practice of a communication that, in the words of de Man, 'puts the original in motion to decanonise it, giving it the movement of fragmentation, a wandering of errance, a kind of permanent exile.'"[5] Bhabha's form of writing mimics the thrust of its content—to be as hybrid and elusive as he says postcolonial theory must be, in order to authentically accommodate all the complexities of the postcolonial position. His arguments are endless refractions through the prism of hybridity.

Certainly, his proposition that existing theories are inadequate to accommodate all the complexities is accurate, but his own theory of postcolonialism is fundamentally unintelligible. Yet his unintelligibility is the distinguishing characteristic of his prose; he writes in a pathology of excess. The Roots, as quoted above in their song "What They Do," describe excessive theorizers as "pretend-to-be cats" who "don't seem to know their limitation" and indulge in jargon free-fall. Richard Rorty recognized this when he described good theories as cleaning agents, descriptions of history that enable us to leave the past with psychological comfort.[6] His standard for a good theory is to check its usefulness to communities.

Theorists of postcolonialism are writing backward toward the era of colonialism without experiencing it, and thus inevitably and predictably sounding unintelligible. Should we jettison the "post" in "postcolonial" and listen to the *currently* colonized populations? Is colonialism still alive, even if in the form of making good Arabs? Are we now merely experiencing different, less identifiable forms of colonialism? Does this excerpt from a song by Jayne Cortez and the Firespitters impress?

> They want the oil not the people
> They want the oil not the people
> They want the oil not the people
> They want the oil not the people
> They want the oil not the people
> They want the oil not the people
> They want the oil not the people
> They want the oil not the people
> They want the oil not the people
> They want the oil not the people
> They want the oil not the people . . .[7]

Give us more than argumentative relativism.

The Importance of Being Unintelligible

Postcoloniality awaits consignment to oblivion.

—RUKMINI NAIR, *Lying on the Postcolonial Couch* (2002)[8]

The Horror! The Horror! Almost a century after *Heart of Darkness* we have returned to that act of living in the midst of the "incomprehensible," that Conrad associated with the production of transcultural narratives in the colonial world. From these disjoined postimperial sentences, that bear the anxiety of reference and representation—"undescribable vividness . . . a materiality of perception, properly overwhelming"—there emerges the need for a global analysis of culture.

—HOMI BHABHA, *The Location of Culture* (1994)

Homi Bhabha asserts that we live in the midst of the incomprehensible. Is there something fundamentally important about being unintelligible, about allowing the presence of unintelligibility to thrive? Is this a way of subverting the dominant culture of clarity and cogency?[9]

The weirdness of Bhabha's English signifies the weirdness of his relation to the subject of colonialism—his own refracted reactions to it as an academic. The form of Bhabha's writing is revelatory of its content. The multiple positions he adopts (his own assertions being obscured by all the others) perform the fragmented or multiple-personaed self that he writes about. The result is a cacophony of arguments, a rag bag of selves that resonates with Salman Rushdie's philosophy of the self. This self is fragmented by multiple loyalties, multiple linguistic commitments, and the multiple anxieties of several histories: the modern and the postmodern self.

Despite his contextualization of this fragmented self, Bhabha's description of the self and his emphasis on hybridity are not particular to colonialist or postcolonialist populations. In his essay "How Newness Enters the World," he asserts that fragmentation is the foundation of an identity crisis and cannot or has not yet been properly represented (yet the entire phenomenon of weird English represents the formation and transformation of hybrid identity): "It is, ironically, the disintegrative moment, even movement, of enunciation—that sudden disjunction of the present—that makes possible the rendering of culture's global reach. And, paradoxically, it is only through a structure of splitting and displacement—'the fragmented and schizophrenic decentring of the self'—that the architecture of the new historical subject emerges at the limits of representation itself, 'to enable a situational representation on the part of the individual to that vaster and unrepresentable totality which is the ensemble of society's structures as a whole.'"[10] Bhabha's description of the emergence of a fragmented self as a synecdoche for society at this moment seems naive. This making of a "new historical subject" lives in the abstract, since the phenomenon of the fragmentation of the self could hardly be called new. Without attention to the particulars of the subject he describes—the concrete details of the situation—the ideas remain in the abstract. Gayatri Spivak, on the other hand, imports the past to support her deconstructive work—and Bhabha's—thereby rescuing him from abstract detachment: "Benita Parry has criticized Homi Bhabha, Abdul JanMohammed, and Gayatri Spivak for being so enamored of deconstruction that they will not let the native speak. She has forgotten that we are natives too. We talk like Defoe's Friday, only much better. Nearly three hundred years have, after all, passed since Defoe's fabrication of Friday."[11] In contrast to Bhabha, Spivak emphasizes talking, and talking better than Friday. Whether her claim is true is subject to question, however; Bhabha's excessively eccentric, impenetrable language in *The Location of Culture* suggests that the source of his unintelligibility is that colonialism is still with us.

Homi Bhabha writes that the term "postcolonialism" makes it possible to conceive of current "neocolonialist" practices. But these prefixes put theorists at a distance from the real issue: Are the current experiences of oppressed people qualitatively different from those of the colonized in different times? Culture may be modern; psychological imperialism exists as much as its physical correlate; and imperialist capitalist practices are increasingly mobile—but the subjectivity of those who are colonized is the desperate pain and darkness that theorists cannot adequately bring into public awareness. Their language is way ahead of their pain. Prefixing cultural practices with a few letters may cause us to think we've changed history—but we've changed only the language, not the practice; "post-" or "neo-" suggests that we are creating new history rather than repeating ourselves after learning nothing. Fear of this truth—that *we have learned nothing*—makes the invention of post-anything appealing. Bhabha's suggestion that we "locate the question of culture in the realm of the *beyond*" is escapist theory, an anaesthetic. He writes that postcolonialism authenticates histories of exploitation, but his description is so distanced from the subjectivity of the colonized that his arguments feel contorted, avoiding a major issue, as if by using excess words he can suppress his emotional response:

> Postcoloniality, for its part, is a salutary reminder of the persistent "neo-colonial" relations within the "new" world order and the multi-national division of labour. Such a perspective enables the authentication of histories of exploitation and the evolution of strategies of resistance. Beyond this, however, postcolonial critique bears witness to those countries and communities—in the North and the South, urban and rural—constituted, if I may coin a phrase, "otherwise than modernity." Such cultures of a postcolonial *contra-modernity* may be contingent to modernity, discontinuous or in contention with it, resistant to its oppressive, assimilationist technologies; but they also deploy the cultural hybridity of their borderline condi-

tions to "translate," and therefore reinscribe, the social imaginary of both metropolis and modernity.[12]

One wants to ask: Do we need a reminder of the "persistent 'neo-colonial' relations"? Postcolonialism, like postmodernism, reminds us only that humanity repeats itself; it is just being articulated by different parties from the ones that spoke before (those either temporally distant or geographically distant from the moment of colonialism). The people who have the most authentic experience of it don't want to discuss it. This is our nemesis: we will always live in the shadow of what we *should have listened to*. Postmodernism posits that the creation of authentically new history is over (everything is recycled) and nostalgia prevails. Postcolonialism shows the privilege of having nostalgia. Without it, there is only empty psychobabble.

Without the possibility of nostalgia (of course, colonized peoples may have personal nostalgias, but a kind of collective nostalgia for their situation cannot surface—only trauma), there is a terrible and curious distance from one's life. Many theoretical texts fixate on this distance. Bhabha's theoretical approaches remove him from the subjectivity of the colonized, even as he tries to explicate it. He blames his own theoretical limits on the language, rather than on his own limited experience:

> The discourse of nationalism is not my main concern. In some ways it is the historical certainty and settled nature of that term against which I am attempting to write of the Western nation as an obscure and ubiquitous form of living about the locality of culture. This locality is more around temporality than about historicity: a form of living that is more complex than "community"; more symbolic than "society"; more connotative than "country";

less patriotic than *patrie;* more rhetorical than the reason of State; more mythological than ideology; less homogenous than hegemony; less centred than the citizen; more collective than "the subject"; more psychic than civility; more hybrid in the articulation of cultural differences and identifications than can be represented in any hierarchical or binary structuring of social antagonism.[13]

Bhabha's frustration with the limitations of language is not unwarranted. There isn't much language that works when a victim articulates sustained acts of endured cruelty. (In the film *Shoah,* it was noticeable that many Holocaust survivors could not speak about their loss.) In this sense Bhabha, Spivak, and other postcolonial writers possess a spiritual valor. But the garbled written results do not represent this spirit; rather, they point to a cultish psychosis. The evil of colonialism survives in the psychosis it generated.

Bhabha also writes about identity and nationality on the margin, in between, still evolving and not located in either past or present. His English possesses the same morphing quality. It is pre- and post-intelligible, defying intelligibility in order to pre and post the subaltern—a figure of speech and not-speech, à la Gayatri Spivak (whose moving essay "Can the Subaltern Speak?" has been the authority in postcolonial discussions since 1988). The problem is that talking about unintelligibility and muteness is most dramatic when illustrated. That is, when we are presented with a woman burning with tape over her mouth, or when we write in an unintelligible way, we enunciate rather than obfuscate our situation. The virtue of Spivak is that she often uses real-life examples to communicate her ideas, especially in her account of the tradition of suttee in "Can the Subaltern

Speak?" She also deconstructs terms to find meaning, while Bhabha erects them without sufficient definition. For example, in *A Critique of Postcolonial Reason* Spivak writes about the violation of translation:

> The structure of translation-as-violation describes certain tendencies within third-worldist literary pedagogy more directly. It is of course part of my general argument that, unless third-worldist feminism develops a vigilance against such tendencies, it cannot help but participate in them. Our own mania for "third world literature" anthologies, when the teacher or critic often has no sense of the original languages, or of the subject-constitution of the social and gendered agents in question (and when therefore the student cannot sense this as a loss), participates more in the logic of translation-as-violation than in the ideal of translation as freedom-in-troping. What is at play here is a phenomenon that can be called "sanctioned ignorance," now sanctioned more than ever by an invocation of "globality"—a word serving to hide the financialization of the globe, or "hybridity"—a word serving to obliterate the irreducible hybridity of all language.[14]

Spivak here reveals the performance of violence through ignorance and uses linguistic carelessness as examples—in particular, the words "globality" and "hybridity." Her assertions also chastise the suggestion of hybridity posited in weird English, and encourage the separation of conceptions of weird English and hybrid English.

Alfred Lopez, in *Posts and Pasts,* ambitiously and honestly tries to map out what postcolonialism is, and succeeds in convincing the reader that it would be easier to describe what it isn't. Lopez writes about the potential contributions of postcolonial writing but does not elaborate in detail: "To the extent that postcolonial studies seeks to affirm and empower the subject-positions of subaltern peoples suppressed by colonial regimes, this question of the other's representation—whether in revisionist historio-graphic discourses, in governing bodies, or in the media—comes to the fore."[15] Later he summarizes his own project: "In these pages I present the postcolonial as a condition, a set of historical and cultural contingencies; and I see postcolonial writings gen-erally as less object than activity, a body of work that seeks to ad-dress these contingencies in the hope of finding ways of think-ing and living in its unprecedented historical moment. In the broadest terms, then, the tasks of postcolonial writing are two-fold."[16] Lopez specifies the two issues as "a reckoning with the colonial past" and "an analysis or articulation of postcolonial di-asporas."[17] He insists that postcolonialism needs historicizing, but he doesn't determine what time frame is required for a sub-ject to be postcolonial. Is it one generation away from the colo-nized condition? Two generations from being colonized seems too far away to engender the term "postcolonial," yet communi-ties remain partially colonized on some level for more than that. But rarely—probably never—do communities emerge unscathed from colonialism. And if we have unrestricted temporal bound-aries, geographies that are considered colonizers might also be included as postcolonial. Perhaps postcolonialism is the condi-tion of the pre-happy and pre-developed country, with a pre-ar-ticulated set of wants. Such a country would also have endured a great deal of post-suffering. It is time we figured out a replace-ment for the "post-" in "postcolonialism."

Rushdie's Unintelligible Polyphony

Suddenly, before I knew why, I felt quite at home. I was in one place that had at least four addresses.

—ANDRÉ ACIMAN, *Letters of Transit* (2000)

Rushdie has given the sub-continent a "voice," not the voices of the vedas but the voice for another sort of people, the voices they speak in when wandering around the streets of their cities, the voices we know so well from playgrounds in so many "English-medium" schools and the voices of the hesitant. These are not the voices of the Mahabharat or the Veda. We are not Vyas, nor are we Tagore, perhaps bits and pieces of them. We are, I am, closer to Rushdie by far. As for Rushdie's alleged pandering "to his Euro-centered readers" one must point out that the average European would find Rushdie very difficult. If anything I'm quite concerned that Rushdie is writing for one specific person, the Urban Indian.

—SUBIR GREWAL (March 8, 1996), www.subir.com/rushdie/
posts/96_02.txt

Salman Rushdie is the icon for postcolonialist unintelligibility.[18] Perhaps it is within fiction that the neurosis of postcolonialism is best expressed; in the form of Rushdie's writing, it is possible to appreciate the layers of psychological complication on an aesthetic level. In his case, "semicolonialism" might offer a better description than "postcolonialism," because the issues which existed within colonialism are still operative. There is still a sense of inferiority to the English that Rushdie sees in Indian culture—and, like Pico Iyer, he parodies it in the cause of eliminating it, of trivializing its importance. He is still amazingly conscious of linguistic elements in the world and how they can be flipped as political currency; and like Bhabha, he uses words as negotiating tools. Rushdie's mission is also the same as Bhabha's, but uses a different route—one which creates a language dense with distractions and digressions, which does not convey one message with more strength than another. He is, like Bhabha, practicing a kind of semantic relativism where no meaning seems to hold more value than another. But unlike Bhabha, Rushdie succeeds in creating an open, semantically experimental and democratic universe with inevitable meaningfulness. Both writers use linguistic excess differently: the effect of Rushdie's linguistic plenty is a dense, rich universe; the effect of Bhabha's theory is confusion, a sense of feeling plenty of desolation. His description of Rushdie's *Satanic Verses* reaffirms this view of the famous exiled writer:

> Rushdie's sin lies in opening up a space of discursive contestation that places the authority of the Koran within a perspective of historical and cultural relativism. It is not that the "content" of the Koran is directly disputed; rather, by revealing other enunciatory positions and possibilities within the framework of Koranic reading, Rushdie performs the subversion of the authenticity through the act of cultural translation—he relocates the Koran's "intentionality" by repeating and reinscribing it in the locale of the novel of postwar cultural migrations and diasporas.[19]

The hybrid self comes alive in Rushdie's work, and remains abstract in Bhabha's texts. In Rushdie's novel *The Ground beneath Her Feet*, readers encounter a dizzying trip through hotel rooms,

Internet sites, and the inner organs of a man's body. Rushdie not only dabbles in experimental Orcish along the ride, but moves the reader through several worlds at hyperspeed, confronting the unintelligibility of existence with multiple narratives rather than theoretical confusion:

> Two hours after I rescued her from the unfathomable chasm of her hotel corridor, a helicopter flew us to Tequila, where Don Ángel Cruz, the owner of one of the largest plantations of blue agave cactus and of the celebrated Ángel distillery, a gentleman fabled for the sweet amplitude of his countertenor voice, the great rotunda of his belly and the lavishness of his hospitality, was scheduled to hold a banquet in her honour. Meanwhile, Vina's playboy lover had been taken to hospital, in the grip of drug-induced seizures so extreme that they eventually proved fatal, and for days afterwards, because of what happened to Vina, the world was treated to detailed analyses of the contents of the dead man's bloodstream, his stomach, his intestines, his scrotum, his eye sockets, his appendix, his hair, in fact everything except his brain, which was not thought to contain anything of interest, and had been so thoroughly scrambled by narcotics that nobody could understand his last words, spoken during his final, comatose delirium. Some days later, however, when the information had found its way onto the Internet, a fantasy-fiction wonk hailing from the Castro district of San Francisco and nicknamed elrond@rivendel.com explained that Raúl Páramo had been speaking Orcish, the infernal speech devised for the servants of the Dark Lord Sauron by the writer Tolkien:

Ash nazg durbatulûk, ash nazg gimbatul, ash nazg thrakatulûk agh burzum-ishi krimpatul. After that, rumours of Satanic, or perhaps Sauronic, practices spread unstoppably across the Web. The idea was put about that the mestizo lover had been a devil worshipper, a blood servant of the underworld, and had given Vina Apsara a priceless but malignant ring, which had caused the subsequent catastrophe and dragged her down to Hell. But by then Vina was already passing into myth, becoming a vessel into which any moron could pour his stupidities, or let us say a mirror of the culture, and we can best understand the nature of this culture if we say that it found its truest mirror in a corpse.[20]

Like Bhabha, Rushdie is an excessively verbose writer. His linguistic virtuosity creates an atmosphere of giddiness and disorientation. Like Bhabha, his words are a shield, a life force, a way of scrambling the reader's argumentative compass; in the above passage we begin with a death in Guadalajara and end up in the metaphor of a mirror. Rushdie's words make readers travel, to both real and imaginary places. He invents words, invents imaginative realms. For example, in *The Ground beneath Her Feet* the main character, Vina, invents her own language: "Chinese khana big mood hai" has the translation "I want a plate of noodles" and "Apun J. R. R. Tolkien's Angootiyan-ka-Seth ko too-much admire karta chhé" means "I like J. R. R. Tolkien." Rushdie's writing is endless, mostly unintelligible chatter. He does not fixate on a single idea; he cannot merely employ a single language. In fact, he moves between ideas and multiple languages like an atom in constant motion, like most of his protagonists. This section will examine Rushdie's experimentation with language, and show that his brand of weird English almost un-Englishes English.

Rushdie's position of exile makes him one of the most memorable writers but also places him in a dangerous Cartesian position where words seem his most vivid reality. Experiencing the fatwa increased the speed of Rushdie's experimentation with mixing languages, with having them build the theater of his life.[21] Traveling and hiding from Muslim zealots, he even began to write in imaginary languages. This is in part derived from his polylingual urban background, but it also manifests itself as verbal self-indulgence. To Rushdie, however, linguistic activity is play: "I think it is typical of Bombay,[22] and maybe of India, that there is a sense of play in the way people use language. Most people in India are multilingual, and if you listen to the urban speech patterns there you'll find it's quite characteristic that a sentence will begin in one language, go through a second language and end in a third. It's the very playful, very natural result of juggling languages. You are always reaching for the most appropriate phrase."[23] Rushdie's language becomes imaginary because it is so infiltrated by other languages and so permeable to new strains that it becomes an impure, unrecognizable creature. In *The Ground beneath Her Feet*, Rushdie parodies the way language can evolve into an over-pidgined, unregulated entity. When so many languages are being used, the original language can be lost in a patchwork of other pieces of language: "Not only in English. Because it was not only me who could prattle on in Bombay's garbage argot, Mumbai ki kachrapati baat-cheet, in which a sentence could begin in one language, swoop through a second and even a third and then swing back round to the first. Our acronymic name for it was Hug-me. Hindi Urdu Gujarati Marathi English. Bombayites like me were people who spoke five languages badly and no language well" (*Ground beneath Her Feet*, 7). Carrying the idea of corrupted language even further, Rushdie shows how individuals can also use a personalized pidgin that defies interpretation. He writes that conversations in families can contain so many linguistic oddities that they become grammatically disobedient. In *The Moor's Last Sigh*, Epiphania and Aurora both exhibit the same family tic of using the suffix "-ofy" after verbs—for example, "startofy," "killofy," "eatofy." Bishnupriya Ghosh points out that these oddities are derived from Indian language: "Hindi and Urdu syntax molds conversations: 'Where is the air to breathe?' says one character, instead of the more standard 'Where is there any air to breathe?' General Hindi phraseology—'hate me, don't me but,' references to 'my goodwife,' idiomatic expressions such as 'wallow-pallow' or 'art-shart'—litters the speech of various characters, while specific accents heard among Goan Christians and Anglo-Indians are mouthed by the narrator's family: 'shutofy' or 'washofy,' for instance, are recognizable constructions that mean 'will shut up' or 'will wash away/out.'"[24] So hybridity occurs on two levels: cultural and familial. Rushdie is aware of the peculiar human drive to develop linguistic tics in order to gain intimacy with others:

> Every family has its own words for things, its own phrases. I wanted to create a family verbal tic. It's interesting to me how much of what it is to be a family is governed by language use. There is that verbal habit, or family vocabulary, but there is also the habit of storytelling; every family has stories about itself. You could argue, in fact, that the collection of stories a family has about itself is actually the definition of the family. When someone joins a family—a child is born, somebody marries into it—they are gradu-

ally told all the secret family stories. And when you finally
know all the stories, you belong to the family.[25]

The inheritance of these linguistic oddities is thus also accompanied by the content of shared history. The linguistic tics
merely expose this shared history and bond. Storytelling is a way
of affirming certain continuities of family and community that
is independent of anything material. This becomes clear in *The
Moor's Last Sigh* when the bonds are tested. The family is safe
from all sorts of threats and surprises—errant politicos, a venge-
ful mother-in-law who wants Aurora's first-born, the birth of the
deformed Moor, and so on. But finally disaster occurs when
someone outside the family, Uma Sarasvati, cracks the code of
the family's language and uses their secrets against them. In
Rushdie's fictional and actual worlds, words have a peculiar way
of allowing human beings to manipulate communities and families. Significantly, it is Moor's words on a tape recorder that
trigger the event of his family's downfall: "She used my words—
my angry, awful, lust-provoked obscenities."[26] Uma uses the arsenal of words that Moor has unintentionally bestowed on her in
order to infiltrate the family trust and banish Moor from his
family.

Just as the family code can be cracked to produce disaster,
linguistic codes can be manipulated to gain acceptance in society. For example, Rushdie shows how the meteoric rise of Adam
Braganza is due to his ability to generate millennium slang,
which is almost incomprehensible. It illustrates how impenetrable people in this community are to each other. Abraham
Zogoiby says, "Modern era . . . Therefore modern lingo. I just
love it!" (*Moor's Last Sigh,* 343). And Moor analyzes this as a future
generation "dedicated to the pursuit of the new, speaking the fu-

ture's strange, binary, affectless speech—quite a change from our melodramatic garam-masala exclamations" (343). Moor satirizes the entrepreneur's "legendary" memos: "'To optimise manpower utilisation, engendering of we-feeling is key,' they typically said. Executives were therefore 'encouraged,' that is, instructed, to spend twenty minutes a week in small groups of ten or twelve, embracing one another. Further 'encouragement' was given to the idea that each employee should offer monthly 'evaluations' of his fellows' strength and weakness—thus turning the building into a tower of hypocritical (overtly huggy-wuggy, secretly stabby-wabby) sneaks" (343). Whether huggy-wuggy or stabby-wabby, the sneaks at least have practices as a community, even if those practices—and their corresponding linguistic descriptions—border on sounding absurd, and demonstrate the distance rather than intimacy of this "we-group." Rushdie parodies jargon by reinventing it in comic forms, sometimes pushing the parody to levels that offend others.

Later Rushdie became conscious of how language determines many forms of community membership. He wrote *In Good Faith* to assuage the Muslim extremists and encourage them to rescind the fatwa. When the gamble failed (they didn't rescind it) and he knew he had made a "stupid mistake," he felt that he "in some way had lost . . . language."[27] He found himself outside the practices of the community, and thus outside the language practices that tie a community together. Losing language and community happen together—but only in certain cases. Thus, Rushdie's exile situation is a sociologically and anthropologically illuminating case: it reveals the role language plays in our communal awareness and functionality. Without communal resonance, language loses its weight, its presence and meaning. Rushdie describes his new language as artificial: "Up to that point, the one thing that kept me going was that I could defend everything I said and I could talk about it in my ordinary language and not have to use any kind of special guarded phrases—you know, just talk."[28] Along with certain kinds of language come responsibilities to certain communities and political forces at work in society. Jargon serves to reinforce the powers in communities that already exist. Thus, language not only exposes the forms of agreement within a community; it is the structure from which the community develops its sense of rationale and justification as it evolves.

Rushdie has experienced his own Cartesian position by writing and angering communities by his solipsistic linguistics, an outgrowth of not having a direct sense of how to use English in a non-English way: "I hope all of us share the view that we can't simply use the language in the way the British did; that it needs remaking for our own purposes. Those of us who do use English do so in spite of our ambiguity towards it, or perhaps because of that, perhaps because we can find in that linguistic struggle a reflection of other struggles taking place in the real world, struggles between the cultures within ourselves and the influences at work upon our societies. To conquer English may be to complete the process of making ourselves free."[29] Rushdie observes a healthier use of English today by the younger generation: "The children of independent India seem not to think of English as being irredeemably tainted by its colonial provenance. They use it as an Indian language, as one of the tools they have to hand."[30] Still, English promises to become more unintelligible and weird in the future. Because English has been used by many different cultures, which have different rules of agreement, the range of meanings for words has increased, expanded. Thus, the relation between signified and signifier has loosened and become less rigid and inflexible, and thus more permeable to other ideas and cultural mediums. It is this permeable linguistic mix that Rushdie advocates as the language of contemporary India and the world, one which mirrors the lack of certainty in the world's unshakable facts and truths:

> Doubt, it seems to me, is the central condition of a human being in the twentieth century. One of the things that has happened to us in the twentieth century as a human race is to learn how certainty crumbles in your hand. We cannot any longer have a fixed, certain view of anything—the table that we're sitting next to, *the ground beneath our feet*, the laws of science, are full of doubt now. Everything we know is pervaded by doubt and not by certainty. And that is the basis of the great artistic movement known as modernism. Now the fact that the Orthodox figures in the Muslim world declared a jihad against modernism is not my fault. It doesn't invalidate an entire way of looking at the world which is, to my mind, the most important new contribution of the twentieth century to the way in which the human race discusses itself. If they're trying to say that this whole process has gone out of the window—that you can't do that, all you have is the old certainties—then yes, I do argue.[31]

Rushdie's picture of the modern age is not bleakly full of doubt but open to change. His appeal to the Muslim zealots that pursue him is to consider his point of view. Certainly, Rushdie may have entertained a naive or restricted sense of reality; but his assassins' appropriation of safe frontiers is too large a compensation for an author's lack of seriousness.

Moor's Temporal Exile

> There is something in the air at the moment—that people
> think everything is speeding up, the pace of life, the rate
> of change, everything just seems to be going zooooom!
> And I thought that if there is this widespread sense of
> the acceleration of things, one way of crystallizing it was
> to make it happen to someone in a very literal way.
>
> —SALMAN RUSHDIE, interview in Salon.com (1996)

The chaos of Rushdie's writing in *The Moor's Last Sigh* enunci-ates the hybridity that Homi Bhabha alludes to in his work. Bishnupriya Ghosh writes that in this novel, "Rushdie's English vernacular records a new vision of India, a global-local post-modern nation whose set of cultural references no longer consti-tutes a stable and homogenous national register."[32] But this novel does more than speak hybridly; it demonstrates the wild-ness of attempting to capture the conditions of living in a fran-tic, global community where time is the most important element but the element that most escapes us. Rushdie introduces the concept of temporal exile in order to illuminate the situation of linguistic exile. His consciousness of the pace of globalization and how it affects the construction of hybrid language runs through *The Moor's Last Sigh*. By bombarding the reader verbally and feeding the reader literary images, Rushdie is able to create an atmosphere where the reader feels the fast pace of life, the speed of oncoming death.

Moor is an apt metaphor for the millennium, both as a narra-tive entity and as a biological one. He is writing to avoid death; and as readers we see how demanding the world is and that it *needs so many* words to rivet anyone, to convince one of the value of the self. Moor, a metaphor illustrating the problem of time for human beings, shows how contemporary civilization is beyond its time technologically and scientifically, but its humanism is underdeveloped. Moor's fast-aging body enables him to have a panoramic set of experiences fast, but his interior is still childlike and in need of care. *The Moor's Last Sigh* conveys the emotional trauma of the exile experience by configuring the exile as a freak and an inevitable skeptic. Moor is a strange, lonely soul who could not feel at home anywhere, someone who longs for belonging, whose words barely moor him to the world.

In the figure of Moor, Rushdie examines the issue of time and what time is like for the exile on a hyperbolic level. Perhaps his experience of time as an exile resembles Moor's; neither observes conventional time. Moor says, "Aurora told me constantly that I must not think of myself as the victim of an incurable premature-aging disorder, but a magic child, a time traveler: 'Baby mine, you just startofied out going too fast. Maybe you'll just take off, and zoom-o right out of this life into another space and time. Maybe—who knows—a better'" (210). In *The Moor's Last Sigh* the "hero" is a six-and-a-half-foot biological mutant; he ages biologically twice as fast as the average human being, and he also has a deformed right "club" hand. But the central theme of the novel is connected to Moor's doublequick lifespan. Rushdie says, "It's all about a guy whose life is speeded up, that we may not have as much time as we think."[33] Rushdie's literalization of this phenomenon and the resulting fixation on time lead to some questions about the effect of time on the plot. Because Rushdie focuses on Moor and not society at large, the reader is privy on a personal level to what the experience of time as "doublefast" can do to the human soul. On an individual level in the case of Moor, the effect of doublefast time is to break down his sense of community. Moor becomes selfish and self-preserving; he allows several people—including his mother, his sisters, and a Japanese art restoration painter, Aoi Uë—to die or suffer before putting himself at risk.

There is a laundry list of common traits that both Moor and Rushdie share. They both have three sisters, although Rushdie is the oldest child in his family and Moor the youngest. Both imagine their father wants to replace them for a more business-minded son, and in Moor's case this actually happens. Moor is dark and deformed; and, given Rushdie's English experiences and experiences in Anglophilic parts of Bombay, Rushdie probably knew something about self-hatred, though he was actually light-skinned. Both were banished; Rushdie wants to be in India but is exiled to England and the West; Moor is never in the right place at the right time, because he is the victim of a biological aging disorder. Both of them have also had their share of dysfunctional relationships, and critics often compare the manipulative Uma Sarasvati, Moor's love, to Rushdie's ex-girlfriend, writer Marianne Wiggins. Both seem to derive pleasure from "destruction"; Wiggins seemed "excited" on hearing the news of the fatwa,[34] and Uma thrives on self-invention and the destructive chaos she wreaks on the Zogoiby family. Small facts also are telling: Moor mentions the "Breach Candy Hospital" (162), which evokes the "Breach Candy Swimming Club" near Rushdie's childhood home in Bombay.

It is not merely an abundance of facts that connect Rushdie's personality to Moor. Rather, there is a sense of personal and emotional investment in Moor that points to an autobiographical relationship. There are certain expressive moments in the novel that seem self-descriptive. The residue from the experience of exile resonates in a hyperbolic sense of insecurity: "What was harder still was the feeling of being ugly; malformed, wrong, the knowledge that life had dealt me a bad hand, and a freak of nature was obliging me to play it out too fast. What was hardest of all was the sense of being an embarrassment, a shame" (*Moor's Last Sigh,* 154). Rushdie writes elsewhere that Moor is conscious of how his "South Indian dark skin" is "so unattractive to society matchmakers" (162). Rushdie writes: "By embracing the inescapable, I lost my fear of it. I'll tell you a secret about fear: it's an absolutist. With fear, it's all or nothing. Either, like any bullying tyrant, it rules your life with a stupid blinding omnipotence, or else you overthrow it, and its power vanishes in a puff of smoke. . . . *I must live until I die*" (164). Moor's narrative soliloquies reverberate with the suffering and disabling effects of being exiled, and hint at the psychological self-hypnosis which Rushdie may have used on himself to deal with his own situation. Rushdie also had to cope with a constant shifting and adjusting; he is said to have moved fifty-six times in one month during the first years of exile.

Moor has the same sentiments of experiencing constant readjustment. The spiritual Moor is outstripped by the biological Moor so quickly that the spirit never gets a respite and is always racing to catch up with bodily transformations: "It seems to me that in my younger self, in that appalling monster in whom a child's mind peered out in confusion through the portals of a young man's beautiful body . . ." (189).

But Moor's life is not simply shorter than the average life; his life is *qualitatively different* from the average life. A sense of outsiderness never leaves him: "For while I might be a perpetual outsider among that racecourse breed, still in my twenty years I had gathered experience at such a rate that I had come to feel that time, in my vicinity, had begun to move at my own, doubled

speed. I no longer felt like a young man trapped inside an old—
or rather, to borrow the lingo of the city's textile industry, 'antiqued,' even 'distressed'—covering of skin. My outer, apparent
age had simply become my age. Or so I thought: until Uma
showed me the truth" (241). In using the words "antiqued" and
"distressed," however, he is alluding not merely to age but to the
old-fashionedness of his outlook and his feeling of being inani-
mate, a piece of furniture. Moor sees his body as furniture, as
uninhabited by a soul and weathered by external forces—not by
his own internal development. In *Crimes of Writing*, Susan Stewart discusses the notion of "distressed" in a way that illuminates
the active way in which one ages an item or character: "'To distress': in common usage (although, curiously enough, not in dictionaries), 'to make old, to antique,' particularly in reproducing
material goods from previous times. Simultaneously, the dictionary definition: 'to afflict, to place in a state of danger or trouble,
bad straits.' In law, to distrain is 'to force by seizure of goods,'
coming from the Latin root dis (apart) + stringere (to draw tight
or stretch): 'to seize and hold property as security or indemnity
for a debt.' In such usage, 'to distress' involves a process of appropriation by reproduction, or manipulation through afflic-
tion."[35] We can import this passage from Stewart to show that it
can also be rich in connotation: one feels that the Moor, like antique furniture, is evolving into a "period" piece: his place in the
world disappears when his family ceases to exist. Aurora's death
signifies the end of an age and ushers in the beginning of a new
one, one ruled by the financial schemes of the likes of Abraham
Zogoiby and his self-appointed successor, Adam Braganza. But
there is also an issue of "anxiety regarding materiality, a hope in
the transcendence of art as either material or concept, a fear of
erasure, a belief in art's capacity to reflect its contextual ori-

gins."[36] Stewart implies that the importation of artifacts is a method of preserving time or transcending history. She says that the formation of genres of this type is connected to this motive: "The desire to produce speaking objects, objects both in and out of time, seems an inevitable outgrowth of this development."[37] Rushdie often describes memory and subjectivity in physical terms. Metaphors and similes pervade his work. He says we can "pickle the past" and that memory can be fragmented like a "broken mirror."[38] He elevates the flaws in our recovered memory:

> I'm not gifted with total recall, and it was precisely the partial nature of these memories, their fragmentation, that made them so evocative for me. The shards of memory acquired greater status, greater resonance, because they were *remains;* fragmentation made trivial things seem like symbols, and the mundane acquired numinous qualities. There is an obvious parallel here with archaeology. The broken pots of antiquity, from which the past can sometimes but always provisionally be reconstructed, are exciting to discover, even if they are pieces of the most quotidian objects. . . . It may be argued that the past is a country from which we have all emigrated, that its loss is part of our common humanity. Which seems to me self-evidently true; but I suggest that the writer who is out-of-country and even out-of-language may experience this loss in an intensified form.[39]

Moor's exile is due to the fact that he is, underneath a distressed skin, the humanist among a lot of people who aren't able to see beyond the conditions of survival. Though he is physically aged by time, Moor remains youthful in spirit, falling in love for the

first time when he is well beyond middle age. The other characters, on the other hand, are corrupted by their selfishness and
anxieties. Unlike Moor, they do not seem to age on the outside
(Aurora and Abraham remain youthful-looking throughout the
novel), but they become enmeshed in dealings of decay and corruption. Abraham creates an empire founded on shady practices
and the drug trade, while Aurora paints her last works in isolation: "Aurora/Axya sat alone in these panels, beside the infernal
chronicle of the degradation of her son, and never shed a tear.
Her face grew hard, even stony, but in her eyes there shone a horror that was never named—as if she were looking at a thing that
struck at the very depths of her soul, a thing standing before her,
where anyone looking at the pictures would naturally stand—as
if the human race itself had shown her its most secret and ter-
rorising face, and by doing so had petrified her, turning her old
flesh to stone. . . . I know that look. She looks as if she might
be coming to pieces. She looks pursued" (*Moor's Last Sigh,* 304).
By the end of the novel, Aurora and Abraham are damaged people, even though superficially they appear to be otherwise; in
contrast, Moor is a wheezing, dying old man on the outside, but
spirited enough to write all of his adventures down. The irony
of the novel is that Moor, though physically and biologically
odd, manages to escape a fate in which he is isolated and alone,
while the other characters, who are provided with great advan-
tages, die feeling misunderstood or under terrible circum-
stances: Uma, Aurora, Mainduck, Aoi Uë, all of Moor's sisters,
and so on. Moor's exile is thus as internal as it is external: it is
his furious construction of narrative that sustains his exile as
much as his doublequick life. Ironically, Moor finally finds his
community through exile: his readers. The task of reconstruction is the way to socialization and reconciliation for Moor; his

narrative is an apology for his own sad role in the life of his family, but also an appeal for the reader to understand him and his world of exile.

Good Vibrations, Bad Vibrations

> I am a modern, and modern*ist*, urban man, accepting uncertainty as the only constant, change as the only sure thing.

> —SALMAN RUSHDIE, *Imaginary Homelands* (1991)

Rushdie, once forcibly in exile, is certain about uncertainty, but perhaps he is only different in degree from global society in constant transition. If we are speaking weird English now, it is because we are busy negotiating the boundaries of language—what to include, and what to abandon. Unintelligible language arises from this uncertainty. In *The Ground beneath Her Feet*, rock and roll and earthquakes materialize the concept of uncertainty within society. In such a society, citizens are alienated exiles who feel deeply alone on an existential level as well as feeling the imminence of physical threats to their unity as a community. Thus, in this epic novel, Rushdie diagnoses society as afflicted by a condition of existence. He writes in this novel, "Suppose the earth itself grew uncertain about us, or rather made up her mind just to open her jaws and swallow us down, the whole sorry lot of us" (*Ground beneath Her Feet*, 573). This is Rushdie's first novel about rock music; he has been accused of being a "phony" for writing it.[40]

Geography and music are Rushdie's themes, and by using them as connections to exile he puts together two different phenomena while sharing linguistic continuity. Both are loud phenomena and both erupt; both cause mobs to form; both are connected to vibrations; both have "scales"; both defy or are anarchic toward the idea of boundaries. Rushdie, by placing the two phenomena adjacent as metaphorical constructs through which to view the notion of exile creation, also shows his linguistic bravado. Language, for Rushdie, allows for the unlikely to be continuous conceptually and linguistically, even if totally separate physically or materially. Rushdie can use the linguistic links that earthquakes and music share to emphasize their destabilizing elements. For Rushdie, the condition of exile equals the condition of destabilization.

Both destabilizing phenomena begin with vibrations. A sense of transience is ubiquitous in the novel. The tone of the novel, structured on supposition and elusive image, is fitting, since the narrator is a photographer. But the elusiveness of images is just one element of the cauldron of doubt in which the novel is placed. There have been other prophets of supposition that are relevant when considering Rushdie's proposition. For example, René Descartes wrote that the world was merely sensory data and material of the mind. In *The Ground beneath Her Feet*, doubt appears to be the ultimate extension of exile: the heroes of the novel are never what they appear to be. The condition of exile is the condition of suspicion of the world.

Constant uncertainty means constant transformation, of both identity and language. Rushdie's idea of literature was that "it is the one place in society where, within the secrecy of our own heads, we can hear voices talking about everything in any possible way."[41] Fixed attachments to any particular place might interfere with this multiplicity of voices. But the existence of doubt, to Rushdie, is a sign of modernism, and to be "nowhere" is the metaphorical state for extreme doubt.

In fact, "nowhere at all" celebrates the Cartesian doubt implicit in all fiction, where the place, characters, and time are invented out of the imagination. Rushdie carries the condition of doubt as far as possible, suggesting that even the quaking of the earth is a fantasy. Perhaps the heroes are also unreal: the photographer's narrative may just be illusion and reality, mere photographic play. Perhaps he is alluding to his own situation of exile from the East, which might have been so traumatic that he still feels disoriented by it. He says: "Disorientation is loss of the east. Ask any navigator: the east is what you sail by. Lose the east and you lose your bearings, your certainties, your knowledge of what is and what may be, perhaps even your life. . . . That's right. The east orients. That's the official version. The language says so, and you should never argue with the language" (*Ground beneath Her Feet,* 176). But, encouraging his own doubtfulness, Rushdie goes on to question: "What if the whole deal—orientation, knowing where you are, and so on—what if it's all a scam? What if all of it—home, kinship, the whole enchilada—is just the biggest, most truly global, and centuries-oldest piece of brainwashing?" Rushdie, continuing on this line of thought, says that maybe "you've got to go through the feeling of being lost, into the chaos and beyond; you've got to accept the loneliness, the wild panic of losing your moorings" (177). Finally he asks the audience to imagine stepping off the edge of the earth, or "through the fatal waterfall" to find "the magic valley at the end of the universe, the blessed kingdom of the air. Great music everywhere. You breathe the music, in and out, and it's your element now. It feels better than 'belonging' in your lungs" (177). It's almost impossible not to think of Rushdie's own experience of being thrust into chaos, away from the community of the East, and finding his element outside of it.

Certainly *The Ground beneath Her Feet* reflects much of the unsteadiness of fame and convention for those who choose the unconventional and transgressive professions: rock stardom, photography, or imitating rock stars. The novel is a story where no conventions seem to hold steady: families are dysfunctional, and individuals morph and transform unpredictably and at lightspeed. *The Ground beneath Her Feet* tries to represent ultimate doubt in practice, or perhaps the precariousness of believing in certainty in a world that doesn't provide it. At the same time, it wants to be a novel about the ultimate, epic love—between Vina Apsara and Ormus Cama, who share "a love so deep that it goes beyond the grave."[42] Rushdie materializes the concept of doubt by presenting a world constantly changing, while juxtaposing it with the enduring love of Apsara and Cama. The novel thus clearly emphasizes that it is the culture which is full of doubt and conspires against the potential of human love.

This pervasive doubt leads to pathology for the characters of *The Ground beneath Her Feet*. The incapacity to feel at home results in an inability to forge a stable identity. Rushdie first introduces Vina as an orphaned, traumatized child whose mother has killed her entire family but Vina, because she could sing. Vina, uncomfortable in the Virginian hills of her childhood, is passed from relative to relative and ends up in Bombay, until she becomes a famous rock star who travels the world. Unlike Moor, who is the victim of ultrafast time, Vina seems to be the victim of *topo-itis*. She despises India and professes to despise everything but the sea: "'I hate India,' my swimsuit queen mentioned savagely as I passed her. 'And there's plenty of it to hate. I hate the heat, and it's always hot, even when it rains, and I really hate that rain.... I hate the languages because they're not plain English either.... Wanna know what I like, what's the only thing I like?' 'Yes, please,' I humbly said. I may even have bowed my head in misery. 'I love the sea,' she said, and ran off to swim. My heart almost burst with joy" (72).

If Moor is psychically unattached to any particular time, Vina Apsara, the character around which *Ground* revolves, is psychically unattached to any material object or any geographic place. Although Moor is a freak, Vina Apsara is a celebrated rock star who is the victim of the world's freakiness, its geographic shiftiness. Her entire family was murdered by her mother, who immediately committed suicide after the killings. Vina, an orphan, is farmed off to different relatives and not accepted or loved until she takes to the stage. Thus, she is a product of exile culture; she is an orphan of mixed extraction and an outcast from two countries, but still a lover of the sea. As Rushdie tells us, "Apsara is derivative of *apsaras,* 'a swanlike water nymph,' in western terms, a naiad" (*Ground beneath Her Feet,* 55). She is a member of a new species of human being who is not defined by nationality, birthplace, or mother tongue, but is an ambiguous, amorphous quantity. If *The Moor's Last Sigh* unfolds how an exile can be resigned and traumatized by banishment, *The Ground beneath Her Feet* is the opposite: the status of exile is glamorized, celebrated, and infused with power. Nevertheless, the continuities which exist in the exile consciousness remain: the undercurrent of anxiety, the caricature-like characterization of the exile, and the urge to reclaim the past or myth in order to provide structure to an unwieldy existence. That the sense of exile is a disorienting existence where even the ground cannot be trusted to be solid is the grand metaphor of this geographically explorative novel, which takes place in America, India, Mexico, and Europe.

The result of Vina's inability to have land legs is that she cannot hold to any lasting identity. Rai will give her names: "Professor Vina, Crystal Vina, Holy Vina, Profane Vina" (*Ground beneath Her Feet,* 339); "Vina in black leggings and a gold breastplate"

(396); "super-charged Vina" (424); Vina "looking her age, with bag-eyed helplessness and wiry dyed red hair" (5); "Vina at twenty-six with an Afro" (223). He summarizes her as "a rag bag of selves, torn fragments of people she might have become. Some days she sat crumpled in a corner like a string-cut puppet, and when she jerked into life you never knew who would be there, in her skin. Sweet or savage, serene or stormy, funny or sad: she had as many moods as the Old Man of the Sea, who would transform himself over and over again if you tried to grab him, for he knew that if you did capture him he would have to grant you your deepest wish" (122). Vina is the metaphoric incarnation of doubt, if doubt is the opposite of steadfast, fixed belief. Vina's association with the sea, the only thing she loves aside from Ormus, represents her comfort zone with doubt. Rai is also a fellow skeptic: significantly, Rai first encounters Vina by the sea, and also seems to have a special attachment to water, which seems to accommodate doubt, unlike land: "I heard a new voice speaking to me, not in any language I had ever learned, but in the secret language of my heart. It was the sea. Its come-hither murmur, its seductive roar. That was the music that could wash my soul. The lure of a different element, its promises of elsewhere, gave me my first intimation of something hidden within me that would pull me across the water, leaving my parents stranded. . . . The sandy shore, on which my barefoot father dug like an overworked undertaker, that beloved homeland, came to seem like a prison to me" (59). Rushdie goes so far as to configure water and land as being in constant interplay, perhaps always encroaching upon each other's territory: "Land, water, water, land" (293). He says in a later passage: "Certain patterns recur, seem inescapable. Fire, death, uncertainty. The carpet whipped out from under us to reveal a chasm where the floor should have been. Disorientation. Loss of the east" (313).

The conflict between the water and the land resembles the conflict between uncertainty and certainty; they are opposites but symbiotic.

> But the inclination towards water and unrootedness seems to be an endemic condition of the millennium age. If one is not anti-community and unrooted, the sense of such a state of mind is contagious, even easy to distribute to the masses. We live in a time of great social change, probably the greatest time of transformation in the history of the human race, one way or another, in which everything—I mean, you wake up every day and the world seems to be a different place. So things—countries appear and disappear; inventions, new technologies arrive which radically alter our way of being with each other in the world. And in that—and I wanted to write about that, this hinge moment in the history of the human race, where things are changing, metamorphosing at the most bewildering speed, and certainly makes us feel uncertain, makes us feel the provisionality of life. And that's what the earthquakes are doing in the book. The earthquakes are trying to suggest that provisionality, the way in which they can do radical change at high speed in things that you take for granted.[43]

Because the landscape of *The Ground beneath Her Feet* changes so frequently, its inhabitants are forced to reinvent themselves quickly in order to survive. "She's twenty-seven years old, and if there's one thing she's learned it's that nothing stays the same for five minutes, not even your goddamn name" (369). Again, in contrast to *The Moor's Last Sigh,* this novel shifts the loci of attention from the emotional state of one exile to the consciousness of the world. The sense of history altering at high speed and

metamorphosing is a universal one, rather than a personal afflic-
tion. Ormus has visions and intuitions of an impending, world-
shaking chaos of mythic proportions which he incorporates into
his lyrics: "The earth begins to rock and roll, its music dooms
your mortal soul, and there's nothing baby nothing you can do.
'Cause it's not up to it's not up to it's not up to you" (390). The
narrator describes Ormus' prophetic visions: The earthquake
songs of Ormus Cama are rants in praise of the approach of
chaos, paradoxically composed by an artist working at the highest levels of musical sophistication. The songs are about the "col-
lapse of all walls, boundaries, restraints" (390).

The presence of doubt creates the possibility of magic and the
supernatural. Rushdie, like Nabokov, may have had a sense of
being a freak of nature, with freaky needs and desires that don't
seem quenchable by his environment and make him feel like an
outsider. He imagines the possibility of a land of exiles, of freaks
who can transform. Ormus' "Quakershaker" songs work strange
phenomena among the audience: "As floodlights rake the crowd,
they reveal abandoned, Dionysiac scenes. . . . When the crowd
roars it is like a lion and beneath the roar there is sometimes
heard a hissing, as of serpents. . . . There is loose talk of bestial
metamorphoses: snakes in the urban gutters, wild pigs in city
parks, strange birds with fabulous plumages perching on sky-
scrapers like gargoyles, or angels" (391). Thus, unlike *The Moor's
Last Sigh*, rather than focusing on a single exile, *The Ground beneath Her Feet* includes those who are on the outside, or who are
moving away from a conservative, mainstream view of humanity.
Rushdie concedes this:

> I wanted to write about the phenomenon of—"outsider-
> ness" is what it's called in the novel. I mean, in which I

would include, you know, displaced people, people who feel outside the mainstream of a culture, you know, minority groups, people who feel alienated, outlaws, gangsters, you know. That whole group of people who don't fit inside the normal frame of conventionally described society because I think, more and more, it's from that group that the nature of the modern, you know, is emerging. I mean, I think this is the great century of migration. It's the first century in which so many people have moved across the face of the earth and ended up in places other than the ones in which they began. And as I suggest in the novel, there are people who are born not belonging. There are people for whom the idea of roots and home is less important than to many of us. And I wanted to write about them.[44]

If the sense of roots and home is on the decline, the need for something else to fill the vacuum is what Rushdie will say is love. Rushdie's narrator will say, "Love is what we want, not freedom"; and Ormus Cama will discover that without Vina's love, he "might go horribly wrong. The idea of family, of community, is almost dead in him. There is only silent Virus and their piano session. Otherwise he has come loose, like an astronaut floating away from a space capsule" (147). This is the only continuity that Rushdie seems to support in his shaken, topsy-turvy, quaking world. For an exile, maybe the most comforting environment is one of doubt—but for the heroine, this world of uncertainties was not enough.

Notes

Introduction

1. My parents planned our Chinese names before we were born. Some Chinese parents choose characters that have poetic resonance or allude to a historical figure; others name their children after plants.

2. Chinese names conventionally contain three characters: a surname, a middle name, and a first name—in this order. The first character (surname) is often the father's surname; the middle character is conventionally uniform among all the children in a family; the last character is unique to each child.

3. My mother said they had planned a fourth child to fill out the character set, but had decided that three was adequate.

4. People in China often asked me why I had such a masculine or neutral *(zhong jian)* name, not knowing that it was linked with my brother's and sister's names.

5. Furthermore, my parents secured loyalty between siblings, at least on a figurative level, since individually we meant nothing (this also affirms the "society over self" formula often said to characterize Chinese ideology).

6. From a genetic standpoint, there is little variance among people of different nationalities and races. See Kwame Anthony Appiah and Amy Gutmann, *Color Conscious* (Princeton, N.J.: Princeton University Press, 2000).

7. Aiwa Ong, David Palumbo Liu, Lisa Lowe, Satya Mohanti, and Manthia Diawara are only a few of the many critics who have provided strong political frameworks for analyzing immigrant and postcolonial works.

8. Benedict Anderson, *Imagined Communities: Reflections on the Origin and Spread of Nationalism* (London: Verso, 1983; rev. ed. 1991), 45. Of course, the ability to transcribe weird English is linked to increased literacy. Thus, the use of weird English in literature is the transcription of a practice that is constantly evolving and that renders its transcription obsolete.

9. When Internet communities were still developing, they resembled early print communities in their ability to disseminate knowledge at a faster rate than human beings were accustomed to. Benedict Anderson writes: "Print-language is what invents nationalism, not *a* particular language per se" (*Imagined Communities,* 134). The Internet has energized use of the vernacular just as the printing press did centuries ago. The Internet contributes to community formation the way periodicals do, only more so, and in multiple formats. Language also functions differently on the Internet; it is more active and alive, since users can be instant-messaging or emailing a response quickly. Thus, formal letters and language are dispensed with as a form of exchange; in their place are emoticons and e-shorthand. Email regularly destroys grammar in favor of efficiency. These language practices also encourage an eccentric vernacular. Though the development of the Internet and the increasing frequency of weird English could in some ways have been a mere happy coincidence, the two are synergistic; the energy of each feeds off the other. There is also a specific Internet language, "leet-speak," a form of written slang that uses nonstandard spellings and that substitutes numerals and symbols for the letters they resemble.

Benedict Anderson, in *Imagined Communities,* describes the way in which the development of print culture served as a tool to create communities and, later, nationalistic sentiment. Print culture, he says, succeeded in unifying fields of exchange and communication, and provided language with a new stability. This stability also contributed to community formation. "These fellow-readers, to whom they were connected through print, formed, in their secular, particular, visible invisibility, the embryo of the nationally imagined community" (ibid., 44). He shows how monolingualism can become a trend in print cultures; such homogenization of language allowed communities a uniform language. In colonized spaces, intelligentsias formed, sometimes accompanied by print-language serials: Young India, Young Java, and Young Amboina are among these groups. These intelligentsias differed from European counterparts because the concept of youth was connected to education rather than to chronological age. "Youth meant, above all, the first generation in any significant numbers to have acquired a European education, marking them off linguistically and culturally from their parents' generation, as well as from the vast bulk of their colonized agemates" (ibid., 119). Serials were a key element in the sustained existence of the intelligentsias, and an effective forum for expression; a single release of a book or journal, for example, would not have permitted this regular form of collective dialogue. The periodical enabled the community to have a fixed definition, a temporally sustained existence, while its expected serial appearance allowed for response from its readers and for adjustments and alterations with each new issue.

Anderson asserts that with the explosion of print culture, some forms of linguistic diversity became extinct: "What, in a positive sense, made the new communities imaginable was a half-fortuitous, but explosive, interaction between the system of production and productive relations (capitalism), a technology of communications (print), and the fatality of human linguistic diversity" (ibid., 42–43). He also suggests that this fatality contributed to the formation of a mass reading public: "The element of fatality is essential. For whatever superhuman feats capitalism was capable of, it found in death and languages two tenacious adversaries. Particular languages can die or be wiped out, but there was and is no possibility of humankind's general linguistic unification. Yet this mutual incomprehensibility was historically of only slight importance until capitalism and print created monoglot mass reading publics" (ibid., 43). For print-language culture, the regularity of serials and the uniformity of monoglot reading publics made community building possible.

Unlike print-language culture, e-language cultures do not encourage monoglot reading publics; they encourage linguistic individualism. Internet communities don't require monoglotism, since they are closer to physical communities than to imaginary ones. Internet exchange can occur with the same timing as the fluid, fast bilateral exchange characteristic of conversation. This makes the Internet community tangible and effable; as a result, language is colloquial and proximate in tone, rather than distant. The imagination stimulated by serials contrasts with the imagination associated with the Internet. A reader's imagination functions differently, more like *mémoire involontaire*; in contrast, an Internet surfer confronts images flashed before the eyes, and these images elicit more visceral and immediate responses than texts do. Jhumpa Lahiri once said that she finds it impossible to use the Internet, because the world is already there at the press of a button, whereas she likes to imagine her worlds.

10. Some writers would take issue with this characterization. In "The Age of White Guilt" (*Harper's* [November 2002], 33), Shelby Steele deftly argues that we are moving from a period of white racism to one of white guilt. Ethnic activism is thus a trend still controlled by the establishment, not truly subversive of it.

11. Gish Jen, "Who's Irish?" *The Beacon Best of 1999* (Boston: Beacon, 1999), 67.

12. Junot Díaz, "The Sun, the Moon and the Stars," *The Beacon Best of 1999*, 101.

13. Ruth Prawer Jhabvala, "A New Delhi Romance," *The Beacon Best of 1999*, 127.

14. Suzanne Kamata, "Driving," *The Beacon Best of 1999*, 177.

15. Jonathan Safran Foer, *Everything Is Illuminated* (New York: Houghton Mifflin, 2002), 1.

16. One example is Daniel Keyes, *Flowers for Algernon* (London: Cassell, 1966), a narrative about a retarded man who becomes a genius through an experimental operation, but later suffers a decline. His linguistic progression from rampantly misspelled English to well-articulated English reflects his evolution into an intelligent man—although the narrative ends in tragedy and his language spirals back to its original form.

17. Gunther Kress, *Early Spelling* (New York: Routledge, 2000), 45.

18. Uriel Weinreich, *Languages in Contact* (The Hague: Mouton, 1970), describes the phenomenon of bilingualism, which resonates with my analysis of weird English.

19. Martin Gustafsson, "Entangled Sense" (Diss., Uppsala University, 2000), 166.

20. Dr. Matthew Albert, an immunologist at the Pasteur Institute, reminded me of the Stroop experiment. In 1935 Jerome Stroop established that there was a distinction between readers' ability to process meaning and their ability to read words. In his experiment, participants were instructed to name each color in a series of colored bars or colored words. The words were names of colors other than the color in which they were written; for example, the word "orange" would appear in a blue font. Participants were instructed to identify the color of a word. Stroop found that the words interfered with the ability to rapidly name the color correctly; participants had an easier time naming the colors of the bars. Scientists have since carried out many variations on this basic experiment—for instance, focusing on geographic directions. See faculty.washington.edu/chudler/words.html#seffect for some examples.

21. Martin Gustafsson, personal communication, March 13, 2003.

22. Cora Diamond, personal communication, Spring 2003.

23. Barbara Wallraff, "What Global Language?" *Atlantic Monthly,* 286, no. 5 (November 2000), 52–64.

24. From www.engrish.com: "The noodles of a phantom with the resistance to the teeth of boast of our shop. The exquisite rainy season which repeated trial and error and was completed. Colorful red pepper of Asia. Domestic careful selection pork with little fat of female liking is used. It has healthy vegetables with salad feeling fully."

25. Authors who use weird English are distinct from modernists because their context is globalization, and their language is a mixture of two rather than an experiment with one. There are some similarities, of course, between the modernists and weird-English authors—for example, self-consciousness about language and about language as the subject of their writing. Such self-consciousness was apparent in modernist writers after World War I. The modernist experiment in language is often attributed to the war's influence, whereas here I suggest that the experimental language of the early third millennium is an expression of repositioning in relation to English. These two historical moments have similarities. The modernist (or post–World War I) writer and the nonnative speaker deeply respect the resonances of linguistic untranslatability and uninterpretability, the modernist for the untranslatability of experience (the horrors of war) and the nonnative for the untranslatability of experience (cultural) and language (foreign). This respect for the interpretation of experience without immediate translatability into words has resulted in experiments with languages, signs, pictures, and collages; it has also allowed for the proliferation of minority, immigrant, and postcolonial voices because it has opened the boundaries of expression. The position and the linguistic impulses of the modernist—the motives that drive such a writer to morph language—resemble those of the immigrant writer who, dissatisfied with the range a nonnative language provides, tailors language to fit his experience.

26. Irvine Welsh, *Trainspotting* (New York: Norton, 1996), 78.

27. Ibid., 89.

28. Only certain parts had subtitles, as if to give the viewer merely a quick lesson in the accent and assume its effectiveness.

29. Of course, film often has greater appeal than books, but in these cases book lovers, too, confessed to this feeling.

30. Irvine Welsh, *Marabou Stork Nightmares* (New York: Vintage, 1995), 58.

31. Lois Ann Yamanaka, "Ten Thousand in the Round," *The Beacon Best of 2000* (Boston: Beacon, 2000).

32. Juliana Spahr, *Everybody's Autonomy* (Tuscaloosa: University of Alabama Press, 2001), 130.

33. Ibid., 131.

34. Jeff also founded and edited *A. Magazine: Inside Asian America,* one of the first Asian American magazines on popular culture.

35. Lisa Yun, personal communication, 2001.

36. Marilyn Halter, *Shopping for Identity* (New York: Schocken, 2000), 9.

37. Although many would say that the trend itself is a strain of racism.

38. Anchee Min, remarks at a symposium sponsored by the *New York Times* (New York, Spring 2001).

39. Stanley Cavell ("Excursus on Wittgenstein's Vision of Language") beautifully explores the ways in which learning a language, acquiring knowledge of a language, is a form of life that is immeasurable according to a kind of academicized vision of language learning, where learning to identify an object is sometimes isolated from learning to interact with the world. Cavell, *The Claim of Reason* (New York: Oxford University Press, 1979).

40. See Doris Sommer, *Proceed with Caution When Engaged by Minority Writing in the Americas* (Cambridge, Mass.: Harvard University Press, 1999), 8.

41. Ibid., 11.

42. Ibid., 9–10.

43. T. S. Eliot's sense of postwar exile was so great that he wrote about the feeling of nonfeeling, the feeling of being "etherized like a patient" ("The Love Song of J. Alfred Prufrock"). Likewise, "The Waste Land" can be read as an extended search for a corpse that exists underground at the beginning of the poem.

44. Edward Sapir, *Language* (New York: Harvest, 1955), 121, 218.

45. Ibid., 215.

46. Ibid., 155.

47. An article in the *New York Times* reported that Chinese also like to be buried outside Chinatown. One of their current favorite burial grounds is now in Westchester.

48. Bill Ashcroft, *Postcolonial Transformations* (New York: Routledge, 2000), chapter entitled "Language."

49. Ferdinand de Saussure was the first to distinguish between *parole* (the individual utterance) and *langue* (language: the system of rules within which the *parole* makes sense). See his *Course in General Linguistics,* trans. Roy Harris (LaSalle, Ill.: Open Court, 1986; orig. French edition, 1916).

50. All quotations from Walcott's poems are taken from *Derek Walcott: Collected Poems, 1948–1984* (New York: Noonday, 1997).

51. Jacques Derrida, *Monolingualism of the Other; or, The Prosthesis of Origin* (Palo Alto, Calif.: Stanford University Press, 1998), 5.

52. Ibid., 23.

53. Ibid., 22.

54. Ibid., 23, 47.

55. Vladimir Nabokov, quoted in Simon Karlinsky, ed., *Dear Bunny, Dear Volodya: The Nabokov-Wilson Letters, 1940–1971* (New York: Harper and Row, 1979), 46.

56. Lawrence Weschler, *Calamities of Exile* (Chicago: University of Chicago Press, 1999).

57. Arundhati Roy, *The God of Small Things* (New York: Harper Perennial, 1997), 170.

58. Derrida, *Monolingualism of the Other,* 65.

59. Ibid., 65.

60. Ibid.

61. Salman Rushdie, *The Ground beneath Her Feet* (New York: Henry Holt, 1999), 124.

62. Wittgenstein, in his work on grammar and language, asserts that the rules of language are ultimately based on the assumption that a community is sharing them and following them. In *Remarks on*

the Foundation of Mathematics, he shows in sections 15–30 that we cannot consider rule-following as an essentially private activity. Martin Gustafsson (personal communication, March 18, 2003) has pointed out the distinction between the solitary and private uses of language. Language is language for communicating in a community of people, and we have not described the rules unless we have described how they function in the community.

63. Eva Hoffman, *Lost in Translation: Life in a New Language* (New York: Penguin, 1990), 97.

64. Iris Murdoch, *The Sovereignty of Good* (New York: Routledge, 1985), 33.

65. Ibid.

66. Stacy Schiff, *Véra: Mrs. Vladimir Nabokov* (New York: Modern Library, 2000), 128.

67. Ludwig Wittgenstein, *Philosophical Investigations,* 3rd ed., trans. G. E. M. Anscombe (New York: Prentice Hall, 1999), sect. 242.

68. Hoffman, *Lost in Translation,* 275.

69. Elizabeth Klosty Beaujour, *Alien Tongues: Bilingual Russian Writers of the First Emigration* (Ithaca, N.Y.: Cornell University Press, 1989), 30.

70. Ibid., 36.

71. Svetlana Boym, "Estrangement as a Lifestyle: Shklovsky and Brodsky," in Susan Rubin Suleiman, ed., *Exile and Creativity: Signposts, Travelers, Outsiders, Backward Glances* (Durham, N.C.: Duke University Press, 1998), 244.

72. Quoted in Brian Boyd, *Vladimir Nabokov: The American Years* (Princeton, N.J.: Princeton University Press, 1993), 35.

73. Trinh T. Minh-ha, *Travellers' Tales: Narratives of Home and Displacement* (New York: Routledge, 1998), 10.

74. Quoted in Paul Skenazy and Tera Martin, eds., *Conversations with Maxine Hong Kingston* (Oxford, Miss.: University Press of Mississippi, 1998), 44–45.

75. Ibid., 75.

76. The classification of Kingston's book *The Woman Warrior* as autobiography has caused great controversy among Asian American writers, who feel that its publisher wanted to cash in on the "authen-

ticity" of the Chinese American experience (insisting on the term "autobiography" and rejecting the term "fiction," which these critics feel is more appropriate). Cynthia Sau-Ling Wong explores the legitimacy of such views, and also offers a look from the other side— i.e., that such criticism may be "measuring *The Woman Warrior* 'against some extra-textual order of fact,' not realizing that this order is 'based in its turn on other texts (dignified as documents)' (Eakin, 23): an ideologically uplifting version of Chinese American history revising earlier racist texts, a version of the Fa Mu Lan legend sufficiently hoary to be considered 'historical'" (Cynthia Sau-Ling Wong, ed., *Maxine Hong Kingston's "The Woman Warrior": A Casebook* [New York: Oxford University Press, 1999], quoting John Paul Eakin, *Fictions in Autobiography*). Ultimately, Wong warns that critics of Kingston "intent on liberating Chinese American writers from one set of constraints" may have "imposed another" (ibid., 162), restricting the written realities that Chinese American writers might claim as their experience.

77. Suleiman, ed., *Exile and Creativity*, 399.

78. Ibid., 401.

79. Minh-ha, *Travellers' Tales*, 16.

80. Ibid.

81. Vladimir Nabokov, *Lectures on Russian Literature* (New York: Harvest, 2002), xi.

82. Vladimir Nabokov, *Speak, Memory* (New York: Vintage, 1989), 125–126.

83. Vladimir Nabokov, *Strong Opinions* (New York: Vintage, 1990), 330.

84. Ibid.

85. Quoted in Brian Boyd, *Nabokov's Butterflies* (Boston: Beacon, 2002), 472.

86. In this case, the imago—or final stage of transformation—is the resulting butterfly.

87. Quoted in Boyd, *Nabokov's Butterflies*, 473.

88. Vladimir Nabokov, *Lolita* (New York: Vintage), 159. A host of connections between Lolita and butterflies have been suggested by Kurt Johnson and Steve Coates: "In English, *nymph* in entomological

terms most often refers to an immature stage of a hemimetabolic insect. . . . *Nymph* can be used as a synonym for *pupa;* and that *nymphe* is simply French for 'pupa' is often overlooked, as Dieter E. Zimmer has pointed out. . . . *Pupa* is also the Latin word for 'doll,' which recalls one of Lolita's nicknames, Dolly. In addition to the obvious mythological associations, a nymphet is a creature that has not reached sexual maturity: Lolita's 'iridescent future' was irreparably blighted by Humbert Humbert." See Johnson and Coates, *Nabokov's Blues* (Cambridge, Mass.: Zoland Books, 1999), 36.

89. Schiff, *Véra,* 128.

90. Elaine Scarry, *On Beauty and Being Just* (Princeton, N.J.: Princeton University Press, 2001), 3.

91. Ibid., 5.

92. Ludwig Wittgenstein, *Culture and Value,* ed. George H. Von Wright, trans. Peter Winch (Chicago: University of Chicago Press, 1984), 48e.

93. Nabokov, *Strong Opinions,* 14.

94. Quoted in Skenazy and Martin, *Conversations with Maxine Hong Kingston,* 126.

95. Arundhati Roy, interview with Reena Jana, Salon.com (September 30, 1997), 2. See www.salon.com/sept97/00roy2.html.

96. Junot Díaz, interview with Evelyn Ch'ien, July 26, 2002.

97. Salman Rushdie, quoted at www.crl.com/~subir/rushdie/uc_maps.html.

98. James Joyce, *Ulysses,* ed. Erroll McDonald and Morris Ernst (New York: Vintage, 1990), 37. Note that Joyce also includes an "ineluctable modality of the visible" (37).

99. Skenazy and Martin, *Conversations with Maxine Hong Kingston,* 147.

100. Elaine Scarry, *Dreaming by the Book* (New York: Farrar, Straus and Giroux, 1999), 2.

101. Edward Said, "Reflections on Exile," *Granta,* 13 (Autumn 1984), 159–172.

102. Primo Levi, *Survival in Auschwitz* (New York: Touchstone, 1995).

103. Josh Skyer, student exam, May 2001, University of Hartford, West Hartford, Conn. Used with permission.

104. The atomistic conception of an individual as unreliant on anyone

else, on any other community, is one that often seems reified in philosophical communities but is too abstract to be tenable. This arose in a discussion with the philosopher Mahlon Barnes—I'm indebted to him for many discussions on the shortcomings of the concept of the atomistic agent. In this book, I separate the importance of the atomic individual in the artistic realm from its importance in other areas.

105. Maxine Hong Kingston, *China Men* (New York: Vintage, 1977), 267.

1. A SHUTTLECOCK ABOVE THE ATLANTIC

1. Most critics might find it difficult to categorize the multilingual Nabokov as a classic immigrant case, but various studies (including mine) demonstrate that his writing was greatly influenced by the fact that he did not live in an English-speaking environment until late in his life. Part of the reason Nabokov is viewed as atypical of many Russian immigrants is that he had a cosmopolitan background. According to many biographical accounts, his parents (Vladimir Dmitrievich, a liberal statesman and jurist, and Elena Ivanovna, an amateur poet) were trilingual in French, English, and Russian; these languages were spoken regularly in the house, but English and French became familiar to the children mostly through literature. Elizabeth Klosty Beaujour, in her extremely helpful book *Alien Tongues* (Ithaca, N.Y.: Cornell University Press, 1989), says that Nabokov read "Wells, Poe, Browning, Keats, Kipling, Conrad, Chesterton, Oscar Wilde, Flaubert, Verlaine, Rimbaud, Chekhov, and Aleksander Blok, and relished the adventures of the Scarlet Pimpernel, Phileas Fogg, and Sherlock Holmes" (86). Nabokov certainly played up his multilingual background but also confessed to feeling crippled in English; on being asked which language he considered most beautiful, Nabokov declared: "My head says English, my heart, Russian, my ear, French" (*Strong Opinions* [New York: Vintage, 1990], 49). In his American years, Nabokov chose English for his later fiction and nonfictional prose (essays on lepidoptera, letters), wrote

sentimental poetry in Russian, and enjoyed French as a Parisien. He also produced some writing in French—for example, one chapter of *Speak, Memory* was originally written in French and later translated for inclusion in the book.

2. Jane Grayson is one critic who has concentrated on the linguistic aspect of Nabokov's writing. She recognizes that his writing intertwines Americanisms, Anglicisms, and Russianisms, in addition to other languages. She writes: "A more serious criticism is that in some of his writing the American vocabulary and up-to-date idiom sits uneasily on top of his essentially literary English prose style. There is in places a noticeable unevenness of style, where old and new elements are not sufficiently blent. But while flavors and lapses can be detected in Nabokov's use of Americanisms, there is no disputing his conscious and scrupulous intention to assume the idiom of his adopted country and become 'an American writer.' All his later works, original writings as well as translations, are stamped with this American style." Grayson, *Nabokov Translated: A Comparison of Nabokov's Russian and English Prose* (Oxford: Oxford University Press, 1977), 192.

3. Jane Grayson describes Nabokov's dilemma euphemistically: "The brilliance of Nabokov's later English style owes not a little to his viewpoint as a foreigner. He sees the English language through different eyes. He sees patterns of sound and potential meanings in words that the native speaker, his perception dulled through familiarity, would simply pass over. He deviates more readily from set modes of expression and conventional registers of style, inventing new and arresting word combinations, employing high-flown, recherché vocabulary." Grayson emphasizes the "foreignness" and "strangeness" (*ostranenie,* or "making strange") of Nabokov's writing—the "fresh, off-centre vision" that Nabokov claimed was central to artistic perception (ibid.).

4. Vladimir Vladimirovich Nabokov was born in St. Petersburg in 1899.
   Michael Wood uses these adjectives to describe Nabokovian English: "mannered, intricate, alliterative, allusive, perverse, hilarious,

lyrical, sombre, nostalgic, kindly, frivolous, passionate, cruel, cold, stupid, magical, precise, philosophical and unforgettable." Wood, *The Magician's Doubts* (Princeton, N.J.: Princeton University Press, 1995).

5. Richard Rorty writes: "Literary language is, and always will be, parasitic on ordinary language, and in particular on ordinary moral language" (*Contingency, Irony and Solidarity* [Cambridge: Cambridge University Press, 1989], 67). But Nabokov's literary language seems to resist this ordinary language, suggesting a reconfiguration of Rorty's statement: ordinary moral language is parasitic on literary language.

6. Nabokov's linguistic creations reflect the most private of imagined worlds, fantasies, and sensations; and the language he employs is so particular and mannered that it is branded "Nabokovian." His works are rich in imaginary geographies and languages. *Pale Fire*'s Zembla and poetic forms; *Lolita*'s celebration of the amoral, anticommunal possibilities in language; and *Pnin*'s illustration of how language resists its user—all of these are Nabokov's linguistic legacies.

7. The way in which my language functions here resonates with the ideas that George Lakoff and Mark Johnson propose in *Metaphors We Live By* (Chicago: University of Chicago Press, 1980). Thanks to Marcia Moen for a conversation about this in 2002.

8. Stanley Cavell writes: "What hides the mind is not the body but the mind itself, his his, or mine his, and contrariwise." *The Claim of Reason* (New York: Oxford University Press, 1979), 369.

9. Laurie Clancy suggests that Pnin is stripped of his interiority: "It is the analytical capacity that leads the narrator to write the novel and so to strip Pnin of his last defense against life, the privacy of his memory." She also implies that Pnin is so abstract that he actually can "transcend his actual existence." Clancy, *The Novels of Vladimir Nabokov* (London: Macmillan, 1984), 123.

10. Stanley Cavell, in *The Claim of Reason,* discusses at length the way in which we can suggest or deny the concept of interior through mindgames and language play: "The *Investigations* takes many ways of approaching ideas which construe the inner life as composed of objects (and if objects then for sure *private* ones). To combat such ideas

is an obsession of the book as a whole. It is as though Wittgenstein felt human beings in jeopardy of losing touch with their inner lives altogether, with the very idea that each person is a center of one, that each *has* a life" (91).

11. In Milan Kundera's novel *The Unbearable Lightness of Being* (New York: Perennial, 1999), Tereza obsesses about having a body like any other, about wishing to make herself distinct. This resonates with my sense of Nabokov as a person.

12. A broken language—a broken English in this case—exposes the problem with relying on language as automatic experiential transfer.

13. In a conversation about the work of George Lakoff and Mark Johnson, Marcia Moen rephrased a view about the omnipresence of the metaphor: some phrases or words are live metaphors, while some go unacknowledged as metaphors when they turn into common parlance (e.g., the phrase "in my mind"). But since language carries the structure of experience from one person to another, it carries a life from one person to another; and so it is important to examine the nature of metaphor for immigrant writers who question the "deadness" of those metaphors that native speakers of English take for granted. Immigrant writers' awareness of this nature deserves attention from critics.

14. In Nabokov's case, the appropriation of English demanded more conscious effort than Kingston's or Díaz's appropriation, since Russian was Nabokov's real native language. It has been argued that his English equaled his Russian—but this is hard to judge. Grayson believes his Russian was "better" than his English (or at least that he was more comfortable with it). "Personally, I would tend to agree with Nabokov that his Russian is superior—if only because it is less uneven and, on the whole, less mannered than his English. However, whatever general view is held of Nabokov's English, it is undeniable that his command of the language has improved over the years and that with time he has evolved a polished and strikingly original prose style" (*Nabokov Translated,* 185).

15. Grayson, *Nabokov Translated,* 190. Grayson writes in great detail

about the linguistic aspects of Nabokov's translations. My emphasis is a subset of her efforts.

16. Ibid., 208.

17. D. Barton Johnson, *Worlds in Regression: Some Novels of Vladimir Nabokov* (Ann Arbor: Ardis, 1985), 9. Nabokov says this in *Drugie Berega* (Other Shores), the Russian version of *Speak, Memory*.

18. See Jonathan Safran Foer, *Everything Is Illuminated* (New York: Houghton Mifflin, 2002), in which Russianisms are no longer in parentheses but part of the body of the text. The reader is forced to work through Russianized English in an act of simultaneous reading/interpretation.

19. Stanley Cavell expounds brilliantly on the problem of the importance of the interior to humanity: it provokes a doubtfulness that we are doomed to live with. "In asking whether there is such a thing as soul-blindness, I do not mean to insist that there are such things as souls, nor that anybody believes there are. But I do, I expect, mean to insist that we may sincerely and sanely not know whether we believe in such a thing, as we may not know whether we believe in God, or in idols. I assume further that one may believe, or protest, that there are souls and yet not know that there are human beings; for that knowledge would require believing that there are embodied souls, something incarnate. And I assume that some people may not believe, or not know, that there are human beings. It may seem that you could believe that the human body is the best picture of the human soul and yet deny that anything corresponds to the picture. My intuition is that this is false, that not to believe there is such a thing as the human soul is not to know what the human body is, what it is of, heir to" (*The Claim of Reason,* 400).

20. Elaine Scarry, *The Body in Pain* (Oxford: Oxford University Press, 1984), connects pained language and its world-destroying features so well that I do not pursue the topic here.

21. Vladimir Nabokov, *Pnin* (New York: Vintage, 1998), 66. Subsequent references to this work will appear in parentheses in the text.

22. Nabokov, *Strong Opinions,* 54.

23. The will to establish a home is connected to the perfection of English. Pnin's self-consciousness and his obsession with annotating and cross-referencing are less a skill than a compensation for being overwhelmed by an environment in which he feels a foreign agent. Such obsessions do not rescue Pnin from disasters, and in fact interfere with his capacity to form a community. Pnin's *über*-competence as a language teacher is almost too much for his university, Waindell, which prefers sugar-coated teaching methods. "As a teacher, Pnin was far from being able to compete with those stupendous Russian ladies, scattered all over academic America, who, without having had any formal training at all, manage somehow, by dint of intuition, loquacity, and a kind of maternal bounce, to infuse a magic knowledge of their difficult and beautiful tongue into a group of innocent-eyed students in an atmosphere of Mother Volga songs, red caviar, and tea; nor did Pnin, as a teacher, ever presume to approach the lofty halls of modern scientific linguistics, that ascetic fraternity of phonemes, that temple wherein earnest young people are taught not the language itself, but the method of teaching others to teach that method; which method, like a waterfall splashing from rock to rock, ceases to be a medium of rational navigation but perhaps in some fabulous future may become instrumental in evolving esoteric dialects—Basic Basque and so forth—spoken only by certain elaborate machines" (Nabokov, *Pnin*, 10). Here, the criticism is that students are learning not the true language but a shallow version of it, conveyed by superficial teaching methods. But Pnin's earnest desire to have students learn "real" Russian is too ambitious for Waindell.

24. Leona Toker, *Nabokov: The Mystery of Literary Structures* (Ithaca, N.Y.: Cornell University Press, 1989), 122.

25. Toker writes: "Pnin's conversations with his Russian friends are rendered in impeccable English, because then it is the narration and the protagonist who perform the translation" (*Nabokov*, 123). Toker, however, does not examine the role of parentheses, which are crucial in deciphering Nabokov's narrative strategy.

26. Toker, *Nabokov*, 123.

27. Ibid., 31.

28. As an exile who created a home out of language, Nabokov was compulsive about developing a language that was distinctly his own. His experience of exile travels into his works. In *Speak, Memory* (New York: Vintage, 1989), he writes: "An exciting sense of *rondina*, 'motherland,' was for the first time organically mingled with the comfortably creaking snow, the deep footprints across it, the red gloss of the engine stack, the birch logs piled high, under their private layer of transportable snow, on the red tender. I was not quite six, but that year abroad, a year of difficult decisions and liberal hopes, had exposed a small Russian boy to grown-up conversations. He could not help being affected in some way of his own by a mother's nostalgia and a father's patriotism. In result, that particular return to Russia, my first conscious return, seems to me now, sixty years later, a rehearsal—not of the grand homecoming that will never take place, but of its constant dream in my long years of exile" (97). During the many years he lived in the United States and Switzerland, Nabokov never bought a home of his own, realizing that "nothing could ever replace Russia" (*Strong Opinions*, 20).

    In *Speak, Memory*, Nabokov calls himself an exile at least three times (97, 276, 288); in *Lolita*, his protagonist seems to speak for him as a *soi-disant* "shabby émigré" (*Lolita* [New York: Vintage, 1989], 196); and *Pale Fire* contains the lines, "No one can help the exile, the old man / Dying in a motel, with the loud fan" (*Pale Fire* [New York: Vintage, 1989], 55).

    Furthermore, Nabokov treasured the Russian language. In *Speak, Memory*, he mentions finding a bookstall in Cambridge which has a copy of *Dahl's Interpretive Dictionary of the Living Russian Language*. "My fear of losing or corrupting, through alien influence, the only thing I had salvaged from Russia—her language—was positively morbid and considerably more harassing than the fear I was to experience two decades later of my never being able to bring my English prose anywhere close to the level of my Russian" (*Speak, Memory*, 265). His simultaneous admiration for and distress about Russian societies is expressed in a volatile mixture of tonally incompatible adjectives, but at other times there is a coherent decoupling of what he feared and what he loved. "The history of Russia (I might, for example, declare) could be considered from two points of view . . . : first, as the evolution of the police (a curiously impersonal and detached force, sometimes working in a kind of void, sometimes helpless, and at other times outdoing the government in brutal persecution); and second, as the development of a marvelous culture" (*Speak, Memory,* 263). Nabokov was considered "un-Russian" by many prominent Russian émigré critics, because he quite openly "evinced no interest in the social, political, moral or religio-philosophical themes (and attendant artistic forms) that characterized many of the most famous works of nineteenth-century literature" (Vladimir Alexandrov, *Nabokov's Otherworld* [Princeton, N.J.: Princeton University Press, 1991], 3). However much he saw his artistic origins in the Silver Age of Russian culture (see Alexandrov, 213), he achieved full artistic being in the United States. Nabokov wanted to write for a twentieth-century audience. His experience of exile also released him from the responsibility of having to set an example for any community. He was famous for inhabiting a range of personalities, from angry professor to playful aesthete, or even classroom flirt (Stacy Schiff, *Véra,* 141). His ability to project a number of moods, from anger (tearing up a book in a lecture), to satisfaction (butterfly-hunting in the Rockies), to the emotional range of *Lolita*—reflected his sense of being exempt from the rules and censorship of any community. Nabokov's real persona was often too elusive to be scrutinized; and he might be dismissed as a member of the "literati" whose lack of self-control could be seen as simply artistic license.

29. Michael Levenson, *The Cambridge Companion to Modernism* (Cambridge: Cambridge University Press, 1999), xii: "What is most notable about the aspiration to exile is how frequently it leads, not to an escape from the community, but to a withdrawal to its interstices."

30. Gennady Barabtarlo writes that Nabokov originally planned to stage

Pnin's death in a tenth chapter of the book. Barabtarlo, *Aerial View* (New York: Peter Lang, 1993), 181.

31. Pnin's conversations with the émigrés are often truncated; he is too agnostic, or socially uncommitted. Emigrés are culturally cordoned off from mainstream America. In fact, the conditions of their experience seem different from those of their own children. The émigrés and their children live in separate universes. "Some parents brought their offspring with them—healthy, tall, indolent, difficult American children of college age, with no sense of nature, and Russian, and no interest whatsoever in their parents' backgrounds and pasts. They seemed to live at The Pines on a physical and mental plane entirely different from that of their parents: now and then passing from their own level to ours through a kind of interdimensional shimmer; responding curtly to a well-meaning Russian joke or anxious piece of advice, and then fading away again; keeping always aloof (so that one felt one had engendered a brood of elves), and preferring any Onkwedo store product, any sort of canned goods to the marvelous Russian foods provided by the Kukolnikov household at loud, long dinners on the screened porch" (*Pnin*, 118). Nabokov adds: "Russian-American life is like a mirage, very intangible and anachronistic. Parents can only occasionally exist for their children through some 'interdimensional shimmer'" (ibid.). The cultural differences seem to have created a time warp that denies coexistence on the same plane. Pnin's awkward interactions with the other Russian émigrés echo some of Nabokov's own sense of estrangement from his local Russian community. Perhaps he suffered the same crisis as Pnin. He was just a different creature from other émigrés, and perhaps his version of Russia was very different from the version of Russia that most other émigrés recalled.

32. Julia Bader, *Crystal Land: Artifice in Nabokov's English Novels* (Berkeley: University of California Press, 1973), 84.

33. Grayson discusses how Nabokov imports the symmetry of Russian linguistic structure into English—for instance, in Nabokov's use of "pairing."

34. Thomas Frosch, "Parody and Authenticity in Nabokov's *Lolita*," *Modern Critical Views* (New York: Chelsea House, 1989), 138: "His displacement of the formula from the literary to the linguistic is instructive. Indeed, both in theory and practice, he is always moving the linguistic, the stylistic, and the artificial to center-stage."

35. Sometimes his special brand of Russianness is termed "Pninian": "At times he graded, as it were, into somebody else, whom Pnin did not know by name but whom he classified, with a bright foreigner's fondness for puns as 'Twynn' (or, in Pninian, 'Tvin')" (Nabokov, *Pnin*, 149).

36. Nabokov also seemed to feel that his individual struggle with becoming fluent in English and adjusting to America was an intensely private affair; mixing with others would not speed up the process but only create a purgatorial, in-between space in which he lingered. Nabokov thought Americans very ignorant about Russians; but he remarked on how distinct he felt Russians were from the standpoint of a Russian émigré. On the other hand, he felt that all émigrés had instinctive radar for forming communities among their own: "One Russian will know another Russian from I do not know what distance. A hundred miles perhaps" (Andrew Field, *Nabokov: His Life in Part* [New York: Viking, 1977], 27). He was also prone to generalize about Russians: "Well—that's just like Russians! They can never, never, never be anywhere on time!" (Nabokov, quoted ibid., 254).

37. Despite expressing love for America, Nabokov sounds most sincere—and most vulnerable—when he asserts his sense of being tied to his Russian identity: "I think in the middle thirties we had just given up the idea of going back. But it didn't matter much because Russia was with us. We were Russia" (quoted ibid., 210). In his personal life, Nabokov was Russian: he spoke Russian at home; his closest friend was his wife, Véra; his favorite translator was his son, Dmitri. He openly expressed his sense of Russian roots: "I owe too much to the Russian language and landscape to be emotionally involved in, say, American regional literature, or Indian dances, or pumpkin pie on a spiritual plane" (Field, *Nabokov: His Life in Part*, 210). Nabokov's life-

long sense of being Russian made him, even in his beloved United States, feel bereft and exiled, and he treated the concept directly in his fiction, titling one of his stories "Exile."

38. They also appear in poems. *Pnin* contains an entire poem in Russian with translation (56).

39. *Tem bolee obidno* is the transliteration for "on top of it all, what a shame," or "all the more vexing," as Nabokov has written here. Yevgeni Borisovich Modin and Mischa Frusztajer provided some of the translations in these endnotes.

40. *Huligani* means "hooligans."

41. "Antique liberalism."

42. To understand this passage fully, one must refer to a poem included earlier in the novel (181).

43. *Chutkiy* means, literally, "joke" or "jokes."

44. Grayson, *Nabokov Translated*, 193.

45. Nabokov, *Strong Opinions*, 10.

46. Nabokov, *Speak, Memory*, 280.

47. Field, *Nabokov: His Life in Part*, 240.

48. Simon Karlinsky, ed., *Dear Bunny, Dear Volodya: The Nabokov-Wilson Letters, 1940–1971* (Berkeley: University of California Press, 2001), 31.

49. Nabokov, *Strong Opinions*, 98, 27.

50. Ibid., 124, 250, 98.

51. Michael Wood writes: "What matters, surely, is that Nabokov in the meantime had found, through his very loss, a fabulous, freaky, singing, acrobatic, unheard-of English which (probably) made even his most marvelous Russian seem poor, and therefore meant that the terrible decision of his early years in America had been right, that the second language could flower from him only at the cost of the first; had to become itself a new first language, a language to write in. Perhaps one cannot love two languages" (*The Magician's Doubts*, 5).

52. Quoted in Karlinsky, *Dear Bunny, Dear Volodya*, 120, 69.

53. Nabokov, *Strong Opinions*, 52.

54. Jane Grayson also mentions that Nabokov adds the suffix "-let" to certain words, Russifying them: in *Pnin*, "townlet" and "bunchlet"; in *Lolita*, "faunlet" (*Nabokov Translated*, 193).

55. Nabokov, *Lolita*, 11. Subsequent references to *Lolita* will be given in parentheses in the text.

56. Nabokov, *Strong Opinions*, 26.

57. Ibid., 149.

58. Karlinsky, *Dear Bunny, Dear Volodya*, 36. Nabokov never shook off his self-image as a clumsy conversationalist, despite the fact that numerous intellectuals thought him a brilliant, highly articulate one. People believed he was a phony. Gloria Fisk emphasizes the performative in Nabokov's character; commenting on a biographical exhibit, she says that it "catches the author in an act of self-creation and shows him as a product, as well as a producer, of fiction. . . . It proves that Nabokov—the master of artifice—was also an artificial man."

59. Nabokov, *Strong Opinions*, xi.

60. Beaujour, *Alien Tongues*, 98.

61. Quoted in Field, *Nabokov: His Life in Part*, 55.

62. Ibid., 12–13.

63. John Hollander, review of *Lolita*, in *Partisan Review* (Autumn 1956), 557–560.

64. Frosch, "Parody and Authenticity in Nabokov's *Lolita*," 138.

65. This is a paraphrase of a passage in Karlinsky, *Dear Bunny, Dear Volodya*, 253.

66. Ibid., 29.

67. Wood, *The Magician's Doubts*, 112.

68. Ibid., 113.

69. Lucy Maddox, *Nabokov's Novels in English* (Athens, Ga.: University of Georgia Press, 1983), 72.

70. Wood, *The Magician's Doubts*, 141, 142.

2. CHINKY WRITING

1. I use the word "language" in preference to "patois," "dialect," "pidgin," or any other conceptualized linguistic derivative. My conception of Chinglish as a language is that it is something other than mere accented English and that it requires translation to be under-

stood as English. Skeptics might say that "why-foo" and "aiya" are interpretable only by people who speak both Chinese and English.

I use the term "semiological theory" specifically to denote a body of work that has emerged in American and European scholarly circles. Ferdinand de Saussure and Charles Sanders Peirce were seminal figures in its development.

Chinglish, unlike Ebonics, has never been the subject of books. Yunte Huang, *Transpacific Displacement* (Berkeley: University of California Press, 2002), has an excellent chapter on the countermocking pidgins of Chinglish. The poets John Yau and Tan Lin use Chinglish in their work and appreciate its potential to create new poetic structures.

I am acutely aware of the Charlie Chan brand of Chinglish that most people would recognize. I am trying to distinguish Kingston's Chinglish and Chinatown Chinglish from Charlie Changlish in order to consider the larger issue of maintaining interpretive connections and harnessing Chinglish for other aesthetic purposes that might strengthen a community. If Chinglish were Changlish, it would be very limited. But it is more than that.

2. Conversations with Tan Lin about Asian American voicelessness have inspired my recharacterization of Asian American linguistic practice.

3. This happens also in reverse, as the artist Xu Bing has shown by writing characters that merely resemble true Chinese characters. He has created art exhibits based on this exercise and has won a MacArthur Award for such efforts. He inspired the designer Vivienne Tam to create a line of clothing with Chinglish characters as pattern. With a similar purpose, Chinglish writers transliterate the acoustic component of Chinese, forcing it into the written structures of English.

4. This does not mean that the ideograph should not be an appropriate locus of meaning. It is to say only that Kingston's own writing reflects a gradual dissociation from emphasizing the ideographic aspect of Chinese.

5. Anyone who has tried to buy stationery or clothes in Japan has been

bombarded by unconventional, highly unorthodox uses of English. Here are two: "Have a doggy day" (stationery) and "Come wake up in the morning father and go drowning with me" (card).

6. Ezra Pound's translations have been criticized casually as misinterpretations of Japanese as Chinese. Yunte Huang, *Transpacific Displacement*, contains a helpful chapter on Pound. But typically Pound is admired more for his efforts to understand Chinese than for the proficiency of his translations.

7. The issue of translation is too massive a theoretical subject to be treated here. See, among many other works, Lawrence Venuti, *The Scandals of Translation* (New York: Routledge, 1998).

8. Lauren Rusk, *The Life Writing of Otherness* (New York: Routledge, 2002), mentions the issue of translation but does not probe it through examples. The claim of otherness implicit in Rusk's title, and her simultaneous exclusion of actual translation, illuminate the problem of disregarding translation in literature. Such neglect produces a sense of otherness that instigates distant, iconographic reading rather than close, accurate reading.

9. For example, Brian Skelly (personal communication, Fall 2002) has detailed some cross-cultural misunderstandings with his wife, who was born in Hong Kong. Brian's wife interpreted "large eyes" as meaning "wide eyes," while Brian thought that "large" in this phrase implied horizontally long. When told to write "straight," Brian's wife thought "straight" implied that the wrist and hand should be perpendicular to each other (because Chinese writing is done with calligraphy brushes, or *maobi*, and the brush is held this way).

10. These sales rankings vacillated wildly, but I monitored the rankings every two days for a month, and the sales of *The Woman Warrior* were always several tens of thousands higher than those of the other two books, which themselves were quite far apart in this respect.

11. For a catalogue of facts about the daunting success of *The Woman Warrior*, see David Leiwei Li, *Imagining the Nation: Asian American Literature and Cultural Consent* (Stanford, Calif.: Stanford University Press, 1998), 57.

12. I use the word "translated" with playfulness. Later I will contend that there is a language, not merely an emotional quantity, to be translated in Kingston's works. This form of analysis has been overlooked in previous treatments of her writing.

13. These critiques are so numerous and so varied that, although valuable, they will not be discussed here. See the works of Patricia Chu, Jeffery Paul Chan, Cynthia Sau-Ling Wong, David Leiwei Li, and Yunte Huang for some of the most recent analyses. Writers like Frank Chin and Jeffery Chan accuse Kingston of distorting Chinese history and legends in her work. Some critics debate whether Kingston's work should be taken as an authoritative or documentary history of Chinese American culture. (Kingston cannot help the fact that her readers automatically grant her authenticity of voice, even if she claims to have had unique, not universal, Chinese American experiences.) From the Chinese American community, criticisms range from dismay at her lack of precision about Chinese American culture to anger that she allowed her work to be classified as autobiography or nonfiction. The same critics defend her as a literary artist, saying that she made bad decisions about how her work is being classified but that she has genuine talent. One writer complains about her lack of precision in translating from English to Chinese: "Kingston, for example, mistranslates the word 'ghosts.' Chinese-Americans call whites *bok gwai*, white devils, as in demons, not ghosts. Ghosts of the dead are not *gwai*, though they could be. *Gwai* are inherently unfriendly. When Chinese-Americans call a white person *bok gwai*, it is an insult. If that person is liked, the term *lo fan* is applied. A *lo fan* is a foreigner. Kingston uses the word 'ghost' in the popular white Christian sense of the word, not Chinese-American. The difference between *lo fan* and *bok gwai* is as obvious to any Chinese-American as the difference between 'mister' and 'asshole.' Of course, it would be difficult to subtitle 'memoirs of a girlhood among assholes'" (Jeffery Paul Chan, "The Mysterious West," letter to the editor, *New York Review of Books,* April 28, 1977). Many critics observe that she appropriates fables and stories to speak to her own

personal experience. After discussing *Eighteen Songs,* Debra Shostak writes: "Kingston picks up on the captive's linguistic isolation, but she alters the experience to speak to her own history" (Shostak, "Maxine Hong Kingston's Fake Books," in Laura E. Skandera-Trombley, ed., *Critical Essays on Maxine Hong Kingston* [New York: Hall, 1998], 60).

Kingston's alterations of myths and legends have provoked dissension and disagreement among many Chinese American critics. There has been a hue and cry over the classification of her work as nonfiction, because some Asian American artists fear that Kingston is selling out. For example, Asian American critics fear that her work is being viewed as simply ethnic biography, rather than as a work of art. Jeffery Paul Chan believes that "a white reading public will rave over ethnic biography while ignoring a Chinese-American's literary art." He fears that there will be a widespread phenomenon where "Chinese-Americans have no authority over the language and culture that expresses our sensibility best—at the same time . . . assuring assimilation" ("The Mysterious West," 85). The kind of assimilation that Chan fears is invisibility.

14. Li, *Imagining the Nation,* 56.
15. Yunte Huang alludes to the distinction that John Guillory makes between "linguistic" and "symbolic capital" to communicate the complicated process of determining standards for canonization—a useful allusion that readers should take as a guide when they make judgments about how to position a book (see Guillory, *Cultural Capital: The Problem of Literary Canon Formation* [Chicago: University of Chicago Press, 1993]). But Huang's analysis of Kingston is too distant, lingering on her "politics" and asserting that she engages in a "positivistic" approach in pursuit of American identity (Huang, *Transpacific Displacement,* 159).
16. Huang, *Transpacific Displacement,* 140. The entire book, which devotes a chapter to Kingston, is helpful and interesting.
17. In critiquing John Yau's poem "Genghis Khan, Private Eye," which is in the series, Huang writes: "Sound and spelling approximations be-

tween grab and grub, sum and some, sum and sub, treat and feet, floor and fours, chow lane and chow mein, fist and first are all characteristic of the kind of pidginization by which Oriental languages have been portrayed in American racist literature. It may recall, for instance, Charlie Chan's 'Allight, boss'" (Huang, *Transpacific Displacement,* 136).

18. Huang quotes Lin Yutang: "I think pidgin a glorious language. It has tremendous possibilities" (ibid., 126).

19. Ibid., 132.

20. Ibid., 159.

21. Maxine Hong Kingston, Interview with Paula Rabinowitz, 1986, in Paul Skenazy and Tera Martin, eds., *Conversations with Maxine Hong Kingston* (Oxford, Miss.: University Press of Mississippi, 1998).

22. Ibid., 75.

23. On the term *différance,* see Jacques Derrida, *Of Grammatology,* trans. Gayatri Chakravorty Spivak (Baltimore: Johns Hopkins University Press, 1998; orig. French edition, 1967).

24. Maxine Hong Kingston, *China Men* (New York: Vintage, 1977), 277.

25. Ibid., 209.

26. Huang, *Transpacific Displacement,* 116.

27. Kingston, *China Men,* 280.

28. Sometimes varieties of Asian-influenced English provoke negative reactions. For example, Lois Ann Yamanaka's pidgin has often been construed as negatively portraying wannabe haole Hawaiian culture.

29. The group I Was Born with Two Tongues, on a spoken-word CD entitled *Broken Speak* (AsianImprov, 2002), plays with uncool and cool Asian-glishes.

30. See Patricia Chu, *Assimilating Asians* (Durham, N.C.: Duke University Press, 2000).

31. Chinese women do not change their names upon marriage. Thus, the evidence of migration takes both the form of the mixture of names as well as the American custom of adopting the husband's surname.

32. Interview with Kay Bonetti, 1984, in Skenazy and Martin, *Conversations with Maxine Hong Kingston.*

33. Ibid., 17.

34. Ibid., 207.

35. In an interview with Michele Janette (*Transition,* 6, no. 3 [Fall 1996], 156), Kingston admits feeling self-conscious about the project of writing Chinglish: "One writer who gave me a lot of permission was Nabokov—because he could do bilingual and trilingual puns, and I thought, 'OK, then I can do it too,' and of course all the time I'm thinking of how most English readers don't know Chinese, and then I think, 'Oh, just do it.'"

36. Ibid., 207.

37. Ibid., 101.

38. Ibid., 78.

39. Ibid., 147.

40. Ibid., 149.

41. It's also useful to note that Kingston's *China Men* is a literal translation from the Chinese. In Chinese, there are no adjectival forms for countries. For instance, the phrases "Italian man," "Englishman," and "American man" would be translated literally from the Chinese as "Italy man," "England man," and "America man."

42. Skenazy and Martin, *Conversations with Maxine Hong Kingston,* 112.

43. Many great authors do this, but Kingston has been excoriated for it, perhaps because the stakes are so high in the formation of Asian American identity.

44. This theory is so famous that I haven't mapped it out here (see Derrida, *Of Grammatology*). But the introduction of the "a" demonstrates the inevitable association, the necessary relationship, of speech and writing in the generation of meaning.

45. Jacques Derrida and C. S. Peirce opened the world to a greater variety of signification than existed in the study of literature and philosophy.

46. It would be possible to extend this argument for several pages, but in the interests of focusing on Kingston I will limit the discussion to this brief and crude treatment of the matter.

47. Ming Gu, "Reconceptualizing the Linguistic Divide," *Comparative Literature Studies,* 37, no. 2 (2000), 101–124. Gu offers a descriptive picture

of the limitations of the pictograph. His insightful thinking stimulated my current ideas about Chinglish.

48. Ibid.

49. Ibid.

50. If you don't want to engage in the complexity of Gu's argument, see zhongwen.com and follow the link, "Are [Chinese] characters pictures?"

51. Archeologist Cherra Wyllie led me to conclude that "logograph" is more appropriate than "ideograph." Frankly, I am not sure what the most appropriate term might be.

52. Maxine Hong Kingston, *The Woman Warrior* (New York: Vintage, 1989), 23.

53. Ibid., 20.

54. Ibid., 35.

55. Ibid., 57.

56. Ibid., 15.

57. Kingston, *China Men*, 20. There's also mention of the ideograph on page 78.

58. Ibid., 37.

59. Of course, finding those occasions where the character's design reflects its meaning is an exercise in itself that many scholars have taken on—especially under the assumption that this is not the backbone upon which Chinese is built. But Kingston doesn't suggest that Chinese is constructed any other way but through ideographic formation.

60. Kingston, *China Men*, 29.

61. I am referring to the film *A Beautiful Mind*, in which mathematician John Nash, diagnosed with schizophrenia, sees equations and codes in the world compulsively.

62. Skenazy and Martin, *Conversations with Maxine Hong Kingston*, 248.

63. *China Men* certainly illustrated progress in incorporating Chinglish, but was by no means free of the ideographic obsession so present in *The Woman Warrior*.

64. Kingston, *China Men*, 241.

65. I am well aware of the ongoing debates about the miscategorization of the book as autobiography.

66. Kingston, *The Woman Warrior,* 53.

67. Tan Lin and King-Kok Cheung are two, but there are countless other examples.

68. We don't have any hesitation critiquing a modernist writer for misusing the English language. It is political correctness, perhaps, that assumes Kingston cannot bear the weight of such criticism.

69. Kingston, *The Woman Warrior,* 165.

70. Countless articles deal with silence. One of the more thorough is King-Kok Cheung, "Articulate Silences," in Cheung, *Articulate Silences: Hisaye Yamamoto, Maxine Hong Kingston, Joy Kagawa* (Ithaca, N.Y.: Cornell University Press, 1993).

71. After 1949, the Communist government set up a committee to study Chinese romanization. The transcription system known as Hanyu Pinyin Fang'an was established in 1958. For many years, Hanyu Pinyin was used mainly to replace Zhuyin Fuhao as a pronunciation guide in elementary schools and in dictionaries. In the meantime, Wade-Giles continued to be used in English-language publications until 1979, when the International for Standardization Organization passed a resolution adopting Hanyu Pinyin as the international standard for Chinese romanization. See www.whiteclouds.com/iclc/cliej/cl4ao.htm.

72. Gilles Deleuze, "He Stuttered," in Deleuze, *Essays Critical and Clinical,* trans. Daniel W. Smith and Michael A. Greco (Minneapolis: University of Minnesota Press, 1997), 108.

73. Interview with Paula Rabinowitz, in Skenazy and Martin, *Conversations with Maxine Hong Kingston,* 71.

74. Interview with Marilyn Chin, ibid., 100.

75. Kingston, *China Men,* 77. Subsequent references to *China Men* will be given in parentheses in the text.

76. I'm thinking here of the Johnny Weissmuller variety, not of Disney's cartoon version.

77. Deleuze, "He Stuttered," 108.

78. Coolie Ranx, Interview with Andrew Magenheim, Teenvoice.com, October 1999.

79. Michael North, *The Dialect of Modernism* (New York: Oxford University Press, 1998).

80. For a contrasting view on the tone of the protagonist, see Li, *Imagining the Nation,* 72: "His self-conscious muttering 'in Chinatown language' thus correlates the loss of a shared linguistic medium with the loss of the immigrant and native-born Asian American connection, losses that were largely the result of exclusion-era social and educational policies."

81. Louis Chu, *Eat a Bowl of Tea* (New York: Lyle Stuart, 1961).

82. Ibid., 87.

83. Ibid., 112.

84. Skenazy and Martin, *Conversations with Maxine Hong Kingston,* 79.

85. Maxine Hong Kingston, *Tripmaster Monkey* (New York: Vintage, 1983), 10. Subsequent references to this work will be given in parentheses in the text.

86. In Chinese culture, humiliation is translated as "losing face."

87. Centuries ago, a well-loved Chinese poet, frightened of government officials, committed suicide. To honor him, villagers threw rice into the river to feed him in the afterlife. Discovering that the rice was becoming a kind of fish food, they wrapped the rice in lotus leaves so it would reach the poet safely.

88. My father used to goad me into finishing my rice by asserting that eating all of one's rice is a way of respecting the farmers who grew it.

89. Interview in Skenazy and Martin, *Conversations with Maxine Hong Kingston,* 61.

90. Skenazy and Martin, *Conversations with Maxine Hong Kingston,* 151.

91. Ibid., 31 (italics added).

92. Ibid., 144.

93. Ibid., 74.

94. Ibid., 39.

95. Ibid., 15.

96. Ibid., 25.

97. Ibid.

98. Ibid., 72.

3. THE POLITICS OF DESIGN

1. On May 13, 2003, Roy also invoked another term: "imperialist democracy." She suggested, "Bring to a boil, add oil, then bomb." Address sponsored by the Center for Economic and Social Rights, delivered at Riverside Church in New York City. See www.cesr.org/roy/royspeech.htm.

2. I hesitate to use "the good" here, which might suggest all sorts of metaphysical stuff I can't address at this juncture.

3. See narmada.org/gcg/gcg.html.

4. Iris Murdoch, *The Sovereignty of Good* (London: Anchor, 1979), 31, 33.

5. Ibid., 5.

6. Arundhati Roy, *The God of Small Things* (New York: Harper Perennial, 1997), 117. The phrase "No Locusts Stand I" appears repeatedly in the novel with regard to the family business; "fishswimming sense" is from page 30. Subsequent references to this work will appear in parentheses in the text.

7. Roy has been interviewed in several publications about her efforts to stop the government from building a dam that would dislocate millions of people (see www.umiacs.umd.edu/users/sawweb/sawnet/arundhati.html). Her essay "The Ladies Have Feelings, So Should We Leave It to the Experts?" (in Roy, *Power Politics,* 2nd ed. [Cambridge, Mass.: South End Press, 2001]) details the oppressive effects of dam building in India, focusing especially on the construction of the Sardar Sarovar Dam.

8. Whereas Rushdie advocates that we move toward a kind of "transnationalism," Roy is extremely nationalistic, particularly with regard to the working and Untouchable class—sometimes even contentiously so. Her novel *The God of Small Things* is one of her least openly political works. Among her other writings are a searing condemnation of nuclear weapons, a cry of protest against the movie *Bandit*

Queen, and a screenplay for *Electric Moon* (which, she declared, lacked the "anarchical quality" she was trying to write into it when it was translated to film). Paradoxically, it is her novel that has sparked the greatest controversy, and not these other works, which bred a small cult following that was nowhere near as large as the audience she possesses now.

9. Roy, *Power Politics,* 11.

10. Arundhati Roy, quoted at website.lineone.net/~jon.simmons/roy/tgost2.htm.

11. Arundhati Roy, quoted at rediff.com/news/apr/05roy2.htm.

12. Quoted in Tamara Straus, "No Small Thing: Arundhati Roy's Cost of Living," *In These Times* (Institute for Public Affairs, Chicago), 24, no. 1 (December 12, 1999). See www.inthesetimes.com.

13. Bill McKibben, "The Enigma of Kerala," *Doubletake* (1995), 5.

14. Ibid., 10.

15. Arundhati Roy, quoted in Maya Jaggi, "An Unsuitable Girl," *Electronic Mail and Guardian,* chico.mweb.co.za/mg/books/aug97/13aug-roy.htm.

16. Arundhati Roy, quoted in R. Madhavan Nair, "In Solidarity," *Frontline* (India), 16, no. 3 (January 30–February 12, 1999), online at flonnet.com/fl1603/16030810.htm.

17. See Gunther Kress, *Early Spelling* (New York: Routledge, 2000), an illuminating collection of thoughts on children's spelling. Kress makes a distinction between accurate spelling and correct spelling.

18. James Phillips, "Peircean Reflections on Psychotic Discourse," in C. S. Peirce, *Semiotics and Psychoanalysis,* ed. John Muller and Joseph Brent (Baltimore: Johns Hopkins University Press, 2000), provided the path to my thoughts here. Phillips cites Peirce as follows: "It is sufficient to say that there is no element whatever of man's consciousness which has not something corresponding to it in the word; the reason is obvious. It is that the word or sign which man uses is the man himself. For, as the fact that every thought is a sign, taken in conjunction with the fact that life is a train of thought, proves that man is a sign; so, that every thought is an *external sign,* proves that man is an external sign. That is to say, the man and the

external sign are identical, in the same *sense* in which the words *homo* and 'man' are *identical*. Thus my language is the sum total of myself; for the man is the thought" (17).

19. Arundhati Roy, quoted at website.lineone.net/~jon.simmons/roy/tgost4.htm.

20. Ludwig Wittgenstein, *Philosophical Investigations*, 3rd ed., trans. G. E. M. Anscombe (New York: Prentice Hall, 1999), 80e.

21. Of course, there are works (such as Elaine Scarry, *Dreaming by the Book*) which emphasize the reading process as physical. But I merely assert that the physical process is perhaps more self-conscious when language becomes unwieldy and we seem to rely on other senses to source information.

22. Ludwig Wittgenstein, *Blue and Brown Books* (New York: Harper-Collins, 1986), 17.

23. Roy was a student at the Delhi School of Architecture for several years, during which she also moonlighted as an architect's artist. She married a fellow student (an American) and left with him to live in Goa and sell cakes on a beach.

24. Wittgenstein, *Philosophical Investigations*, 197.

25. Martin Heidegger, *On the Way to Language,* trans. Peter D. Hertz (New York: Harper and Row, 1971), 119.

26. Gayatri Spivak, "The Burden of English," in Carol A. Breckenridge and Peter van der Veer, eds., *Orientalism and the Postcolonial Predicament: Perspectives on South Asia* (Philadelphia: University of Pennsylvania Press, 1993).

27. Anita Desai, *Clear Light of Day* (New York: Mariner, 2000).

28. Arundhati Roy, "The End of Imagination." See disarm.igc.org/oldwebpages/ROY.html.

29. See www.geocities.com/SoHo/CoffeeHouse/7417/roy/ar_onnd.htm.

30. I address this in a passage about the children's discomfort with Miss Mitten, a teacher who is disturbed by their backward-written English and who says they have "Satan in their eyes."

31. Steven Pinker, *The Language Instinct: How the Mind Creates Language* (New York: Perennial, 2000).

32. Judith Butler, *Excitable Speech* (New York: Routledge, 2001), 2. This

beautifully theorized book about language, and language that hurts, is underrepresented in my discussion here. But I wanted to show that the kinds of questions we face about injurious language in the United States are not immediately translatable as useful in interpreting postcolonial works.

33. Elaine Scarry, *The Body in Pain* (New York: Oxford University Press, 1984), 53.

34. Butler, *Excitable Speech,* 2.

35. Ibid., 28.

36. Heidegger, *On the Way to Language,* 130–131.

37. Jean-Jacques Rousseau's *Essai sur l'origine des langues* (Essay on the Origin of Language) includes an account of a man using metaphor to describe his encounter with a bear.

38. David Crystal, *Cambridge Encyclopedia of the English Language* (Cambridge: Cambridge University Press, 1995; paperback ed. 1997), 360.

39. Raja Rao, quoted ibid.

40. Braj B. Kachru, *The Indianization of English: The English Language in India* (Delhi: Oxford University Press, 1983).

41. At times, Roy prods her readers to comprehension of her Indian words, like the idea that "kutty" signifies "small," but often she allows her Indian words to provide the reader merely with the sounds of Malayalam. Sometimes this results in misinterpretation by critics. For instance, Alice Truax committed an obvious gaffe when she referred, in the *New York Times Book Review,* to the "withering" of the "Kochamma family"—mistaking "Kochamma" for a surname. This kind of slip is a reminder that words have different arrangements in various languages, and that even in a work written mostly in English we cannot trust our English-derived linguistic instincts to give us meaning.

42. Arundhati Roy, interview with Reena Jana, Salon.com (September 30, 1997). See www.salon.com/sept97/00roy2.html.

43. Arundhati Roy, quoted at website.lineone.net/~jon.simmons/roy/tgost6.htm.

44. Arundhati Roy, quoted at website.lineone.net/~jon.simmons/roy/tgost2.htm.

4. "The Shit That's Other"

1. Junot Díaz, interview with Evelyn Ch'ien, July 26, 2002.

2. Early editions of Díaz's story collection *Drown* included a glossary, but current editions do not.

3. Junot Díaz, interview with Evelyn Ch'ien, July 26, 2002.

4. Junot Díaz, interview with Silvio Torres-Saillant and Diógenes Céspedes, "Fiction Is the Poor Man's Cinema," *Callaloo*, 23, no. 1 (Winter 2000). I would like to thank Ginger Thornton for providing me with a transcript of the interview.

5. Ibid.

6. Junot Díaz, *Drown* (New York: Riverhead, 1997; orig. pub. 1996). Idem, "The Sun, the Moon and the Stars," *The Beacon Best of 1999* (Boston: Beacon, 1999). Idem, "The Brief Wondrous Life of Oscar Wao," *New Yorker* (December 25, 2000). Subsequent references to these works will be given in parentheses in the text.

7. Junot Díaz, interview with Evelyn Ch'ien, July 26, 2002.

8. Here, Spanish words are italicized because they are written words or proper names, but not because they are Spanish.

9. Junot Díaz, interview with Michael O. Collazo, Part 1, *Grafico*. See jan.ucc.nau.edu/~jdb36/diazinterviews.html.

10. Lawrence Venuti, *The Scandals of Translation* (New York: Routledge, 1998), 11. Venuti's book, which addresses issues of professionalism in translation, is provocative but takes a very different approach from the one I use here.

11. Ibid., 31.

12. Lahiri's refined prose, in her collection of short stories *Interpreter of Maladies*, is a counterpoint to the undecorated prose of Díaz.

"I translate, therefore I am": Jhumpa Lahiri, "To Heaven without Dying," *Feed* (July 24, 2000), feedmag.com. See www.umiacs.umd. edu/users/sawweb/sawnet/books/jhumpa_lahiri.html. The essay deals with translating South Asian culture into English. Lahiri writes: "Rendering an Indian landscape into English . . . is one thing. Dialogue is wholly another. Because Bengali is essentially a spoken language for me, because it occupies such an aural presence in my mind, forcing my Bengali characters to speak a tongue they either can't or wouldn't speak in a given scene is one of my most daunting challenges. It is a disorienting and at times highly dissatisfying thing to do. I must abandon a certain sense of verisimilitude in the process, a certain fidelity. It is something of a betrayal" (4). Lahiri does acknowledge—in common with Díaz—the impossibility of "real" translation. Later in the essay, she writes: "In my dictionary, the biblical definition of 'translate' is 'to convey to heaven without death.' I am struck by the extent to which this decidedly Western, non-secular definition sheds light on my own personal background of Eastern origin. For in my observation, translation is not only a finite linguistic act but also an ongoing cultural one. It is the continuous struggle, on my parents' behalf, to preserve what it means to them to be first and forever Indian" (5). Lahiri's compromise here is surprising and contrasts sharply with Díaz's statements. I expected her to discuss the impossibility of translation—and how illuminating the biblical definition is in this respect—rather than confirm its reality.

13. Junot Díaz, interview with Terri Lynn Platt, *Meridian,* 7 (Spring 2001).

14. This is not a new idea. See Jean-Jacques Rousseau, *On the Origin of Language* [Essai sur l'origine des langues], trans. John Moran (Chicago: University of Chicago Press, 1986), 16: "Anyone who studies the history and progress of the tongues will see that the more the words become monotonous, the more the consonants multiply; that, as accents fall into disuse and quantities are neutralized, they are replaced by grammatical combinations and new articulations. But only the pressure of time brings these changes about. To the degree that needs multiply, that affairs become complicated, that light is shed, language changes its character. It becomes more regular and less passionate. It substitutes ideas for feelings. It no longer speaks to the heart but to reason. Similarly, accent diminishes, articulation increases. Language becomes more exact and clearer, but more prolix, duller and colder. This progression seems to me entirely natural."

15. Díaz, interview with Terri Lynn Platt. Still, on a personal level, Díaz feels attached enough to English to take *Drown*'s epigraph from Gustavo Pérez Firmat: "The fact that I am writing to you in English already falsifies what I wanted to tell you. My subject: how to explain to you that I don't belong to English, though I belong nowhere else."

16. Díaz, interview with Terri Lynn Platt.

17. Arundhati Roy says something very similar ("I like the way it looks on the page"). See Chapter 3.

18. Díaz, interview with Terri Lynn Platt.

19. Ibid.

20. Ibid.

21. See Russell Potter, *Spectacular Vernaculars* (Binghamton, N.Y.: SUNY Press, 1995), 57–58: "On the one hand there are hegemonic vernaculars, such as 'Received Standard English' (the term that postcolonial critics use to highlight the arbitrary status of the privileged 'standard' dialect of English); posed against them, appropriating and subverting their claims to 'standard-ness,' are what I would call resistance vernaculars, since even to speak these vernaculars is in a crucial sense to make inroads against the established power-lines of speech." In his brilliant, fun book, Potter writes historically and socially about the positioning of hip-hop vernaculars.

22. My students—some from Edison, New Jersey (Díaz's hometown)—used these words to express their enthusiasm for Díaz's work. Some were Latinos and Latinas; some weren't.

23. Junot Díaz, interview with Pablo Peschiera, *Gulf Coast* (University of Houston), May 2002.

24. Bert Wang, "Asian for the Man," *Yellow Peril* (CD, 2000).

25. Junot Díaz, interview with Evelyn Ch'ien, July 26, 2002.

26. Ibid.

27. Junot Díaz, quoted in Maximo Zeledón, "Dominican Dominion: An Interview with Junot Díaz," *Frontera Magazine* (1998), fronteramag.com. See jan.ucc.nau.edu/~jdb36/diazinterviews.html.

28. Henry Miller, *Tropic of Cancer* (New York: Signet, 1995), 24.

29. The appropriation of rap by nonminority singers such as Eminem points to attitudes that class is superseding race as a way of being that feels on the margin.

30. DMX, Wu Tang Clan, and Public Enemy, for example, have their own beats.

31. One critic advised me not to make too clear a distinction between my writers as eye people or ear people, since some are clearly both. In Chapter 2, I show that Chinglish can be a visual or an aural phenomenon (Vivienne Tam versus Wittman Ah Sing), and that even within weird Englishes care has to be taken not to overemphasize one sensibility. In Díaz's work, however, because Spanish uses roman letters, it may be redundant to focus on its visual elements.

32. Junot Díaz, interview with Evelyn Ch'ien, July 26, 2002.

33. Ibid.

34. Ibid.

35. Miller, *Tropic of Cancer*, 80.

36. Bomfunk MCs and Ice Cube (among other groups) have said this.

37. Nicholas Lezard, article in *The Guardian,* July 10, 1997, feature page.

38. Díaz was born in Santo Domingo, Dominican Republic, the third child of five. His parents were from farming communities in the country and migrated to the city to find work. His father became a cobbler and later joined the military, and his mother worked in a chocolate factory. Díaz says that, in hindsight, his childhood experiences seem like "science fiction" because of the immense amount of suffering within the community, even though he didn't know of a life outside. He still wakes up with memories whose truth he can't believe, and says his whole family suffers from post-traumatic stress disorder: "I plan my day around meals" (quoted in article by Candida Crewe, *The Times,* November 23, 1996).

39. Junot Díaz, interview with Alexandra Lange, "Speaking in Tongues," *New York Magazine.*

40. Junot Díaz, interview with Evelyn Ch'ien, July 26, 2002.

41. Díaz, quoted in David Stanton, "Junot Díaz: On Home Ground," *Poets and Writers,* 26, no. 4 (August 1998).

42. Quoted in Zeledón, "Dominican Dominion: An Interview with Junot Díaz."

43. Junot Díaz, interview with Michael O. Collazo.

44. Junot Díaz, interview with Evelyn Ch'ien, July 26, 2002.

45. Ibid.

46. Ibid.

47. Jürgen Habermas, "On Leveling the Genre Distinction between Philosophy and Literature," in Habermas, *The Philosophical Discourse of Modernity*, trans. Frederick G. Lawrence (Cambridge, Mass.: MIT Press, 1987).

5. Losing Our English, Losing Our Language

1. Derek Walcott, "The Antilles: Fragments of Epic Memory," Nobel Lecture (1992). See www.nobel.se/literature/laureates/1992/walcott-lecture.html.

2. The best theory brings hope into the discursive zone and subjects acts of evil to linguistic control, recasting such events as September 11, 2001, colonialism over the decades, and other seemingly unnarrativizable acts of cruelty into discursive entities. If philosophy is "clean-up," then maybe it is required to revive humanity after an occurrence of evil. Narrative brings a dark vision of humanity into the discursive zone. (What did Conrad's phrase "The horror! The horror!" offer us, but a way to understand the evil of colonialism?) Evil is in the sentences we create; it is conceptual. Without it, we have the black hole of unhappiness and violence without a name or a shape. Sentences give a shape, an identity, to what might be random disasters, and also provide us with the possibility of human participation. The positive side of theory is that it contains the possibility of hope: theorists envision ever-evolving notions of what should be. Theory—in the most positive self-reflexive sense—can explain human behaviors and build a wall between the past and present, thus preventing recurrences of evil.

3. Homi Bhabha, *The Location of Culture* (New York: Routledge, 1994), 1.

4. Ibid.

5. Ibid., 228.

6. Richard Rorty, seminar in Modern Studies, University of Virginia, Fall 1995.

7. Jayne Cortez and the Firespitters, "They Want the Oil," *Women in E Motion* (CD, 1992).

8. Nair describes the language of postcolonialism as so abstract and indifferent that it is inevitably doomed to disintegrate in our discourse. "Put it this way: postcoloniality is a condition in which the memory of colonization ensures that nothing in the presently inherited structures of action and speech can be taken at face value. Being postcolonial means being forced to read ironically—always." Rukmini Nair, *Lying on the Postcolonial Couch: The Idea of Indifference* (Minneapolis: University of Minnesota Press, 2002), 245.

9. Again, to cite the insightful Nair: "Always, always, the language of the innermost recesses of the postcolonial chamber, the sanctum sanctorum of institutional power, is a language of loss. Writing about the manifestations of indifference as rhetoric in a temporarily unstable postcolonial context troubled by vague forebodings of amnesia has revealed to us several times over how blatantly guilt from a colonial inheritance sticks to all privileged paper pushers, not least the clerks of academia, cool analysts of crisis. As I write I obviously manufacture the very material of indifference, designed to destroy, which I seek to deconstruct. Indifference—the essence of terror, inhumanity, antimemory" (ibid., xxxi).

10. Bhabha, *The Location of Culture,* 51.

11. Gayatri Chakravorty Spivak, *A Critique of Postcolonial Reason* (Cambridge, Mass.: Harvard University Press, 2002).

12. Bhabha, *The Location of Culture,* 6.

13. Ibid., 140.

14. Spivak, *A Critique of Postcolonial Reason,* 164.

15. Alfred Lopez, *Posts and Pasts* (Binghamton, N.Y.: SUNY Press, 2000), 22.

16. Ibid., 6.

17. Ibid., 7.

18. Rushdie was born in India, two months before India's first day of independence, and shared his boyhood with three younger sisters. His father, Anis Rushdie, held a degree from Cambridge; his wealthy Muslim family surroundings, the Windsor Villa, symbolized his link to an Anglicized Bombay: "Down below, off Warden Road, were the shops: Chimalker's Toyshop, Reader's Paradise, and the confectioners Bombelli's, with their delectable One Yard of Chocolates. There was also the Breach Candy Swimming Club, even after Independence a segregated hideaway for Brits, 'where pink people could swim in a pool the shape of British India without fear of rubbing up against a black skin'" (Rushdie, quoted in Ian Hamilton, "The First Life of Salman Rushdie," *New Yorker* [December 25, 1995–January 1, 1996], 90). He attended the Cathedral and John Connon School, where Christian practices were observed even though the school was, according to Rushdie, only about 2 percent Christian. He confesses that the words of the Lord's Prayer didn't go very deep: "I didn't know what 'World without end' meant at all" (quoted ibid., 93). Sameen, the eldest of his sisters, says that her studious, law-abiding older brother was "every parent's dreamchild" (ibid.).

The young Rushdie read both popular and classical literature and went to the Bombay talkies to see many Bollywood productions. He left for Rugby when he was thirteen with a sense of optimism: "It felt as exciting as any voyage beyond rainbows" (ibid.). Unfortunately, the excitement turned into disillusionment rather quickly. Rushdie was repeatedly called a "wog" by his schoolmates, and in a Mock General Debate about tightening immigration laws he was told that he was a "peculiar brownish color" (ibid.). Periodically his essays were torn up, and his Indian-accented English was the butt of jokes (ibid.). Nevertheless he stayed in England, which suggests that the racist environment did not turn him entirely away from British culture. He is said to have been desperate to return to India. But his parents had moved to England and his father insisted he go to Cambridge, which he attended from 1965 to 1968 and where he read history at King's College. During these years, Rushdie discovered an interest in acting and theater, which offered a liberating bohemian atmosphere.

After graduating, Rushdie was encouraged by his parents to move to Karachi, where his father planned for him to take over the business of running a towel factory. He refused, and worked at a Pakistani television service instead. After a play he wrote for the service—*The Zoo Story*—was heavily censored, Rushdie decided to return to England and live, together with his sister Sameen, in a house in Fulham. Return to England seemed to mark his first literary attempts and a greater emotional investment in a country that had disappointed him. He began his first novel, *The Book of the Pir,* and appeared periodically as an actor in the productions of Oval House in Kennington. He worked at a small advertising agency, Sharp McManus, and later left to finish his novel, which he couldn't persuade an agent to represent. He then worked at Ogilvy and Mather as a copywriter. Rushdie's two marriages were to non-Indians who were quite distant from South Asian culture. Despite his Anglicized exterior, Rushdie still seemed to think of India with a strong sense of emotional attachment.

Yet Indian culture was not so distant physically in London; the immigrant population formed an India inside the city. In *Imaginary Homelands: Essays and Criticism, 1981–1991* (London: Granta Books, 1991), Rushdie writes: "Britain is now two entirely different worlds, and the one you inhabit is determined by the color of your skin" (102). Rushdie's assertion implies a distinction between geographic separation and exile: exile is not simply a state of struggling in a physical space but a way of relating to physical space as a *world.* Space can be appropriated as an area of ethnic contestation, or it can be shared. For Rushdie, a split subjectivity is the result of this unnecessary contestation. He observes this in the area of assimilation: the unity of subjectivity is denied because real assimilation is not permitted in England: "The phrase that really gets me angry is this thing about being 'more English than the English.' It is used as if it should be offensive. I point out to these people that if there was an English person living in India who adopted Indian dress, who had learnt to speak Urdu or Hindi or Bengali fluently without an accent, nobody would accuse him of having lost his culture. They would be flattered and pleased that the language had been acquired so efficiently. And they would see it as a compliment to themselves. But they wouldn't accuse him of having betrayed his origins" (Hamilton, "The First Life of Salman Rushdie," 102).

The issue of betrayal is one that Roy and Díaz encountered when they became famous writers in English. In Rushdie's case, the environment of racism and the divide between Indians and English motivated his participation in projects creating jobs for Bangladeshi immigrants in 1977. It also made him more conscious of the power of perception. Hamilton writes that even in England his "'writing self' was somewhere else—in India" ("The First Life of Salman Rushdie," 102). Rushdie's description of migrancy prefigures his own later sense of exile: "To migrate is certainly to lose language and home, to be defined by others, to become invisible or, even worse, a target; it is to experience deep changes and wrenches in the soul. But the migrant is not simply transformed by his act; he also transforms his new world. Migrants may well become mutants, but it is out of such hybridization that newness can emerge" (*Imaginary Homelands,* 210). Migration, in fact, may or may not lead to exile. Exile means losing not simply a language but a more complicated set of feelings, accompanied by the fixation on the phenomenon of losing language and using it to create a new home. But the seeds of Rushdie's exile are planted by his migration from India to England. He writes: "The Indian writer, looking back at India, does so through guilt-tinted spectacles (I am of course, once more, talking about myself. I am speaking now of those of us who emigrated . . . and I suspect that there are times when the move seems wrong to us all, when we seem, to ourselves, post-lapsarian men and women. We are Hindus who have crossed the black water; we are Muslims who eat pork. . . . Our identity is at once plural and partial" (*Imaginary Homelands,* 15). For

Rushdie, the first experience of exile motivated him to understand and probe the history of colonialism and the existence of internal exile among the Indian population in England. This prepared him for his second phase of exile—a condition that made him more aware of the unbreakable bonds between words and their meanings. This increased his appetite for playing with multiple languages, but it also made him less naive about the power of language and its political attachments.

19. Bhabha, *The Location of Culture,* 226.

20. Salman Rushdie, *The Ground beneath Her Feet* (New York: Henry Holt, 1999), 6. Subsequent references to this work will be given in parentheses in the text.

21. Here is the fatwa, as issued by the Ayatollah Khomeini: "I inform all zealous Muslims of the world that the author of the book entitled *The Satanic Verses*—which has been compiled, printed, and published in opposition to Islam, the Prophet, and the Qur'an—and all those involved in its publication who were aware of its content, are sentenced to death. I call on all zealous Muslims to execute them quickly wherever they may be found, so that no one else will dare to insult the Muslim sanctities. God willing, whoever is killed on this path is a martyr" (Hamilton, "The First Life of Salman Rushdie," 113). The fatwa is viewed as a symbol of hatred and censorship, as well as a symbol of passionate religious faith. It depends whom you ask. Nevertheless, the literary worlds Rushdie created have already outlived the fatwa, lifted in 1995. Rushdie is an outsider to a culture he writes about, and the fatwa confirmed this. He experienced the consequences of writing from a naive perspective about another community's reality. He writes, "The use of fiction was a way of creating the sort of distance from actuality that I felt would prevent offence from being taken. I was wrong" (*Imaginary Homelands,* 409). Rushdie is still puzzled about what he intended to write and what was interpreted: "*He did it on purpose* is one of the strangest accusations ever leveled at a writer. Of course I did it on purpose. The question is, and it is what I have tried to answer: what is the 'it' that I

did? What I did not do was conspire against Islam; or write—after years and years of anti-racist work and writing—a text of incitement to racial hatred; or anything of the sort. My golem, my false Other, may be capable of such deeds, but I am not" (ibid., 410).

Rushdie's appropriation of a religious history must be susceptible to outside criticism; his work must be judged according to how it interacts with the religious histories that it wants to debunk, or simply mock. Rushdie's urban sensibility had its own limited view of reality: the city. His failure to move outside the circles of cosmopolitanism into the inner chambers of religious provincialism composed, in part, the source of his troubles. A strong argument against Rushdie came, surprisingly, from a non-Muslim. Because the fatwa brought Rushdie fame that he made no effort to shun, some critics believed him to be an opportunist who desired to write a book that would provoke Muslim attention. Roald Dahl writes: "With all that has been written and spoken about the Rushdie affair, I have not yet heard any non-Muslim voices raised in criticism of the writer himself. On the contrary, he appears to be regarded as some sort of hero, certainly among his fellow writers and the Society of Authors, of which I am a member. To my mind, he is a dangerous opportunist" (Dahl, letter to the editor, *Daily News,* March 1, 1989). Dahl implies that Rushdie committed an act of spiritually inappropriate behavior. But did Rushdie's work fall below a standard of spiritual seriousness that literature, in Dahl's eyes, should adhere to? Rushdie's work has often been accused of being too "sensational" or humorous to be a part of the corpus of high literature. But Dahl seems to mean something else: his implication is that an aesthetic act is opposed to opportunism. But significantly—and I believe this is a serious oversight on his part—he does not consider Rushdie's simple, and not necessarily willful, absence of knowledge.

Rushdie, in an interview in the *New York Times Book Review,* said that he viewed the affair as a "clash of languages." But it is clash of contexts that makes those utterances intelligible. There are certain forms of life that give meaning to certain utterances, and threatening the validity of the utterances is a way of suggesting that the forms of life they belong to should disappear: "It strikes me that a religious belief could only be something like a passionate commitment to a system of reference. Hence, although it's belief, it's really a way of living, or a way of assessing life. It's passionately seizing hold of *this* interpretation" (Ludwig Wittgenstein, *Culture and Value,* trans. Peter Winch [Chicago: University of Chicago Press, 1984], 64e). Rushdie refused to see the continuity between the seriousness of his own convictions and that of others. Furthermore, he might have committed the sin of being too strident, too lodged in the truth of experience. We might say that he approached a subject *empirically which acquired its meaning from the spiritual and religious standpoint.* In *The Satanic Verses,* he effectively emptied the meaning of the history of Islam, from the point of view of those who had this faith. The erasing of meaning itself, along with the strident high-mindedness of the intellectual junkie, are what Dahl speaks to. And Rushdie's own words about his exploration of Islamic history indicate this aspect of his enquiry as scientific and intellectual, but not conscious of the religious or spiritual side: "The interesting thing about Mohammed is that there is objective information about him other than the sacred text. It seemed to me, when I studied it as a historian, that that makes this whole phenomenon a historical as well as a spiritual one, and the relationship between the people involved is absolutely fascinating. Islam is, after all, one of the greatest ideas that ever came into the world—I supposed the next idea of that size would have been Marxism—and the chance to study the birth of a great historical idea is interesting. The one thing you learn as a historian is just how fragmented and ambiguous and peculiar the historical record is. So I thought, well, let's not try and pretend to be writing a history. Let's take the themes I'm interested in and fantasise them and fabulate them and all that, so that we don't have to get into the issue: did this really happen or did it not?" (quoted in Lisa Appignanesi and Sara Maitland, eds., *The Rushdie File* [Syracuse: Syracuse University Press, 1990], 22). For a writer, this explanation is sen-

sible, even convincing. But Rushdie's wish to "fabulate" is a challenge to believers who view their version as truth, an objection to not
only their faith but ultimately their form of life. For those who are
divided on the question of religion, the dispute arises from having
different forms of life, not simply contrary intellectual opinions.
Wittgenstein says, "I think differently, in a different way. I say different things to myself. I have different pictures" (*Culture and Value*, 55).
Again, the prominence of images (from someone who was exposed
to many cultures and languages) emerges here, and Wittgenstein
shows how the way in which a statement is uttered can be missed
by someone who is not in the same realm of agreement. For instance, he imagines a believer and a nonbeliever holding forth in a
discussion on their beliefs. In response to the believer's testament of
faith, Wittgenstein, taking the role of the nonbeliever explaining absence of belief, says, "And then I give an explanation: 'I don't believe
in . . . ,' but then the religious person never believes what I describe. I
can't say. I can't contradict that person. In one sense, I understand
all he says—the English words 'God,' 'separate,' etc. I understand. I
could say: 'I don't believe in this,' and this would be true, meaning I
haven't got these thoughts or anything that hangs together with
them. But not that I could contradict the thing. You might say:
'Well, if you can't contradict him, that means you don't understand
him. If you did understand him, then you might.' That again is
Greek to me. My normal technique of language leaves me. I don't
know whether to say they understand one another or not. These
controversies look quite different from any normal controversies.
Reasons look entirely different from normal reasons" (*Culture and
Value*, 55). Wittgenstein's thinking contrasts with Rushdie's because
he sees the possibility for superstition to serve as foundations for
action, community building, and forms of life. For Wittgenstein,
we cannot discuss religious issues in normal language, or at least
express such beliefs with what we might regard as the normal technique of language. If Muslim reactions are taken into account,
Rushdie did not know the rules of that community and how lan-

guage—specific vocabulary, proper names—worked within that community. A Muslim writes: "Even more shocking and saddening at the same time is the communication gap between the Muslim community and the so-called intelligentsia. There is no mental rapport, no instantaneous recognition of pain, no spontaneous sharing of anguish. Our country is divided in many ways, but can it survive such a psychological barrier? Can it overcome these intellectual divides that seem to preclude any possibility of speaking to each other in the language of the heart? It's unbelievable that what pains one section gives pleasure to the other. Are we really so estranged from each other?" (Appignanesi and Maitland, *The Rushdie File,* 37).

From the Muslim point of view, the disagreement runs deeper than the sorts of words involved—though for Rushdie the argument is about the physiognomy of the words. Rushdie speaks of the difference between the sacred and the profane in the context of intellectual curiosity, while the emphasis for the Muslim writer is faith-based. From this view, the sacred is something that cannot be questioned and is represented by the "language of the heart"; it is not something that should be tested by intellectual interrogation. From the religious point of view, it is perhaps impossible to define the sacred in terms of any language. Conversely, for Rushdie, language reveals the extent of knowledge: we do not know more than we can express. For the Indian-born author, language should not be limited from conveying what others view as transcendent: phenomena are all describable in linguistic terms; there are no moral boundaries that exist outside language. The Muslim extremists would beg to differ: they believe in moral and immoral uses of language. Nevertheless, they seem alive to linguistic power; it created the specter of death for Rushdie and is a testament to the strength of language. The fatwa's existence makes arguments about the morality or immorality of using language beg the question.

22. Rushdie says, "The city as reality and as a metaphor is at the heart of all my work" *(Imaginary Homelands)*.

23. Salman Rushdie, "The Salon Interview: Salman Rushdie" (1996). See www.salon.com/06/features/interview.html.

24. Bishnupriya Ghosh, "An Invitation to Indian Postmodernity: Rushdie's English Vernacular as Situated Cultural Hybridity," in M. Keith Booker, ed., *Critical Essays on Salman Rushdie* (London: G. K. Hall, 1999), 139.

25. Rushdie, "The Salon Interview."

26. Salman Rushdie, *The Moor's Last Sigh* (New York: Vintage, 1997; orig. pub. 1995), 320. Subsequent references to this work will be given in parentheses in the text.

27. Salman Rushdie, interview with David Cronenberg, "Cronenberg Meets Rushdie," *Shift*, 3, no. 4 (June–July 1995). See www.david cronenberg.de/cr_rushd.htm.

28. Ibid.

29. Rushdie, *Imaginary Homelands*, 17.

30. Ibid., 64.

31. Rushdie, quoted in Appignanesi and Maitland, *The Rushdie File*, 25.

32. Ghosh, "An Invitation to Indian Postmodernity," 130.

33. Rushdie, "The Salon Interview."

34. Hamilton, "The First Life of Salman Rushdie," 101.

35. Susan Stewart, *Crimes of Writing* (Durham, N.C.: Duke University Press, 1994), 68.

36. Ibid., 67.

37. Ibid.

38. Rushdie, *Imaginary Homelands*, 11.

39. Ibid., 12.

40. Salman Rushdie, interview with Melinda Penkava, National Public Radio (NPR), May 3, 1999. See discover.npr.org/features/feature. jhtml?wfId=1049585.

41. Rushdie, *Imaginary Homelands*, 429.

42. Rushdie, NPR interview with Melinda Penkava, May 3, 1999.

43. Ibid.

44. Ibid.

Index